W9-DJN-177

WITHDRAWN

A Century of the Symphony

Richard E. Mueller

Book Design and Layout
by
Carol Brown Corey

KNIGHT PUBLISHING COMPANY
3552 CRITTENDEN
ST. LOUIS, MISSOURI 63118

TABLE OF CONTENTS

ACKNOWLEDGMENTS

There are a number of persons without whose assistance this book would not have been possible. The staff of the St. Louis Symphony Orchestra lent constant and enthusiastic help. They gave me complete access to materials which were indispensable in my research. I want to acknowledge all of the individuals and institutions whose names appear in the bibliography and picture credits; authors who were responsible for sources which I used, and those who were so generous with their time in granting me interviews regarding their associations with the history of the orchestra. I am especially indebted to my friend, Dr. William J. Miller, whose unlimited expertise and interest contributed so much to this project from its inception.

Preface

St. Louis, founded in the eighteenth century, became one of America's major cities because of its strategic location and its role in the development of the American frontier. Through the years of its growth as a transportation and industrial center it attracted people who found time to develop an interest in cultural activities. Among the citizens of St. Louis who patronized libraries, museums, theaters, and good architecture, there were those who loved good music.

One of St. Louis' greatest cultural institutions is the St. Louis Symphony Orchestra, founded in 1880, and thereby being the second oldest permanent symphony orchestra in the United States; second to the New York Philharmonic. The centennial anniversary of such a civic asset is a time to celebrate the existence of a great musical organization, to contemplate its contributions to its city, region and nation, and to project its future. It is also a time to take a fond look back; to reminisce and recall favorite concerts and musical personalities. It is a time to remember those special times and to bring them together in pictures and words before they escape us completely.

The main thrust of this book is the period in the Symphony's history when Vladimir Golschmann was its conductor. He was on the podium from 1931 to 1958; quite a long tenure for an orchestra leader. That time-period is just far enough back in our memories to evoke thoughts of nostalgia for a time when many present-day St. Louis music lovers were beginning to attend the orchestra's concerts. It is hoped that this volume provides some entertainment to those who remember the times of music amidst the grim events of the Depression and war years; and to those, also, who did not know the Golschmann era firsthand. It is also hoped that the many people who like St. Louis history, exclusive of any musical interest, will find enjoyment here.

Admittedly, there are omissions in this work. The period in the orchestra's development over the last twenty years receives just surface treatment. And some phases of the period under consideration are not developed fully, or perhaps not at all. These will have to be treated elsewhere.

But if *A Century of the Symphony* aids in reliving enjoyable past firsthand experiences and in kindling interest in current and future activities of the orchestra, it will be successful.

My gratitude to
Gertrude and Paul Mueller
for their help and encouragement
in so many ways

A
Century
of the
Symphony

Richard E. Mueller

Golschmann

The patrons who attended the presentation of Handel's *Dettingen Te Deum* by the St. Louis Choral Society on March 24, 1881 heard the first performance of what later became the St. Louis Symphony Orchestra. For many years, however, serious music already had had an important status in St. Louis.

St. Louisans listened to small theatre orchestras as early as 1819; and choral groups performed at the Roman Catholic Cathedral. In 1837 "The Celebrated Prague Company of Nine Professors of Music from Europe" visited the city, and afforded music patrons their first chance to hear ensemble music of a high caliber. [1]

The first local orchestra was that of the Missouri Musical Fund Society, formed in 1838; its purpose probably being to raise money for needy musicians in the area. [2] In 1845 local music lovers founded the Polyhymnia Society with the intent of providing vocal and instrumental music for St. Louis. Although its concerts were well-attended, the orchestra was disbanded about 1855. In 1853 the Germania Orchestra visited the city and presented to St. Louisans for the first time the complete Beethoven Second Symphony.

Left. The "Old St. Louis Little German Band" was just one of the many early musical organizations of St. Louis before the establishment of the Symphony. (St. Louis Public Library)

Mendelsohn Musical Society

Above. The Mendelssohn Musical Society was one of many groups which supplied St. Louis with serious music around the turn of the century. (Missouri Historical Society)

9

One of the organizations which brought music to St. Louis in the nineteenth century. (Ernst C. Krohn Special Collections, Gaylord Music Library, Washington University, St. Louis, Missouri)

Where people of German background settled, singing societies almost inevitably followed. St. Louis was no exception, and during the mid-nineteenth century St. Louisans established such groups, including the St. Louis Saengerbund. In addition, the city hosted a number of famous soloists, including sopranos Jenny Lind and Adelina Patti, and the great Norwegian violinist Ole Bull. Of a Jenny Lind concert in 1851 one writer commented, "The city was on tiptoe and ready to do honor to the most marvelous singer on earth, superior to any bird nature can produce..." [3]

For a decade after 1859 St. Louis music lovers could attend concerts by the Philharmonic Society, under the direction of Eduard de Sobolewski, August Waldauer, and Egmont Froehlich. Sobolewski, a native of Koenigsberg and a personal friend of Mendelssohn and Schumann, did much for the cultural atmosphere of St. Louis. In the words of the historian Thomas Scharf:

> To Mr. Sobolewski is due the credit of first gathering into close and really harmonious relationship whatever was of real worth in our musical circles. His selections of musical compositions were guided by sound judgment and refined taste, while the performances themselves became genuine artistic unities through the inspiration of rare directive power. [4]

This old daguerreotype is of Jenny Lind, the "Swedish Nightingale." Her concerts always attracted much attention. (Missouri Historical Society)

The celebrated violinist Ole Bull contributed to the musical life of St. Louis before the founding of the Symphony. (Missouri Historical Society)

10

The announcement of the first concert of the St. Louis Philharmonic in 1860. (Missouri Historical Society)

August Waldauer helped establish the St. Louis Musical Union, which in 1890 merged with the St. Louis Choral Society. (Missouri Historical Society)

Members of the St. Louis Philharmonic Quintette Club sometime during the late 1800s. (Ernst C. Krohn Special Collections, Gaylord Music Library, Washington University, St. Louis, Missouri)

A rehearsal of the St. Louis Philharmonic, about 1930, with Frank Gecks conducting. (Missouri Historical Society)

Waldauer, a German native, was a violinist and composer, as well as conductor. He led several local theater and opera orchestras, as well as the Philharmonic. Froehlich, a native of Stuttgart, was a composer as well as the leader of several local singing groups. He was also music supervisor of the St. Louis public schools for a time.

St. Louisans attended an especially distinguished performance when Theodore Thomas and his "Grand Concert Organization of Forty Eminent Musicians, Comprising all the Celebrated Soloists of his Grand Orchestra," first visited the city in 1869. The local music public anxiously awaited concerts in the city for the next several years. The Thomas orchestra participated in the festival programs dedicating the Exposition Hall on Olive Street, now the site of the main public library, in 1885. Thomas, a competent violinist, became the first conductor of the Chicago Symphony.

After the demise of the Philharmonic in 1870 (it has since been revived) an amateur group called the "Haydn Orchestra" performed serious music from 1871 to 1880, and the "St. Louis Grand Orchestra," a group of fourteen musicians, played at the outdoor Schnaider's Garden for several summers after 1880.

Theodore Thomas and his orchestra highlighted the musical seasons of the 1870s. (Washington University)

Egmont Froehlich conducted the St. Louis Philharmonic Society in the 19th century. (Wash. University)

Beer baron Adolphus Busch was a prominent supporter of the early Symphony. (Anheuser-Busch Inc.)

Schnaider's Garden was a favorite spot to listen to music on St. Louis summer evenings. (Missouri Historical Society)

It is to the year 1880 that we may trace the origin of what today is the St. Louis Symphony Orchestra. For on September 1 of that year, local music enthusiasts founded the St. Louis Choral Society, and in the spring of 1881 the organization presented two concerts, performing the afore-mentioned *Dettingen Te Deum* by Handel. The organist for the occasions was Edward M. Bowman, theoretician and co-author of the *Bowman-Weitzmann Manual of Musical Theory.* During the next season the Society presented four concerts with a membership of ninety singers and accompaniment by thirty-five instrumentalists.[5] The conductor of the Choral Society was Joseph Otten, a German church organist who remained in St. Louis with the organization until his resignation in 1894. Otten increased the membership of the chorus to three hundred in 1883, and through his devotion, the Choral Society became a permanent asset to the cultural life of St. Louis. Frequently during those early years Otten's singing group collaborated with Theodore Thomas in such presentations as Handel's *Messiah.*

In 1884 the St. Louis civic leader Robert Brookings headed the organization and strengthened the financial situation of the Society. He was a wealthy hardware manufacturer and president of Washington University's board of trustees. His money enabled the Society to expand its repertoire, and by the late 1880s the Choral Society presented mixed choral and orchestral concerts.

In 1890 the St. Louis Choral Society merged with the St. Louis Musical Union. The former conductor of the Philharmonic, August Waldauer, helped establish the Musical Union in 1881 with initial capital of $8,000.[6] The Musical Union, numbering fifty-four players,[7] played its first concert at the Mercantile Library Hall in November 1881. Its organizers wanted to establish a series of winter concerts, as opposed to the normal summer fare which was somewhat common in St. Louis music circles in those days. They succeeded in establishing the largest orchestra in St. Louis up to that time.[8]

Throughout the 1880s the Musical Union presented about six concerts per year, and with the completion of the 1889-1890 season, Joseph Otten's St. Louis Choral Society absorbed the Musical Union. Thus, after the merger in 1890, St. Louis' most

ST. LOUIS
CHORAL-SYMPHONY SOCIETY.

The guarantee fund for the Choral and Symphony Concerts, for the Season of 1891 and 1892 has, up to the present time, the following signatures:

JAS. L. BLAIR.	WM. E. GUY.	MRS. MARY C. McKITTRICK.
JOHN N. BOFFINGER.	HY. C. HAARSTICK.	WM. F. NIEDRINGHAUS.
HOWARD BENOIST.	WM. A. HARGADINE.	N. O. NELSON.
ROBT. S. BROOKINGS.	E. A. HITCHCOCK.	AMADE V. REYBURN.
A. BOECKLER.	EZRA H. LINLEY.	MRS. CAROLINE O. SHICKLE.
JAS. H. BROOKMIRE.	WM. J. LEMP.	E. C. SIMMONS.
A. D. COOPER.	GEO. E. LEIGHTON.	JOHN Q. ADAMS SMITH.
CHARLES CLARKE.	JOHN R. LIONBERGER.	BYRON SHERMAN.
WAYMAN C. CUSHMAN.	J. E. LIGGETT.	CHARLES H. TURNER.
MRS. JUSTINA CATLIN.	WM. McMILLAN.	JAMES TAUSSIG.
GEORGE S. DRAKE.	GEO. D. MARKHAM.	CLAUS VIETHS.
FRANCIS A. DREW.	HUGH McKITTRICK.	W. H. WATERS.

ROBERT S. BROOKINGS,
President.
A. D. CUNNINGHAM, SECRETARY.

JOSEPH OTTEN,
Conductor.
HUGH McKITTRICK, JR, TREASURER.
J. P. GRANT, ACCOMPANIST.

BOARD OF DIRECTORS:

RICHARD PERRY,	OTTO BOLLMAN,	HENRY S. POTTER,
GEO. D. MARKHAM,	A. T. GRINDON,	JAMES M. BULL,
R. D. KOHN,	D. H. CLARK,	A. D. CUNNINGHAM.
A. P. HEBARD,	HUGH McKITTRICK, JR	

TWELFTH SEASON.

Third Symphony Concert,
MISS ADELE AUS DER OHE (Pianist).
SOLOIST.
AT
MUSIC HALL,
TUESDAY EVENING, FEBRUARY 2, 1892.

Above and following page. A selection of the programs used by patrons of the Symphony down through the years shows the organization's evolution from the St. Louis Choral Society to the St. Louis Symphony Orchestra. (Ernst C. Krohn Special Collections, Gaylord Music Library, Washington University, St. Louis, Mo.)

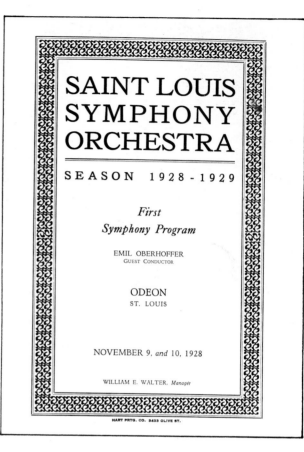

ST. LOUIS CHORAL SOCIETY,

ASSISTED BY THE

"Male Chorus of the Liederkranz.

TENTH SEASON—FIRST CONCERT.

✳BERLIOZ'✳

Damnation of Faust,

AT MUSIC HALL,

Monday Evening, December 2nd, 1889.

MR. JOSEPH OTTEN, — — — Conductor.

⟋SOLOISTS.⟍

MR. WILLIAM LUDWIG, Baritone (as Mephistopheles).
MME. ADELAIDE MULLEN, Soprano (as Marguerite).
MR. HENRY BEAUMONT, Tenor (as Faust).

Saint Louis
Choral-Symphony
Society   MR. ALFRED ERNST, Conductor.

Programme
One

Thursday
November 27
1902

1902-1903

Twenty-Third
Season

THE ODEON
GRAND AND FINNEY AVENUES

LAMBERT-DEACON-HULL PRINTING CO. ST. LOUIS

14

Civic leader Robert Brookings helped to strengthen the financial situation of the Symphony. (State Historical Society of Missouri)

Joseph Otten directed the St. Louis Choral Society and the St. Louis Choral-Symphony Society from 1880 to 1894. (St. Louis Symphony)

important musical organization became known as the St. Louis Choral-Symphony Society; Joseph Otten remained as conductor. Wealthy brewers like Joseph Griesedieck and Adolphus Busch, and prominent Jewish merchants, like the Epstein brothers, financially supported the Choral-Symphony Society. In the words of a member of the orchestra during that time, "Jewish money was the biggest support of the orchestra." [9]

With the merger of the two musical organizations, orchestral and choral concerts alternated at the Exposition Hall on Olive Street. Frequently the audiences filled only one-fourth of the hall,[10] perhaps due to the unfavorable economic situation in the nation at that time, plus a lack of interest in the programs. Those years proved difficult for the musicians in another way. In the 1890s the pay per concert was eight dollars, with three dollars for each rehearsal (which were infrequent). [11] But the musicians enjoyed some compensations. As one observer noted, "Mostly Germans in the old orchestras....They used to have big social evenings with a keg of beer and an old Dutch lunch because the Germans like them. Musicians' picnics were lots of fun." [12]

Alfred Ernst, a temperamental German, conducted the St. Louis Choral-Symphony Society from 1894 to 1907. (St. Louis Symphony)

15

The directors of the Choral-Symphony Society reduced the number of concerts each season due to a lack of funds. Because of this problem the conductor of the society, Joseph Otten, decided to resign. In 1894 a new man arrived and replaced the capable first conductor of the organization which later became the St. Louis Symphony Orchestra.

The Choral-Symphony Society turned for leadership to another native German. Alfred Ernst, in 1894 a 26-year-old bearded pianist, remained in the city as conductor until 1907. Ernst occasionally displayed much anger in his attempts to increase the proficiency of his singers and players. At the rehearsals he frequently cursed the men, and on one occasion he described the sound of the orchestra as "cats and chickens screeching in the basement."[13] On another occasion he told the orchestra that the timpani sounded like the "thumping of a toilet seat."[14] Some contemporary accounts charged that the conductor was guilty of not studying the scores sufficiently, and that he relied too heavily on improvised techniques which he assumed the players could follow.[15]

During the early years of Ernst's tenure, the organization tended to do mostly choral works, but as time went on, it performed more strictly orchestral pieces. One contemporary commentator noted,

> It is a well known fact that instrumental concerts...are as a rule not well patronized...As soon as it is known that only "mysterious" symphonies and "learned" overtures are offered, they take it for granted that such concerts are not intended for them.[16]

Thus, Ernst faced the problem that has plagued most subsequent conductors: how to expand the repertoire and still please the music patrons.

The Choral-Symphony Society employed two hundred voices and fifty-five players during the 1900-1901 season, and during that season the organization performed three oratorios, three symphonies, two popular concerts, and two concerts featuring instrumental soloists.[17] Between 1903 and 1907 the Society presented only six concerts each regular season.[18] We may gain some understanding of the financial difficulties during that time by noting that in one year in the early 1900s, the expenses of the Society ran to $20,000, twice the amount of its income. By contrast, during the same time period the orchestra in Cincinnati spent $31,000, that of

The Mercantile Library building served as the location of concerts by the St. Louis Musical Union. (Missouri Historical Society)

Pittsburgh spent $77,000, the one in Chicago spent $250,000, and in Boston one man gave $250,000 to put the orchestra on a paying basis.[19]

With the coming of the World's Fair to St. Louis in 1904, the St. Louis Choral-Symphony Society took part in the festivities. The instrumentalists played at the attraction called the Tyrolean Alps, and Ernst provided his services as conductor of the large Symphony Orchestra which performed at Festival Hall. That orchestra drew its members from orchestras all over the United States, and it included some musicians from the St. Louis Choral-Symphony. The choral members of the Society were also involved with the Fair activities. On opening day, April 30, some of them sang as part of a chorus composed of various St. Louis groups. The program on that occasion included two works written especially for the opening of the Fair, with the music supplied by the Sousa Band. The musicians who played at the Fair had a contract that called for a minimum of forty-five dollars per week for six-day weeks and four-hour days.[20]

At the conclusion of the 1906-1907 season, Alfred Ernst returned to Germany to devote his full time to opera. The next season marked a watershed for the premier musical organization of St. Louis. A new conductor came to St. Louis for the opening of the 1907-1908 season--Max Zach. The St. Louis Choral-Symphony Society therewith changed its structure. The choral portion of the Society disbanded, and the new name of the organization was the St. Louis Symphony Society. The orchestra increased from fifty-two to sixty-four musicians under the new conductor.[21]

Max Zach, born in what is now Poland, came to St. Louis from the Boston Symphony where he had been first violist and conductor of the famed "Pops" concerts in that city. Zach, the first nationally known conductor to lead the St. Louis orchestra, was quite the stern taskmaster. He had his batons hand-made by a local artisan, and he often broke two or three of them during rehearsals. His great discipline and dignity pleased the players as the goateed and bespectacled maestro led his musicians to a greater musical proficiency. Zach did not seem to convey a great deal of warmth to the audience, nor did he excel in his presentation of the romantic repertoire, but he increased performances of the great classical masters, and gained the respect of musicians and patrons alike, as evidenced by the many capacity audiences at the hall.

With regard to the repertoire during the Zach

Much of the musical activity of the World's Fair centered around the Tyrolean Alps. (Missouri Historical Society)

Max Zach, the first nationally recognized conductor to lead the St. Louis Symphony, presided over the organization from 1907 to 1921. (St. Louis Symphony)

Festival Hall at the 1904 World's Fair was the scene of large orchestral performances. (Photo courtesy Harry M. Hagen)

years, 1907 to 1921, he was one of the country's first conductors to perform the entire cycle of Beethoven symphonies,[22] and he stimulated St. Louis' interest in the music of Tchaikovsky. [23] Zach introduced the works of a number of American composers to St. Louis audiences; such composers as Chadwick, Converse, MacDowell, Carpenter, Goldmark, and Hill. In 1917 the works of American composers constituted twelve per cent of the St. Louis Symphony programs, the highest percentage of any orchestra.[24] And Zach conducted a number of his own compositions at the Sunday "pops" concerts, which the audiences enjoyed.

During the Zach tenure the Symphony inaugurated the policy of making tours to towns in Missouri and neighboring states in order to acquaint more people with the Symphony. The St. Louis business community supported that kind of endeavor, for in 1916 the Business Men's League raised money to send the orchestra on a tour of cities in the St. Louis trade territory in order to bring good will to the city. In a letter to Columbia, Missouri, making arrangements for a trip to that city, a Symphony spokesman wrote, "The Board of Management of our orchestra association have just decided to give a series of three or four symphony concerts in the smaller cities of this state, and the citizens of Columbia are marked out as possible victims."[25] In a trip to Camp Funston, Kansas, during World War I to entertain the soldiers, the "victims" were probably the members of the orchestra, as the men played in a place where the outside temperature was eighteen below zero.[26] The musicians were also under heavy guard because so many of them were German-born. A highlight of that particular concert was the appearance of Mme. Ernestine Schumann-Heink with the orchestra, whose sons fought on both sides of the war.

The legendary Mme. Ernestine Schumann-Hienk appeared with the orchestra during World War I. (Missouri Historical Society)

Max Zach and the orchestra at the Musicians Union Hall on West Pine during the 1908-1909 season. (Missouri Historical Society)

John Philip Sousa directed the St. Louis Choral-Symphony at the 1904 World's Fair. (Missouri Hist. Society)

The tours attracted some favorable responses from the critics, as evidenced by a review by a Chicago critic after a visit by the Symphony to that city:

> The concert was a welcome one. The St. Louis orchestra was well worth hearing and we hope that now that they have found the way here they will come again. The audience was most cordial in its applause for Mr. Zach and the men and did all in their power to persuade them to another visit.[27]

The Symphony continued to tour during the following years, and the practice became an important part of the activities of the St. Louis Symphony.

One of the most amusing and dramatic events that occurred during the Zach period was the confrontation between the conductor and the pianist Vladimir de Pachmann during the latter's appearance with the orchestra in the 1911-1912 season. Zach was well aware of the reputation of de Pachmann as an eccentric artist who delighted, during performances, in conversing with the audience about his own superior ability. He frequently played the piano beyond his allotted time, all the while commenting aloud in English, French, Russian, or German. During a particular concert with the Symphony, de Pachmann, after finishing his scheduled solo piece, remained at the piano and said to the audience, "Messieurs et dames, the great de Pachmann will now play for you, as you have never heard the piano played." [28] At the conclusion of one encore the stagehands tried to remove the piano as Zach had

Among the great artists who appeared at the old Odeon Theatre were Enrico Caruso, Feodor Chaliapin (here dressed for his part in **Mefistofele**), Mary Garden, and Amelita Galli-Curci. (Missouri Historical Society)

The old Odeon Theatre was the home of the St. Louis Symphony until the move to Kiel Auditorium. (Missouri Historical Society)

ordered. But the audience started to scream, "We want de Pachmann!" When the conductor mounted the podium in an effort to resume the program, the audience continued its chanting, and Zach threw down his baton and stalked off the stage. Later Zach said, "I may have been hasty, but I cannot lend myself to buffoonery in a symphony concert. If people want clowning, let them go to a circus." [29]

This incident occured at the Odeon Theater on North Grand and Finney Avenues, the home of the St. Louis Symphony from the time it was built just before the 1904 World's Fair until the musicians moved into the new Kiel Auditorium in 1934. Great singers like Nellie Melba, Luisa Tetrazzini, Mary Garden, Geraldine Farrar, Amelita Galli-Curci, Ernestine Schumann-Heink, Marcella Sembrich, Feodor Chaliapin, and Enrico Caruso entertained at the theater. The dancers Anna Pavlova and Vaslav Nijinsky performed on the Odeon stage, and Roald Amundsen, Will Rogers, Eugene Debs, Emma Goldman, and many famous statesmen lectured there. And, of course, some of the greatest instrumentalists of the musical world performed on its stage, either in concert with the St. Louis Symphony or in recital. Many music patrons remember the Odeon fondly for its beauty, fine acoustics, and intimate atmosphere. After several fires, it was razed in the mid-1930s.

Of course, the Symphony Society concerned itself with matters of finance during those years. Throughout its history, the organization usually found difficulty in paying the bills and gathering enough money to guarantee the next musical season. In 1916 Mrs. George Parker gave twenty-five shares of American Radiator stock to the Symphony Society. The gift served as the first substantial endowment for the organization.[30] And in 1920 a group of dedicated women organized the Women's Committee of the Symphony Society, later called the Women's Association. This organization has played a vital role in increasing support of the orchestra by sponsoring annual season ticket drives, scholarship awards to deserving young musicians, concerts for students, as well as providing various social activities for women involved.

The interior of the Coliseum, at Washington and Jefferson Avenues. The Symphony occasionally played special concerts here. (Missouri Historical Society)

During the time when their permanent home was the Odeon, the Symphony also occasionally performed at the Coliseum, at Washington and Jefferson Avenues. The seating capacity was greater at the Coliseum, and it was used for occasional free public concerts, or when the Symphony musicians were hired to accompany an outstanding visiting soloist apart from their regular subscription series.

The Coliseum was the site of many special Symphony concerts in the early part of this century. (State Historical Society of Missouri)

Thus, the Symphony developed well under the leadership of Max Zach. The progress and popularity of the orchestra were the themes of a letter to a local newspaper by George Markham, one of the leading sponsors of musical activities in St. Louis for many years:

> The growing ticket sales and hearty applause at concerts favor the contention that Mr. Zach is a success in St. Louis. Certainly he is doing all that in him lies to please our public and perfect our orchestra. He tries to bring to our problem all the light gained from experiments made in other cities by other conductors. If you could poll the ticket buyers you would find that Mr. Zach had as high a percentage of commendation and enthusiastic support as have other conductors in other cities tested in the same manner. Mr. Zach's increasing freedom and temperament in leading, now that he feels that orchestra to be capable, secure and responsive, will draw increasing popularity as his conducting gives greater and greater pleasure.[31]

After a brief illness, Max Zach died in St. Louis in February 1921. The assistant conductor, Frederick Fischer, and three guest conductors, Rudolph Ganz, Theodore Spiering, and Dirk Foch conducted the orchestra during the remainder of the 1920-1921 season.

Rudolph Ganz conducted the orchestra permanently the following season. He had especially impressed the women on the Board of Control with his elegant and urbane manners, even though he enjoyed a reputation as a pianist rather than as a conductor. A native of Zurich, his past was steeped in personal associations with musical greats such as Brahms, Ravel, and Bartók. He had been a student with Albert Schweitzer at the Conservatory of Music in Strasbourg, and a pupil of the great pianist Ferruccio Busoni.

In the opinion of many observers at the time, the Symphony Society made a mistake when it chose Ganz as the leader of the orchestra. He earned $15,000 a season, more than twice the salary of

Rudolph Ganz, conductor of the Symphony from 1921 to 1927, introduced much new music to St. Louis and started the student concerts. (St. Louis Symphony)

Frederick Fischer was the orchestra's assistant conductor from 1907 to 1931. He was succeeded by Scipione Guidi. (St. Louis Symphony)

Zach,[32] whereas he did not possess the conducting skill of his predecessor. Before his first concert he reportedly told the St. Louis musicians, "Gentlemen, the orchestra is not my instrument, so please do your best and we will learn together." [33] Certainly, Ganz was not the conducting technician that Zach had been, and on several occasions when the members of the orchestra finished playing, Ganz kept swinging his arms because he could not follow the score correctly. He improved with experience, however, while many of the musicians admired him for his gentle and courteous manner.

To Ganz's great credit, he introduced new music to St. Louis audiences: Schoenberg, Stravinsky, Mahler, Respighi, Honegger, Richard Strauss, and Vaughan Williams.[34] Ganz introduced to American audiences, as well, the compositions of Debussy and Ravel.[35] He genuinely loved contemporary music, and he did not seem to mind the occasional hostility which the patrons directed toward his programs. In fact, he actually invited the audience to hiss any modern works that they disliked. But strangely, the percentage of American music in the repertoire actually decreased during the Ganz years, to about five per cent of the programming,[36] a more normal percentage for American orchestras.

After six seasons in St. Louis, Ganz left the orchestra due to local dissatisfaction with the programming of modern music and his failure to develop as a conductor. One critic has written, "When Mr. Ganz departed, public interest was at a low ebb and the orchestra was probably the worst in the country."[37] But Ganz did return to St. Louis later as guest piano soloist. He also guest-conducted various orchestras around the country, and for a time he was conductor of the New York Philharmonic Young People's Concerts. He also served as director of the Chicago Musical College of Roosevelt University.

But the greatest legacy that Ganz left to St. Louis was the children's concerts. These events have become an important part of the cultural life of St. Louis under subsequent conductors, and many of the later subscribers to the Symphony recall with fondness their experiences of going to hear the St. Louis Symphony play; many young people in St. Louis developed an interest in music because of the efforts of Rudolph Ganz. He had a commendable rapport with the young people, and he taught those audiences the workings of the orchestra by having the various principals in the orchestra demonstrate their instruments to the students. Then when the students later heard the instrument which had been featured, they were encouraged to clap to show that they recognized its sound. When at times the young people became obstreperous and resorted to shouting and throwing paper airplanes at the stage, Ganz, instead of becoming angry, said to them: "Shoot some more. Any more? Please shoot them!" [38] The reverse-psychology usually succeeded in quieting the disturbance. When Ganz resigned in 1927, the following editorial appeared in a local newspaper:

> To the schoolboy and schoolgirl of St. Louis, every creed and color, Rudolph Ganz brought the message of good music. And he brought it, not in the atmosphere of an irksome or perfunctory duty, but with the genius and elan of a rare privilege. Our beaux and belles of the 1940's will pay him homage. He has set their feet on luminous ways. [39]

23

With the beginning of the 1926-1927 season the Symphony Society employed several guest conductors for four years. Eugene Goossens, Emil Oberhoffer, Bernardino Molinari, Carl Schuricht, Willem Van Hoogstraten, Enrique Fernández Arbós, George Szell (who made his American conducting debut in St. Louis), and the man who served permanently for the 1931-1932 season, Vladimir Golschmann, all conducted on a temporary basis between 1927 and 1931. A series of guest conductors stunted the development of the orchestra, demanding the permanent services of one individual who could constantly instruct and lend support to the musicians. At one point the guest conductor Molinari castigated the musicians in Italian. When he finished, an interpreter announced to the orchestra, "The Maestro says you all stink."[40] He also remarked that "the first violinists of the orchestra should be second violinists, and the second violinists should be in jail." [41] Such sentiments did not always make for the best music. The orchestra required permanency, and in 1931 the Symphony Society hired a man who later established a record for length of service as permanent conductor of a major American symphony orchestra.

Among the guest conductors employed by the orchestra between 1927 and 1931 were Emil Oberhoffer, Eugene Goossens, Enrique Fernández Arbós (here pictured with his wife), and George Szell. (Missouri Historical Society; George Szell: The Cleveland Orchestra)

CHAPTER II

VLADIMIR GOLSCHMANN: THE MAN AND HIS MUSIC

The St. Louis Symphony named Vladimir Golschmann as the new permanent conductor for the 1931-1932 season, a man whom *Time* magazine once described as a "Parisian to his tapering finger-tips."[1] His parents, natives of Russia, had emigrated to Paris separately, where they married and had four sons. Vladimir, the eldest, was born on December 16, 1893. His father made a name for himself as a writer, mathematician, and translator.

Young Vladimir commenced study of the piano at four and the violin at seven. At the age of ten, he wrote, "I love piano and I love violin but I want to become a conductor."[2] At the age of twelve he joined a semi-professional orchestra at the Sorbonne church as a second-violinist. As a boy he attended many concerts in Paris. He developed rapidly as a musician, and attended Buffon College and pursued musical training at the *Schola Cantorum*.

As a young man interested in the arts, Golschmann immersed himself in the Paris atmosphere of Debussy and Ravel, and the Cubist painters. He joined the Sechiari Orchestra and played with the *Concerts Rougé*.

As noted, Golschmann wanted to conduct, and he received his opportunity through his relationship with a wealthy Parisian patron of the arts, Albert Verley. Verley was a chemical engineer and perfume manufacturer who had been a pupil of the composer Erik Satie. Verley also composed, and he wanted to find someone to play his own compositions for the piano and violin. In 1919, upon the recommendation of Satie, Verley gave young Golschmann the money to start his own orchestra in Paris, the performances of which became known as the Concerts Golschmann. The concerts were famous in the musical circles of Paris, and Verley awarded prizes for the composition of modern music; one such award went to the composer Arthur Honegger in 1921, whose work, *Pastorale d' été*, Golschmann presented. The orchestra also played some of the works of the patron Verley, including the première of one of his *Pastels sonares*.

The Concerts Golschmann took place at the *Salle des Agriculteurs* and later at the *Salle Gaveau*. The young conductor managed the whole operation himself; he ordered the posters and even sold tickets for the concerts.

The programs for the performances leaned toward the modern musical literature, with special emphasis on the works of the "French Six." This school of composers, followers of Erik Satie, included Darius Milhaud, Arthur Honegger, Francis Poulenc, Louis Durey, Georges Auric, and Germaine Tailleferre. The audiences did not hesitate to vociferously demonstrate their feelings about the controversial compositions. Of one performance of Darius Milhaud's *Four Studies for Piano and Orchestra*, Golschmann later said,

> As soon as I started, the audience began to riot. The pianist turned pale, turned white, turned green. I could not even hear the work myself, but I finished it. Then I turned to the audience and said, "I think it is perfectly wonderful that there is so much life, so much artistic vitality, here. But may I suggest that you first listen to the work and then show your reactions? After the intermission we shall play it a second time and I expect you to hear it through!" They listened in absolute silence to the end. Then pandemonium broke loose![3]

Unfavorable audience reaction to new music was something that Golschmann experienced throughout his career.

The Concerts Golschmann proved a success, and one critic wrote of the conductor, "Here is an unknown, who will soon be known all over the musical world." [4] Because of his fame from the Concerts Golschmann, the French government appointed him director of the *Cercle musical* at the Sorbonne.

Igor Stravinsky admired Golschmann's talent and introduced him to the great dancer Sergei Diaghilev, who hired him as conductor of the Ballet Russe. Golschmann won personal acclaim with that company for his presentation of Stravinsky's *Le Sacre du printemps*. He conducted the Ballet Russe all over France and Europe, with great dancers such as Anna Pavlova. He then assumed the role of permanent conductor of the Scottish Orchestra in Glasgow and Edinburgh.

Golschmann first journeyed to the United States as a violinist in 1918 with the touring Paris Conservatory Orchestra. Some of his best friends in Paris were Americans, among them the composers George Antheil, Aaron Copland, and Virgil Thomson. Golschmann conducted the Paris premiere of George Gershwin's *Concerto in F*. He loved their kind of music, and he dreamed of one day conducting in America. His opportunity came when he conducted the Swedish Ballet on tour in the United States in 1923. The public and critics did not respond well to that company's presentation of modern ballet, but whatever disappointment Golschmann may have felt must have diminished when the New York Philharmonic invited him to be their guest conductor. Golschmann's reception in New York brought a spectacular response from music patrons. [5]

The manager of the New York Philharmonic, Arthur Judson, called the young Frenchman in Paris and told him of his recommendation of Golschmann to be one of the guest conductors for the St. Louis Symphony during the period after the Rudolph Ganz resignation. He said to Golschmann, "Are you a good conductor?" Golschmann replied, "What's the use of answering that? Let the St. Louis people hear me and decide for themselves." [6] In January and February 1931 the 37-year-old French conductor appeared in St. Louis for four concerts with the Symphony. The programs included works by Vivaldi-Siloti, Beethoven, Richard Strauss, Wagner, Mozart, Rabaud, Rimsky-Korsakov, Scarlatti, Ravel, Dvořák, Debussy, Liszt, and two friends of the conductor, Erik Satie and Arthur Honegger. His reception in the city influenced the Symphony Society to hire him permanently for the 1931-1932 season. Of that occasion, Golschmann later told a St. Louis audience, "Never will I forget my happiness when I was asked to be your conductor. I promised myself I would do my best, that I would improve the orchestra, that I would make you proud." [7] As subsequent history proved, he succeeded.

Regarded as a man of great charm, wit, elegance, and culture, someone once said of Golschmann, "Even the ashtrays in his home are in perfect taste." [8] His interests were varied. One author wrote of him,

> Golschmann's chief joy is in encounters with human beings. He talks science with scientists, journalism with reporters, world affairs with politicians. He has ideas about art, city planning, sports, travel, engineering. He is an avid collector of modern paintings, of African and archaic Greek Sculpture. He talks his head off and is glad to listen to anyone else talking *his* head off. [9]

Golschmann's collection of paintings ranked as one of the most eminent in the country. He had pictures by Braque, Miró, Matisse, Rouault, Modigliani, and about twenty-five works by his friend Pablo Picasso. The artist and the conductor visited each other during many summers in France. Many of Golschmann's friends in St. Louis shared his interest in collecting, and he was probably responsible for the fact that much good art came to St. Louis while he lived in the city. During his travels around the world he frequently visited museums. On a visit to the New York World's Fair in 1939 he wrote to St. Louis friends about an exhibit,

> It is one of the greatest exhibits I have *ever* seen. You may cry when you see the Van Goghs. He is great among the greatest and greater than we ever imagined.....If you do not see it, *never talk again to me*. [10]

Vladimir Golschmann as he looked in 1931, the year he becam conductor of the St. Louis Symphony. (St. Louis Symphony)

When Golschmann retired, his collection of forty works by Picasso and Braque went on public display for the first time, at Washington University.

Golschmann and his beautiful and charming French wife, Odette, delighted in returning to Paris nearly every summer. The conductor (who did not favor the *1812 Overture* because it symbolized a French defeat) demonstrated his love for his native city in a letter during one such visit,

> Rain or no rain, Paris is still marvelous. ....This is my hometown, where I was born, where I have spent my childhood, a city in which I can drive as well as any taxi driver; a city which I know so well and which I love so profoundly. To enjoy it, I do not have to spend evenings in night clubs and to rush during the day from a museum to a swanky restaurant. To wander on the quay of the Seine has more charm for me than to sit down at the terrace of a Montparnasse Cafe. [11]

The Golschmanns loved to visit their apartment in Paris, and to spend holidays on the French Riviera. On one such vacation he wrote,

> To us, St. Tropez, Cannes, Juan-Les-Pins does not only mean swimming twice a day in the heavenly Mediterranean, but also the joy of meeting again many American and French friends and the joy of visiting with one of the greatest artists who ever lived, with Picasso. As always with him, we will have the grandest time. It is hard to realize that a man of such immense fame can be as unassuming as he is. [12,]

Golschmann displayed truly eclectic interests. He loved to go to sporting events, especially to see the St. Louis Cardinals play baseball. When his brother René was released from a German prison camp during World War II and arrived in St. Louis to visit with Vladimir, René said of St. Louis and his brother, "It is my one hope that their baseball team will be able to win the flag, whatever that is, because it apparently means so much to them." [13] Years after Golschmann left the permanent conducting job in St. Louis, he returned for one of several visits to the city and was eager to watch a heavyweight prize fight on closed-circuit television.

And he enjoyed the game of poker. The orchestra tours afforded good opportunities to play the game with the musicians. One of his friends said, "He's too reckless to be a good player. But he sure puts a lot of life in a game." [14]

The Golschmanns enjoyed going to parties, and they frequently hosted their friends at their succession of fashionable apartments during the time that they lived in St. Louis. Vladimir, with his touch of a French accent, always had many witty stories and jokes to tell. The stylish couple seemed to enjoy life in St. Louis, even though they naturally wanted to go back to France as often as possible.

Most of the musicians who worked with Golschmann during his long tenure in St. Louis recall him fondly. Of course, there were occasional personality conflicts with the players, but generally the conductor and his orchestra got along quite well. [15] Golschmann frequently invited some of the

27

members of the orchestra to his parties, and occasionally gave books or other thoughtful gifts to the musicians. The rehearsals usually went smoothly, and as one musician said of the conductor, "Golschmann gets good discipline without blowing his top."[16] One observer wrote, "At rehearsal, wearing a sweater and smoking many cigarettes, he directs on the principle that better results are achieved by treating the musicians like human beings than by edifying them with bursts of temperament."[17] Rather than force a musician, who was either not feeling well or knew his part after years of experience, to rehearse a familiar passage, Golschmann, on more than one occasion, excused a musician from the rehearsal.

Even during the times when the conductor was not entirely pleased with a particular rehearsal, he exhibited more wit than anger. Once when a wind player was playing ahead of the rest of the musicians, Golschmann halted the orchestra and said to the offending musician, "When you get finished, don't go home, wait for the rest of us. I want to talk to you."[18] During a rehearsal of Prokofiev's *Alexander Nevsky* Golschmann said to the orchestra, "The Russians are supposed to win this battle. The way you play it, they are losing it." And during a play-through of Ravel's *Daphnis and Chloe* he said to the musicians, "Chloe is supposed to throw herself into Daphnis' arms here. Now maybe these sounds coming to my ears are your ideas of making love. Mine is different."[19]

Vladimir Golschmann's talents included an ability to provide balanced programs. He tried to incorporate a variety of composers' works into his performances. As he once said,

> In Europe one hears a great deal of national music. But here! Everyone knows Wagner, and Brahms, Debussy and Ravel, Vivaldi and Resphigi, Falla and Tchaikovsky, and a conductor of a major orchestra has to be able to do the whole lot.[20]

If a program included a somewhat slow-moving piece, Golschmann tried to include an exciting, fast-moving work in the same program. He also did his best to include at least one twentieth-century work on each program. He thought that by programming in that way he could interest more people in the newer compositions. Of that task he said,

> I don't mean that I want to drag music through the gutter. I hate that sort of thing with a mighty hatred. But I am trying to get rid of the concept that the concert hall is a churchly place, where you must go in your best bib and tucker, sit perfectly straight, keep a stiff upper lip, and then go straightly home.
>
> And I think I can do that without playing cheap music. The secret...is the

Rehearsal time with Vladimir Golschmann usually proved to be a pleasurable experience for most of the members of the orchestra. (St. Louis Symphony)

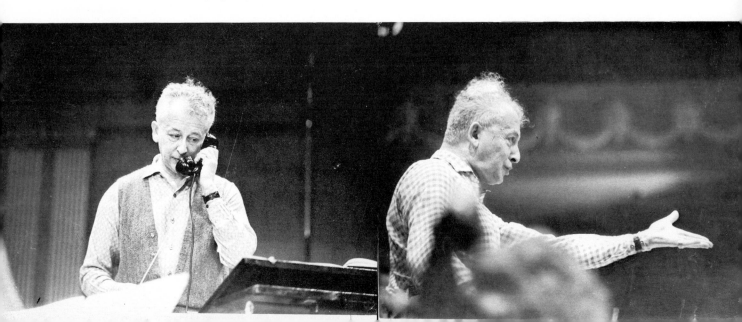

ability to make good programs. Varied, amusing programs.

I consider a man a fool to play ultra-modern music before an audience which still has its classics to learn. And equally I think it stupid to force a mixed audience to listen to a long program all of one sort of music. I have yet to eat a good dinner which was a succession of meat courses.

My plan is to play "serious" things...at will, and to let the audience relax by hearing after them something equally good, but in a less demanding genre. And to hunt out, and play, music that is a little off the beaten path. [21]

And about the fact that audiences usually wanted to hear the old masterpieces, he said,

You go to a play and you do not expect that it should be Shakespeare. You are satisfied if you are entertained. But in music, everything must be a masterpiece. It is immediately compared to Beethoven and Brahms. Why should this be? Why shouldn't people be just as interested in the output of contemporary composers as they are in new plays and new books? [22]

As an example of the conductor's effort to present balanced programs, he even included one standard work on the program of a 1938 "Music of Our Time"

concert so that, in Golschmann's words, "those who come will meet an old friend." [23] But the subject of contemporary music was a controversial one. As previously noted, Golschmann contended with unfavorable audience reaction to new works even as a young conductor in Paris. Throughout his tenure as conductor of the St. Louis Symphony the local newspaper critics generally complained that he did not include enough contemporary music on his programs. As one critic wrote, "A little more tolerance on the part of the audience is...in order. But audiences cannot show even tolerance unless they are given the opportunity." [24] The critics believed that when Golschmann did offer contemporary works, they were brief, inconsequential ones, offered only to appease patrons who were interested in something new. The conductor, however, believed that he presented new works of substance. He once said,

When I go to a composer and tell him we want to play one of his pieces I'm not interested when he drags out a large number of unplayed numbers and tells me we can have the première. Of such pieces there are too many first presentations and often no seconds. I want a piece that is worth playing. St. Louisans don't care if someone in Kalamazoo has heard it a few weeks before. [25]

It is, of course, impossible to please all of the listeners. One interested patron wrote to a local newspaper,

> Golschmann reserved for himself the doubtful distinction of letting loose... more loud and less excusable racketty fustian and discordant foolishness than was ever before projectiled against the auditory nerve-system of a hardly baffled audience. I can well understand why our "permanent" conductor resorts to these crazy moderns for program material. It's for a smoke-screen, with which he can obscure his lack of understanding of the classics. [26]

One episode perhaps best illustrates Golschmann's attitude about the introduction of new music to the repertoire. He once talked to a record collector who told him that a certain tempo Golschmann had taken seemed a little too fast; he told the conductor that he knew what he liked. Golschmann replied that it was more a case that the man liked what he knew. [27]

It is not surprising that Vladimir Golschmann loved to conduct the works of the modern French composers. He carried the memories of his Paris youth with him throughout the rest of his life, and reflected his French background while on the podium at St. Louis and while guest-conducting in the major musical cities of the United States and the rest of the world. At one point during the 1930s the St. Louis Symphony presented the works of Ravel and Debussy and other French composers one and one-half times as often as the orchestras in New York, Boston, Chicago, Cincinnati, Philadelphia, and Minneapolis.[28] Many observers would agree that his rendering of the modern French compositions represented the highlight of his years in St. Louis.

Golschmann also excelled at conducting Haydn and Mozart. A former member of the Symphony said that some of the Mozart performances were the best interpretations of that composer done anywhere in the country.[29] He also loved to conduct Brahms, and as his experience in St. Louis increased, he included more works of American composers in his programs. Other composers who appeared in the St. Louis

repertoire with some frequency during the Golschmann years included Mendelssohn, Tchaikovsky, Prokofiev, and Shostakovich. And, as noted, Golschmann favored the works of many less famous contemporary composers, including the Polish composer Alexander Tansman, whom Golschmann befriended during his years in Paris.

It is generally agreed that Golschmann did not particularly enjoy conducting the works of Beethoven and Wagner. Especially the latter, even though Lauritz Melchior once commented that Golschmann was one of the five great Wagnerian conductors in the world. [30] He did not generally excel at conducting operatic scores, and to say that he disliked appearing with singers is an understatement. Many observers use the word "hate" when they describe Golschmann's opinion of most of the singers with whom he conducted. Perhaps this is because many singers do not follow the conductor closely, and tend to feel a kind of "separateness" from the orchestra. Once a Swedish Wagnerian singer from the Metropolitan Opera, at the conclusion of her performance, approached Golschmann and lifted him off the podium when he refused to take a bow with her. He didn't like her anyway, and her attempt to irritate the conductor greatly succeeded. [31]

In 1949 a national magazine asked Golschmann for his opinion of ten musical selections he would choose for a beginning record library. He named Bach's *Suite in B Minor*, Mozart's *Symphony No. 40*, Beethoven's *Symphony No. 3*, Berlioz' *Symphonie Fantastique*, Schubert's *Symphony No. 7*, Brahm's *Symphony No. 4*, *Pictures at an Exhibition* by Moussorgsky-Ravel, Debussy's *Nocturnes*, Suite No. 2 from *Daphnis and Chloe* by Ravel, and Stravinsky's *Le Sacre du printemps*. [32] In his choices he reflected some of the composers whose works he most liked to conduct.

If one word can be used to describe the effects of Vladimir Golschmann's conducting on the St. Louis Symphony Orchestra during most of his tenure between 1931 and 1958 it might be "refinement," or perhaps "finish." Leonard Bernstein said that he chose the St. Louis orchestra to record his *Jeremiah Symphony* in 1947 because it had a certain "finish." [33] The St. Louis music critic Thomas

Vladimir Golschmann traveled the world in fulfilling his guest conducting assignments. (St. Louis Symphony)

Golschmann received the honorary degree of Doctor of Music from the University of Missouri in 1954. (St. Louis Symphony)

A broken foot was no reason for Golschmann to interrupt his busy schedule. (St. Louis Symphony)

The Maestro and some of his musicians. Left to right: Salvatore Campione (double bass), Victor Hugo (viola), Elmer Gesner (percussion), Golschmann, Karl Auer (double bass), Joseph Carione (trumpet and cornet), Clarence Gesner (clarinet), Carlos Camacho (clarinet), and Max Steindel (cello). Picture was taken about 1950. (St. Louis Symphony)

Sherman wrote, "Golschmann has special qualities of refinement and plasticity. He has a better ear for tone quality than for precision...." [34] One veteran member of the orchestra said that Golschmann was the most talented and the most sensitive of the conductors under whom he played. [35] Golschmann carefully chose his principal players, because they had to know what the conductor meant by his movements and nuances. He made technical mistakes because he geared his conducting to the reactions he received during the performances from the audience. [36] In other words, we might describe Golschmann as a very "impressionistic" conductor; he tried to grasp just what the composer of a particular piece of music wanted to convey to the audience, and he based his performances on the mood and spirit of a given audience. Thus, no two performances were alike. The success of the concerts depended on the ability of the musicians to know almost instinctively what sounds and moods the conductor wanted conveyed to the audience.

During Golschmann's time as conductor of the St. Louis Symphony Orchestra he frequently served as guest conductor for the major American orchestras and those abroad. During his first year as permanent conductor of the St. Louis Symphony he conducted the New York Philharmonic, as a guest conductor temporarily substituting for Arturo Toscanini. One New York critic wrote of his "youthful enthusiasm that stirred the audience," and of his knowledge of "how orchestral effects are obtained." [37] Another wrote of his "well-placed emphases" and his "brilliant" style.[38] Of Golschmann's guest-conducting of the Philadelphia Orchestra in 1935, substituting for Leopold Stokowski, a critic wrote,

> Mr. Golschmann has a modest, engaging manner and an imaginative and frequently individual approach to the compositions. His conductorial technique is hardly above average, nor is he free from mannerisms, but he was generally able to make himself understood, and the orchestra, in turn, played magnificently for him. [39]

The critics in Chicago also usually admired Golschmann's performances when he appeared in that city. After a concert that the visiting St. Louis Symphony played in 1937, one critic described his performance with the orchestra as "poetic, dramatic, exciting and thrilling." He also wrote, "The knowing audience made much of Golschmann, who...possesses elegance, verve, with restraint of manner and a sense of dramatic value which made itself felt but not ostentatiously visible." [43] Another critic wrote, "He has subtlety, keen insight and the ability to perceive the composer's structural intentions...What more can an interpreter do than this?" [44] And after a 1939 concert in Chicago, a reviewer wrote,

> Mr. Golschmann is no exponent of the dead pan school of conducting. He looks likable and approachable at all times, and the sincerity and intelligence indicated by his manner extend to his musical as well as his stage personality.
> Mr. Golschmann can turn a phrase in an intoxicating manner, can subtly intensify a quality of feeling by a slight change of pace, can give a passage a thrilling rhythmic urgency by a series of delicately handled accents. [45]

And of his performance in Philadelphia, another critic wrote, "The guest conductor showed himself to be a musician of unquestioned feeling, intelligence and sincerity, and with a very complete knowledge of the works which he interpreted." [40] Another wrote, "This keen, understanding musician indicated that he is able to accomplish many of the intricacies of the baton with the skill and capability that has marked his success in other cities." [41] Still another reviewer accurately described the Golschmann style, after the conductor appeared with the Philadelphia Orchestra in a 1954 summer concert, "Long admired by Dell audiences, Golschmann has always impressed as a captor of the nuance, a conductor ready to enhance a composer's melodic passages with a rich and penetrating translation." [42]

While many of Golschmann's observers noted his nuances and subtlety, still others remarked about his clarity and technical precision. After the conductor's guest appearance with the Musician's Symphony Orchestra in New York in 1933 Olin Downes wrote, "Mr. Golschmann quickly showed what a conductor who has real technical knowledge, an exceptionally clean beat, and the nature of a sensitive and enthusiastic musician can accomplish with imperfect material." [46] And on the occasion of the St. Louis Symphony's first appearance at Carnegie Hall, in 1950, a Boston reviewer wrote of the conductor, "Mr. Golschmann's style is straightforward to a degree; his signals are always clear, his ideas lucid rather than emotional, his interpretative bent orderly and disciplined rather than informed with fervor or heat." [47]

Naturally, Golschmann relished such compliments, especially from critics in cities of some of America's major orchestras. As noted, Golschmann travelled throughout the United States and the rest of the world to fulfill his guest conducting engagements. His appearances at a series of concerts in Caracas, Venezuela in 1951 attracted the largest crowds ever assembled in that city for such events. [48] And the compliments which the reviewers wrote of him when he went on these excursions also brought indirect attention to the St. Louis Symphony. Of a request from Israel that he appear as guest conductor in that country, he wrote, "I will gladly do it because I believe that this invitation is not only a compliment to me but to our orchestra and to our entire organization." [49]

As an example of the strenuous travel activities which Golschmann undertook during most of his tenure with the St. Louis Symphony, we may observe that during May and June 1956 he appeared in Spain and Paris with the National Orchestra of Madrid. In July he conducted the Lewisohn Stadium concerts in New York. October of that year saw him with the Paris Conservatory Orchestra and the Brussels Philharmonic. In November he conducted the Colonne Orchestra in Paris, and after that he appeared with the Boston Symphony in Baltimore. Then in mid-December it was time to conduct the St.

Louis Symphony. It seems as though he thrived on such activity, and, as usual, the reviewers rewarded him with laudatory notices. After an appearance with the National Orchestra of Madrid in 1954 a Spanish critic wrote of him, "He has conquered our public and he leaves us in a triumphant blaze of glory." [50]

Thus, Vladimir Golschmann, while conductor of the St. Louis Symphony Orchestra from 1931 until 1958, enjoyed the praise and esteem of music lovers in the United States and abroad. Those who appreciated his efforts bestowed many awards and honors on him. [51] And people justifiably admired him for characteristics not related to the world of music. The author Hope Stoddard expressed the sentiments of many when she wrote of him, "Certainly, though a member of a calling particularly conducive to one-sidedness, he has retained balance, breadth of outlook, a sense of humor, and an ever fresh taste for life." [52] Vladimir Golschmann's name is, of course, associated with the St. Louis Symphony Orchestra. Now we may examine the activities of the orchestra which shared in the praise of its conductor.

CHAPTER III

ST. LOUIS
AND ITS SYMPHONY
DURING
THE
GOLSCHMANN
YEARS

When Vladimir Golschmann joined the St. Louis Symphony on a permanent basis for the beginning of the 1931-1932 season, he joined an orchestra of seventy-eight regular players. On the occasion of the first rehearsal for that season, the orchestra's manager, Arthur J. Gaines, said to the musicians,

> This year we are starting out with clean pages. What is to be written on them during the ensuing season is up to you. I will be satisfied with writing nothing less than that the St. Louis Symphony is the best orchestra in this country. [1]

Many St. Louis music lovers shared the manager's optimism about the future.

The new conductor brought fourteen new musicians with him in 1931, including a new concertmaster, Scipione Guidi. [2] The new concertmaster also became the new assistant conductor. Guidi was, perhaps, the most distinguished concertmaster in America. He was born in Venice, Italy and studied at the Milan Conservatory. He established his own string quartet, and in 1921 went to New York as concertmaster for the Philharmonic. Guidi appeared as violin soloist with that orchestra on numerous occasions and brought into his repertoire practically every great work written for solo violin with orchestral accompaniment. Shortly after his arrival in St. Louis, Guidi said,

The task which Conductor Golschmann and I have to face, in view of the Symphony Society's determination to build up one of America's greatest orchestras here, is to create through personnel and training a permanent ensemble of the highest rank.

It is not enough, I understand, that the orchestra's program be interesting and well presented, but there must be a building for the future. [3]

The music critics of three of the major local newspapers joined in the optimistic atmosphere of the new season. The opening program offered Weber's Overture to *Der Freischütz*, Brahms's *Symphony No. 2*, Richard Strauss's *Tod und Verklärung*, and Rimsky-Korsakoff's *Russian Easter Overture*. Hume Duval of the *St. Louis Globe-Democrat* called the first concert "a gala program masterfully conducted and admirably played." He continued,

> It was apparent to every listener that a great change has come over the St. Louis Symphony. The improvement is sufficiently great to satisfy the most critical observer....The orchestra has in Vladimir Golschmann a conductor who is capable of bringing out the best there is in the musicians, and in Scipione Guidi a concertmaster who is an inspiration to each of his fellow members. [4]

Oscar Condon of the *St. Louis Times* wrote,

> We record with a deep sense of satisfaction, the auspicious launching of the fifty-second season of the St. Louis Symphony Orchestra at the Odeon yesterday afternoon. The stage in festal attire, decked with shrubs and greenery, the occasion differed in several respects from the inaugurals of past seasons. First there seemed more feeling of security as to the orchestra's future, in knowledge that it is again to be guided by a permanent conductor along a charted course, bound for a definite goal.

Arthur Gaines was the Symphony's manager when Vladimir Golschmann arrived in St. Louis in 1931. (St. Louis Symphony)

Scipione Guidi joined the orchestra as concertmaster in 1931, the same year that Vladimir Golschmann became permanent conductor. (Missouri Historical Society)

Cellist Max Steindel was one of the most prominent members of the orchestra; he was a member for over forty years. (Missouri Historical Society)

Secondly, we heard an orchestra far superior to that of last season, and furthermore, the opening was attended by the largest afternoon subscription audience in the history of the organization....

Golschmann scored a triumph for his initial effort in his new appointment and was recalled many times by the enthusiastic audience. Concertmaster Guidi was an inspiration to the men and the beautiful tone he drew from his priceless instrument heard in isolated solo passages, was that of a master. [5]

And Thomas Sherman of the *St. Louis Post-Dispatch* wrote, "Under the direction of Vladimir Golschmann...the improved virtuosity of the orchestra soon became apparent. The playing was livelier, smarter and more resilient..." [6]

The Symphony played eighteen pairs of subscription concerts that season, on Friday afternoons and Saturday evenings. Later during the Golschmann period the orchestra played Thursday evening and Sunday afternoon concerts. Some of the world's outstanding soloists appeared with the orchestra during Golschmann's premier season, including pianists Myra Hess, Ossip Gabrilowitsch, Edgar Shelton, and Vladimir Horowitz. Violinists Albert Spalding, Adolf Busch, and Samuel Dushkin appeared, and Jeannette Vreeland, John Charles Thomas, Paul Althouse, and Friedrich Schorr sang with the orchestra. [7] Two of the orchestra's own members appeared in solo roles during that season--Scipione Guidi and the principal cellist during much of the Golschmann era, Max Steindel. In addition to being in the cello section of the orchestra, Steindel also served as personnel manager during the entire Golschmann period. He came from a very musical family in Germany, and was a genuine favorite among the St. Louis music patrons. Other members of the orchestra who served with him remember him as a brilliant musician and a perfect gentleman.

Golschmann's first season with the symphony was an auspicious one, and as one critic wrote at its conclusion,

> Mr. Golschmann leaves his audience and his orchestra in better shape than it has ever been. The audience is larger and, on the whole, more responsive and more sensitive musically. And Mr. Golschmann bears the unmistakable stamp of its approval. [8]

Surely one of the marks of an important orchestra is the degree to which it involves itself in the life of its community. It must participate in community events and share with other cultural institutions in the quest to improve the quality of life in its area. The Golschmann period was a time when the St. Louis Symphony accomplished these goals.

In 1932 the Symphony performed at the Washington University Field House in a special concert with a University choral group in celebration of the bicentennial of George Washington's birth and the seventy-fifth anniversary of the founding of Washington University. The next year the orchestra presented a "promenade" concert at the National Flower and Garden show at the St. Louis Arena. The audience strolled among flowers and splashing fountains as the musicians rendered a variety of popular pieces. Eleven thousand people attended the "Good Neighbor Concert" at the Convention Hall of Kiel Auditorium in 1937, as the General Motors Concert Company sponsored a special program for people in the St. Louis area who had contributed to the cause of music in the community. Singers Grace Moore and Richard Tauber appeared on the program, and Milton Cross announced the activities to a national radio audience.

The Symphony helped launch the annual United Charities campaign in 1939 with a special "Religious Mobilization for Charity" concert. A choir of four hundred voices from various local churches and temples participated. During World War II the orchestra participated in a number of patriotic concerts sponsored by various governmental and charitable organizations such as the Navy and the USO. One such concert in 1942, which one thousand sailors attended, included prayers for victory and peace by Protestant, Catholic, and Jewish clergy. In 1943 the orchestra presented a special concert commemorating the tenth anniversary of the establishment of diplomatic relations between the United States and the Soviet Union. The musicians played works by Russian and American composers,

During World War II Golschmann took the orchestra to Fort Leonard Wood for performances. These pictures show the orchestra in rehearsal and part of the attentive audience during the 1942-1943 season. (St. Louis Symphony)

and the audience stood for the playing of the "National Anthem" and the *"Internationale."* And Metropolitan Opera tenor Giuseppe di Stefano sang with the Symphony at a special 1949 concert in honor of the twenty-fifth anniversary of the founding of Fontbonne College.

The Symphony participated in an especially important event in 1951, when the United Nations sponsored a concert in commemoration of Human Rights Day. Various celebrities participated in the nationally broadcast event from Kiel Auditorium, including narration by Lynn Fontanne, Jose Ferrer, and Rex Harrison. Uta Graf, Elena Nikolaidi, Robert Rounseville, and William Warfield formed the quartet for the "Ode to Joy" section of Beethoven's *Symphony No. 9,* and the audience heard a recorded speech by Mrs. Franklin D. Roosevelt.

In an effort to bring good music into St. Louis industrial plants and business places, the orchestra offered, in 1954, a series of concerts at such places as the Edison Brothers Stores office in downtown St. Louis at the noon hour. Employees of various businesses listened to the music as they ate lunch. The year 1956 saw the Symphony perform at the Mid-America Jubilee on the St. Louis riverfront, under the direction of Edwin McArthur, the musical director of the Municipal Opera. And during the same year the orchestra offered a special concert sponsored by the Central Trades and Labor Unions

of St. Louis, which presented the International Ladies Garment Workers mixed chorus.

By appearing on radio and television an orchestra can gain further recognition, and thereby bring good music to people who might not otherwise be able to attend concerts. The St. Louis Symphony appeared on radio before the Golschmann era began, but during his tenure this practice continued and served to increase the reputation of the orchestra. The Symphony made its first international radio broadcast in 1933, when people across the United States and Canada listened to a concert from the

(**Above**) Harry Farbman, the Symphony's concertmaster from 1942 to 1961. (St. Louis Symphony)

Four of the Symphony musicians in the early forties. Left to right: Concertmaster Harry Farbman, Irvin Rosen, Max Steindel, and Herbert Van den Burg.
(Missouri Historical Society)

Edward Murphy was a horn player in the Symphony almost continuously from 1930 to 1966. He also served as assistant conductor in the sixties. (St. Louis Symphony)

In addition to the regular subscription and special events concerts, the Symphony offered several popular concerts each season. Normally the assistant conductor presided over these "pop" concerts. With the commencement of the 1942-1943 season, the assistant conductor, and concertmaster, was Harry Farbman. He was born in Cincinnati and studied under the great violinist, Leopold Auer. Before joining the St. Louis Symphony, Farbman played with the Mutual Broadcasting Orchestra under Alfred Wallenstein, and was concertmaster of the National Symphony Orchestra in Washington, D. C. While playing with the St. Louis Symphony, he also headed the St. Louis String Quartet and the twenty-piece Farbman Sinfonietta, which appeared frequently on local television. He and his wife, the concert pianist Edith Schiller, frequently appeared together in St. Louis.

The popular concerts afforded an opportunity to attract people to symphony music who might not otherwise attend the more serious programs of the regular series. One patron, who attended one of the "pop" concerts, wrote to a local newspaper,

> I heard my first Symphony concert last night and it opened up a new world to me...I have no music background...but all my life I had an idea that Symphony concerts were a dull ordeal if you hadn't been educated up to them...It was one of the great experiences of my life. I heard things in that music that I had never heard in any other music. [9]

Not all patrons reacted so enthusiastically. When the Symphony proposed a series of "pop" concerts in 1937 at which beer would be served, someone drew up a resolution of protest "in the interest of our youth" and "all music lovers who wish to enjoy the symphony orchestra without the degrading association of beer." [10] But generally, the popular concerts were well-received. A 1942 "pop" concert drew the largest audience in the history of Kiel Auditorium up to that time with an all-Tchaikovsky program. At one such concert in 1956, the audience saw the world

Odeon Theater. And during the 1934-1935 season the orchestra played a series of Monday evening concerts over the NBC radio network. The same network chose the St. Louis Symphony to appear on its "Orchestras of the Nation" series in 1946. This involved two Saturday afternoon concerts of one hour's duration in a series featuring America's best orchestras. For the first of the concerts the musicians played Couperin's Overture and Allegro from *La Sultane*, Schoenberg's *Verklärte Nacht*, and Tchaikovsky's *Francesca da Rimini*.

The Symphony was one of the first major orchestras in the United States to appear on television. In 1949 the orchestra presented, in a locally televised concert, Vitale's *Chaconne*, Brahms's *Symphony No. 1*, and excerpts from Schubert's *Rosamunde*. Golschmann's last regular appearance with the Symphony, in 1958, was also televised locally.

Members of the orchestra perform under the direction of William Heyne in a Bach Festival Concert.
(Ernst C. Krohn Special Collections, Gaylord Music Library, Washington University, St. Louis, Missouri)

première of a movie entitled *Mike*, the story of the experiences of a Laborador retriever. Edgar M. Queeny, the chairman of the board of Monsanto Chemical Company photographed and produced the film and the orchestra played the musical accompaniment. And in what surely was one of the most unusual displays of special effects for a concert, the professional bowler Don Carter rolled a bowling ball across the stage in front of the musicians during a 1955 popular concert in order to imitate the sound of dwarfs playing ninepins in Ferde Grofé's *Hudson River Suite*.

In addition to these novelties, the management of the Symphony occasionally asked the patrons to make suggestions for future programs. In 1933, the management submitted a list of twenty symphonies, sixteen overtures, and forty-five miscellaneous pieces from the orchestras repertoire of the previous two seasons for consideration. The patrons chose works by Ravel, Franck, Wagner, and Beethoven.

In 1933 the Symphony provided the music for dance concerts of the Ballet Russe de Monte Carlo. It was the first time that the ballet company appeared in America with the full complement of a major symphony orchestra. The company appeared many times afterward with the Symphony. In the 1940s the Symphony Society sponsored appearances in St. Louis of the Metropolitan Opera of New York. The

Symphony did not participate in performances, but guaranteed the company financially for each appearance. The Metropolitan included St. Louis on its spring tours annually until the early sixties.

The Symphony organized its own chorus (appropriately, since the organization began as a choral society) in 1934, under the direction of William B. Heyne. In that year the St. Louis Symphony Chorus began singing two pairs of concerts with the orchestra each season. The two hundred-voice chorus served without pay, but the Symphony Society disbanded the chorus in 1938 due to the cost factor. (Happily, the orchestra has recently revived the practice of using its own chorus.) In 1938 the management decided that the music patrons preferred straight orchestral works. But in 1951 the orchestra joined forces with the Bach Choir, also under the direction of William B. Heyne, for the performance of a pair of Bach concerts.[11] This began a tradition of cooperation between the Symphony and the Bach Society which has produced many fine choral concerts.

As previously noted, one of the most important traditions that began before Vladimir Golschmann arrived on the scene was the orchestra's performance of student concerts. During the Golschmann period the tradition continued. Occasionally, private citizens sponsored student attendance at the regular

Views of the Opera House of Kiel Auditorium during a student concert in the 1944-1945 season.
(Above photo courtesy Charles Trefts Photograph Collection, State Historical Society of Missouri;
photo below courtesy St. Louis Symphony)

concerts by paying for a block of seats to be used by interested students from local schools. After one such act of generosity by a St. Louis businessman, a student wrote to the Symphony Society,

> I hope that you will thank the person, who so generously donated these tickets, for us. We take every opportunity we can to hear good music, and attending concerts of the St. Louis Symphony is always a thrill for us. [12]

Usually the Symphony journeyed to city high schools for about three concerts for high school students each season. The St. Louis Board of Education sponsored these. And normally the orchestra played at the symphony hall in a few concerts for elementary and high school students each season. The Women's Committee sponsored the concerts at the hall. Usually Golschmann conducted the high school concerts and the assistant conductor handled the elementary school performances. At one such grade school concert in 1953 which Harry Farbman conducted, the program consisted of Weber's Overture to *Oberon*, Schumann's *Traumerei*, a passage from Mendelssohn's *A Midsummer Night's Dream*, the allegretto from Shostakovich's *Symphony No. 5*, and the "Hoe Down" section from Copland's *Rodeo*. And during the same year Golschmann conducted the orchestra in a high school program of the first movement of Haydn's *Concerto in D* (with the orchestra's Dodia Feldin as the cello soloist), Weber's Overture to *Der Freischütz*, the third and fourth movements of Brahms's *Symphony No. 4*, a passage from Debussy's *Children's Corner* suite, and Rimsky-Korsakoff's *Capriccio Espagnol*. In a 1955 student concert, 8-year-old Trudi Buxton was piano soloist, the youngest artist ever to perform

Maestro Golschmann signing autographs after a student concert. (St. Louis Symphony)

with the orchestra.

It is a matter of opinion whether or not Golschmann really liked conducting the student concerts. The students were usually restless during the last piece on the program, and one year Golschmann abolished the paper programs to eliminate the rustling noises from the audience. But most observers agree that the conductor handled the concerts well. During one such concert, one of the first violinists let loose of his bow, and it flew under the skirt of one of the supervising nuns in the audience. The musician went down to the audience to retrieve his bow, and the orchestra continued to play through the entire incident.

The Superintendent of Instruction for the St. Louis public schools summed up the significance of the student concerts when he said,

These musical programs have given much satisfaction to those who had the privilege of hearing them. Through them, the orchestra also has contribu-

ted definitely to musical interest in the high schools and has helped materially to elevate the student body standards of musical appreciation. It not only helps the schools in their enlistment of community support, but...we are warranted in believing that a deeper public interest in that type of music will become increasingly characteristic of the people of our community. [13]

The Symphony not only elevated the musical education of the area elementary and high schools students, but offered splendid ticket prices to students for the regular subscription series.

Soldan High School student Harold Zabrack was the soloist during one of the orchestra's student concerts in 1944. (St. Louis Symphony)

Beginning with the 1934-1935 season, the Symphony occupied Kiel Auditorium. The orchestra left the Odeon Theater due to its small size, and because of complaints that it was becoming a "firetrap." The new city-owned Municipal Auditorium, named for former mayor Henry W. Kiel, appeared to be just what the Symphony needed, even though it was not owned by the orchestra, requiring the Symphony Society to pay rent. The orchestra used the Opera House of the auditorium (it also contained an Exposition Hall and a Convention Hall), with a seating capacity of about 3,500. At first most observers thought that the acoustics would be at least satisfactory, but as time elapsed, many patrons noticed that there were several "dead" spots in the hall. The Symphony Society found at least a temporary solution to the problem when the conductor Leopold Stokowski designed a special shell for the stage area of the Opera House in 1936. But many people continued to complain in later years about the poor acoustics, the large capacity of the hall (sell-out crowds were unusual in such a large hall), [14] and the inavailability of the auditorium for rehearsals. Toward the end of the Golschmann period, the lack of adequate parking space and the distance from many of the patrons' homes created problems.[15] Many complained of the sounds of boxing matches, basketball games, and other events elsewhere in Kiel while trying to listen to symphonic music in the Opera House.

Dedication ceremonies of the new Kiel Auditorium, which served as the permanent home of the Symphony from 1934 to 1968. (Photo courtesy Harry M. Hagen)

One of the most interesting aspects of the history of the St. Louis Symphony Orchestra deals with its activities away from its St. Louis home. As noted, the orchestra started touring well before the 1930s, but during the Golschmann period it reached new heights in this field. Usually, the orchestra embarked on two or even three tours each season, and the musicians usually enjoyed the experiences. Many of them say that they gave some of their best performances on the tours due to the fact that they played many of the same pieces repeatedly on a given tour. The orchestra traveled to all parts of the United States except the Far West during those years, with special emphasis on the Midwest and South. And, with the exception of part of the World War II period, when the orchestra curtailed or halted its touring activities, the musicians set out aboard train cars, and later buses, for several weeks to bring good music to many cities which did not have permanent orchestras.[16] As a typical example of the kinds of places to which the musicians traveled, the 1956-1957 season saw the Symphony visit Decatur, Illinois; Columbia, Missouri; Louisville, Kentucky; Charleston, Huntington, and Lynchburg, West Virginia; Bristol, Tennessee; Pensacola, Florida; the Texas cities of Houston, Dallas and Fort Worth; Fayetteville and Hot Springs, Arkansas; Jackson and Greenville, Mississippi; and Baton Rouge, Louisiana.

Perhaps the most important of the tours was the one in 1950 to Boston, New York, and Washington, D. C. The orchestra had never visited those cities before, and Golschmann had said that he would never take the orchestra to New York until he was confident that it could give an excellent performance. That tour was a great success. The three leading music critics of Boston gave fine reviews after the performance, and one wrote, "On the whole this was a most agreeable afternoon and the people of St. Louis are to be congratulated on their orchestra and its dynamic leader."[17]

At Carnegie Hall in New York the orchestra played Manuel Rosenthal's *Magic Manhattan*, Couperin's *Overture and Allegro*, as orchestrated by Darius Milhaud, Schoenberg's *Verklärte Nacht*, Dances from de Falla's *The Three-Cornered Hat*, and Mozart's *Symphony No. 40*. Of the performances, Olin Downes of the *New York Times* wrote,

> The St. Louis Symphony Orchestra, Vladimir Golschmann conductor, gave a concert tonight in Carnegie Hall, playing a curiously assorted program, playing it with such liveliness and musicianship that it fascinated an audience which packed the hall, from start to finish.
>
> There are orchestras more extensively financed than this one, which have more first-class virtuoso players. But most of the firsts of the St. Louis orchestra appear to be players of exceptional capacity, who never play in a merely routine manner and who are obviously drilled in a most painstaking manner by Mr. Golschmann. It is a very efficient ensemble...In the sum of it, the tone is warm and lyrical; the strings do not merely execute, they sing; the articulation and phrasing have distinction.[18]

As *Time* magazine wrote of the occasion,

> Even the Manhattan critics conceded that the sensitivity and sonority of St. Louis' band measured up mighty close with the East's big three; the Boston, the Philadelphia and the New York Philharmonic-Symphony.[19]

The presence at the concert in Washington, D. C. of many political celebrities added to the excitement of the occasion. President and Mrs. Truman, Missouri Senators Kem and Donnell and their wives, General Harry Vaughan, the presidential advisor, presidential press secretary Charles Ross, and several ambassadors and cabinet members attended the performance. The orchestra played the ballet suite from *Cephale and Procris* by Grétry, as orchestrated by Felix Mottl, Rachmaninoff's *Symphony No. 2*, Vitali's *Chaconne*, Debussy's *Prelude to* the *Afternoon of a Faun*, "The Walk to the Paradise Garden" from Delius' *A Village Romeo and Juliet*, and the Dances from *The Three-Cornered Hat* by de Falla. Reviews in Washington were also favorable.

The tours usually gratified the musicians. The audiences in the many college towns which the orchestra visited appreciated their work, and the musicians performed in a more relaxed and informal manner than they did in the concert hall at home. Sometimes conditions on the tours were not the most physically comfortable, as when the orchestra encountered an occasional blizzard. But it was during times like that when the musicians especially appreciated the talents of the management at planning properly and getting everything to move smoothly. Probably the hardest-working member of the orchestra on the tours (and at other times as well) was the man who served as the librarian during the entire time when Golschmann was conductor-- Elmer Gesner. He frequently spent nearly every waking moment organizing the scores and making sure that everything was in order for the concerts, at home and on the road. And while he was the librarian, he also served as the principal percussionist in the orchestra. [20] The whole orchestra appreciated his constant energy and thoughtfulness.

Some rather strange things happened on the tours. [21] At one town, due to confusion in scheduling, no audience appeared for the concert. At another, the committee which had arranged for the orchestra to play told the management that there was no money to pay the musicians. They played as scheduled. Frequently, various tardy musicians leaped to the platform of the moving train in order to join their colleagues for the ride to the next town. A member of the cello section, Gustaf Keller, carried a rope with him on tour and tied it to his hotel bed. He then hanged the other end out of the hotel window so that he would have an easy means of escape in case of fire in the night. [22]

The conductor usually enjoyed the tours as much as the players. But he sometimes tired of the monotony and lack of excitement in some of the small towns. [23] He occasionally displayed some anger over

Violist Herbert Van den Burg on tour with the Symphony. (St. Louis Symphony)

Cellist Max Steindel and percussionist Elmer Gesner on one of the Symphony's many tours. (St. Louis Symphony)

Some of the female members of the orchestra during the early fifties. Left to right: Leah Krolick (violin), June Rotenberg (double bass), Lucy Baicher (violin), and Gertrude Buttrey (viola). (St. Louis Symphony)

45

incidents that occurred on tour. Once when the announcer of a program told an intermission audience how wonderful the next orchestra to appear in the town would be, Golschmann raced through the second half of the program in about half its normal playing time. He did the same when another announcer in another town mispronounced his name. During a Southwestern tour Golschmann was to deliver a luncheon talk to a group of music patrons. The train arrived late and a group of flustered women met him and took him to the meeting where they constantly referred to him as "Dr. Goldman." He ignored the mistake in names, but after he talked to them about music, the chairwoman said to him, "Dr. Goldman, it is indeed surprising to hear a scientist so interested in the arts. But we are a trifle disappointed that you did not discuss the care of babies as you promised." The real Dr. Goldman, a pediatrician, mistakenly went to the group of music lovers where he was called "Mr. Golschmann." [24]

Mrs. Herbert Van den Burg says goodbye to her husband and Edward Murphy. The orchestra gave some of its best performances while on tour. (Edward Murphy)

Members of the orchestra waiting to board a train for a tour. At left are Max Steindel (cello) and Joseph Carione (trumpet). Carlos Camacho is in the middle holding his clarinet case. (St. Louis Symphony)

The reviews that the critics gave the orchestra during the historic first trip to Boston, New York, and Washington, D. C., were typical of those they gave in other cities of the country. After a 1938 concert in Chicago, Herman Devries wrote,

> The St. Louisans, in their annual visit to Chicago have never failed to impress us as a body of fine players but at yesterday's concert it became evident that a complete change had taken place, so marked as to call forth the highest encomiums for an orchestra that now ranks with any of the finest in the world. [25]

And after a 1942 concert in Memphis, a reviewer commented on the importance of such events to that part of the country,

> Second only to the wide dissemination of symphonic interest through the radio, the Golschmann-St. Louis performances in Memphis have done more to make the Mid-South conscious of good orchestral music than all the other factors combined. They have rendered a signal service both to music and to us whose appreciation thereof has been enriched through their efforts. Tonight we shall therefore bid the maestro and his men a most fond and fervent farewell, hoping that time and circumstance shall speed the day of their return to the Memphis schedule. [26]

Vladimir Golschmann attending the celebration of the orchestra's recording at the German House in St. Louis in January of 1959. (St. Louis Symphony)

Some of the members of the string section hard at work during rehearsal. (St. Louis Symphony)

A celebration of the Symphony's recording with Columbia Records in 1957. The last three men on the right are Mayor Raymond R. Tucker, Vladimir Golschmann, and Mitch Miller (a Columbia executive). (St. Louis Symphony)

Dallas critics wrote of the Symphony, "As long as it plays as it does and what it does, the Symphony continues to give St. Louis cultural suzerainty in the whole Mississippi valley." [27] And, "The orchestra is a superb musical ensemble, easily a peer of the best in the country." [28] A Houston critic wrote in 1936, "Never have we experienced such a thrill as when we heard the St. Louis Symphony orchestra concert Monday evening." [29] Thus, the practice of touring the United States increased the reputation of the Symphony and brought good music to many American people.

Another indication of an orchestra's prominence is the frequency with which it makes recordings. It is somewhat of an honor for a major record company to invite an orchestra to participate in a series of recordings. This usually enhances the reputation of the orchestra and creates favorable publicity for the city in which the orchestra resides. The St. Louis Symphony made many records during the Golschmann period--with Columbia, Capitol, and RCA-Victor. [30] Some of the notable soloists who recorded with the Symphony were Leonard Pennario, Arthur Rubinstein, and Nathan Milstein. As noted, Leonard Bernstein chose the Symphony to record his *Jeremiah Symphony* in 1947, and Bernstein himself conducted. Of that recording, Thomas Sherman wrote, "On the whole the effect is impressive." [31] The orchestra in 1945 made the first long-playing record of Tchaikovsky's *Swan Lake.* Again, Sherman wrote of the recording, "The whole body of sound has vitality, all of the various choirs are well projected and the strings are particularly gracious." [32]

Several of the members of the orchestra during that time commented on the problems of making recordings. Edward Shalett, a violinist during the 1930s, said,

I had my most grueling experience of a lifetime when we made our records... the size of the orchestra made it necessary that we play on the concert stage, not in a sound-proof studio. It was necessary to make two unmarred recordings of everything we played. We had to play the Beethoven *Seventh Symphony*, which takes about fifty

minutes, six or seven times. Something would happen every time--a violinist accidentally would hit the stand with his bow or somebody would kick a stand. Then, on our best effort, the noon factory whistles blew and spoiled the recording. [33]

Golschmann frequently displayed much anger when a noise occurred during a recording session. On one occasion, after the orchestra played a certain piece about eight times because of a "ticking" sound, Golschmann discovered that the offending sound came from his own wristwatch, so he took the watch off and smashed it on the floor. [34]

Under the direction of Vladimir Golschmann the Symphony continued to attract the world's leading solo performers. It was one of the first orchestras in the United States to schedule Arthur Rubinstein, Robert Casadesus, Leonard Bernstein, Nathan Milstein, Isaac Stern, Helen Traubel, and other outstanding artists. The violinist Milstein was one of Golschmann's best personal friends, and starting with Golschmann's second season in St. Louis, he appeared with the orchestra on numerous occasions throughout the conductor's tenure. Milstein had the reputation of a good-natured complainer, and Golschmann and the musicians enjoyed his antics and good humor. Once during rehearsal with the orchestra he sat in the violin section without Golschmann's knowing about it. Everyone thought it was amusing when the conductor discovered the new addition to his orchestra. Some of the other violinists who appeared with the orchestra were Yehudi Menuhin, Fritz Kreisler (about whose performance of the Brahms concerto Thomas Sherman wrote, "It was a musical event of the first importance. It was also an artistic triumph for all the participants), [35] Jascha Heifetz, Isaac Stern, Samuel Dushkin, Mischa Elman, Zino Francescatti, Efrem Zimbalist, Ruggerio Ricci, and, as noted, Albert Spalding and Adolf Busch.

When Symphony patrons of those years talk about their memories of the soloists who particularly impressed them, they most often mention Sergei Rachmaninoff. He appeared with the orchestra throughout the 1930s, and his presentation of his *Rhapsody on a Theme of Paganini* in St. Louis was one of the first times he performed it in America. He was physically very striking, and he was as warm and human a man as he was a magnificent artist with the piano. Of a 1938 performance, Reed Hynds of the *St. Louis Star-Times* wrote,

> When the stiff, tall form of Sergei Rachmaninoff came onto the stage at Municipal Auditorium yesterday afternoon, the Symphony Orchestra concert audience knew at once that here was an occasion. The immense dignity of the man, his austerity and the world-weary look of his face, promised it. Applause beyond that of a perfunctory greeting rang out.
>
> He was in excellent form, sweeping up and down the piano with ease...and producing again that astonishing array of tonal color which has made his concerts special joys to the ear. [36]

During one concert with the Symphony, one of the musicians played the wrong note, and Rachmaninoff, rather than draw attention to the offending player, himself repeated the incorrect note at the piano. [37]

Arthur Rubinstein gave numerous recitals in St. Louis and appeared with the Symphony almost on an annual basis from 1937 to the end of the Golschmann period. Patrons remember his brilliant and theatrical performances with great admiration. They also remember the visits of Robert Casadesus (and his wife and son), Arthur Schnabel, Vladimir Horowitz, Rudolf Serkin, Myra Hess, Jose Iturbi, Eugene List, Paul Wittgenstein (who played Ravel's *Concerto for the Left Hand*, written especially for him), and two close personal friends of Golschmann's, Alexander Tansman and Darius Milhaud. [38] The appearance of these as well as other world-famous pianists gave the St. Louis audiences opportunities to hear some of the best musicians in the world.

Another of those who made frequent appearances with the orchestra was the cellist Gregor Piatigorsky. In 1955 he and Isaac Stern performed the Brahms *Double Concerto* with the Symphony. Of Piatigorsky's first appearance with the orchestra Thomas Sherman wrote, "It was one of those rare phenomena--a perfromance so satisfying that it was almost impossible to imagine it in another way." [39]

And, even though Golschmann did not particularly enjoy working with most singers, some of the greatest opera personalities appeared with the Symphony during his tenure. The long list includes Lotte Lehmann, Marguerite Piazza, Eleanor Steber,

Timpanist William Erlich was a member of the orchestra for over thirty years. (St. Louis Symphony)

Fritz Kreisler played the Brahms and Mendelssohn violin concertos with the Symphony during the thirties. (St. Louis Symphony)

Ezio Pinza, Lily Pons, Mario Lanza, Gladys Swarthout, Lawrence Tibbett, Lauritz Melchior, Jan Peerce, Beverly Sills, Leonard Warren, and two native St. Louisans, Marion Telva and Helen Traubel. While not as important a musical event as when those formerly mentioned sang, a 1949 appearance of Margaret Truman with the Symphony caused much publicity. She sang respectably, and Thomas Sherman commented after the performance,

> In sum, she sang agreeably and with taste. So far as stage presence is concerned, she has little to learn. She carried herself with poise, smiled enough but not too much and kept still while singing. The Symphony Orchestra also participated. [40]

During the times when Vladimir Golschmann conducted orchestras in other parts of the United States and the world, the Symphony Society hired various guest conductors to direct the orchestra. The guest-conducting duties included directing the orchestra at regular subscription concerts, "pop" concerts, and various other special concerts. Some of the conductors were Thomas Schippers, Jascha Horenstein, Georg Solti, Erich Leinsdorf, Charles Munch, Leopold Stokowski, Arthur Fiedler, Andre Kostelanetz, Fritz Reiner, and Sir Thomas Beecham. A number of outstanding musicians whose fame rested more with their composing than with their conducting also came to St. Louis to conduct the orchestra in renditions of their own works. Outstanding composer-conductors included George Gershwin, Virgil Thomson, Hector Villa-Lobos, Sergei Prokofiev, Sigmund Romberg, and Igor Stravinsky. [41]

Between 1931 and 1958 the orchestra presented the premier performance of many musical works, which enhanced the reputation of the orchestra and its conductor. Some of the performances were the first presentations of the works in the United States,

Arthur Rubinstein as he looked when he played the Mozart **Concerto No. 23** and Chopin **Concerto No. 2** with the orchestra in 1946. (Missouri Historical Society)

Yehudi Menuhin played the American première of the Robert Schumann "lost" violin concerto with the St. Louis Symphony in 1937. (St. Louis Symphony)

Concertmaster Harry Farbman, Golschmann, and principal cellist Edgar Lustgarten in the late forties. (St. Louis Symphony)

and others constituted world premières.[42] A number of works by recognized "masters" appeared on the programs, including the world première of Bach's *Partita in E minor* (as orchestrated by Claude Levy), and his *"Wachet Auf, Ruft Uns Die Stimme"* ("Sleepers, wake, a voice is calling") orchestrated by Amadeo de Filinni. The latter work was a chorale-prelude for the organ. Two American premières of works by Domenico Scarlatti appeared on the programs, including his *Toccata, Bourrée and Gigue* and *Concerto No. 5 in D minor for String Orchestra with Piano.*

In 1937 the orchestra and Yehudi Menuhin presented the American première of Robert Schumann's "lost" violin concerto (*Concerto in D minor*). The composer wrote the work in 1853, the year before he went insane. He gave the score to the violinist Joseph Joachim, who never played it and requested that its première be delayed until a century after Schumann's death, which would have been 1956. A German publisher found the score in the Berlin State Library and sent a copy to Menuhin. Joachim's son and Schumann's daughter agreed to permit Menuhin to play it. The world première of the work was to be played in London and the American première in St. Louis, but because of Adolf Hitler's intervention, the world première occurred in Berlin with Hitler in attendance and with Menuhin as soloist. Menuhin finally played the piece for the first time in America, with a piano accompaniment, in New York. But in St. Louis the violinist played the work with the orchestra. After all of the publicity and politics, the critics gave the work mediocre reviews, and what was to have been a major musical event turned out to be a good deal less than that. [43]

The orchestra presented, for the first time anywhere, Bela Bartók's *Mikrokosmos Suite* (arranged for orchestra by Tibor Serly) and the American première of Bartók's *Divertimento for String Orchestra*. It also presented the world première of *Five Preludes* by Dmitri Shostakovitch (as arranged for orchestra by Lan Adomian from Shostakovitch's *Twenty-four Preludes* for the piano). In 1956 the orchestra played American premières of Dmitri Kabalevsky's Suite from his opera *Colas*

Breugnon, and a work called *Rossiniana*, a suite freely transcribed from Rossini's *Les Riens* by Ottorino Respighi.

As previously noted, Vladimir Golschmann received much assistance early in his career from his Parisian sponsor, Albert Verley. Thus, under the direction of Golschmann, the orchestra presented world premières of some of Verley's compositions, including his *Cloches dan la vallée, Pastel Sonore,* and *Chanson Tourangelle.* Golschmann also presented world premières of works by his friend Darius Milhaud. The composer wrote his *Fanfare* especially for the sixtieth anniversary of the St. Louis Symphony, and the orchestra gave the première of the work in 1940. The orchestra also presented the world première of Milhaud's transcription and arrangement of Francois Couperin's *Overture and Allegro.* And the composer's *Concerto for Marimba and Vibraphone* received its première in St. Louis in 1949. This work was commissioned from Milhaud by a member of the orchestra's percussion section, Jack Conner. It was the first time that a major orchestra performed a work for those instruments at a subscription concert. Golschmann further demonstrated his love for modern French music by conducting for the first time in America the "Symphonic Suite" from the ballet *Phedre* by Georges Auric.

Golschmann's friend, Alexander Tansman, dedicated several of his works to the St. Louis Symphony and to its conductor. Some of these compositions, which the orchestra played for the first time anywhere, were Tansman's *Deux Moments Symphoniques*, his transcription of Bach's *Tocata in D minor*, his *Variations on a Theme of Frescobaldi*, and his *Ricercari.* Golschmann commissioned the last two works; the *Ricercari* for the seventieth anniversary of the orchestra.

As part of its sixtieth anniversary celebration, the Symphony offered a prize of one thousand dollars to an American whose symphonic composition was accepted by a panel of three judges including Golschmann, Rudolph Ganz, and Eugene Goossens. The panel chose Antoni van der Voort's *Sinfonietta*, and the orchestra played the work for the first time in 1940. [44]

Other American works that received their première in St. Louis include Morton Gould's *Anniversary Quadrille*, which the composer wrote especially for the seventy-fifth anniversary of the orchestra, and Erich Korngold's *Concerto in D Major for Violin and Orchestra.* Jascha Heifetz played the concerto at the 1947 première, and of the event Korngold said, "It is needless to say how delighted I am to have my concerto performed by Caruso and Paganini in one person: Jascha Heifetz." [45] One of Golschmann's best American friends from his early years in Paris was George Antheil. The composer dedicated several of his works to Golschmann, and the St. Louis Symphony played them for the first time. The orchestra gave the first playing of the Nocturne from *Decatur at Algiers* in 1944, and the waltzes from *Spectre De La Rose*, a concert version of waltzes from a movie which Antheil scored, in 1948. In 1950 the orchestra performed the world première of Antheil's *Tom Sawyer, A Mark Twain Overture*, which the composer dedicated to Golschmann and the Symphony on the seventieth anniversary of the orchestra.

Golschmann and the St. Louis Symphony also gave the first performance of several works by native St. Louisans Albert Stoessel and John Kessler. In 1938 they performed the Suite from the opera *Garrick* by Stoessel. Compositions by Kessler include his *Poems for Orchestra*, the *Two Symphonic Sketches: Avalon*, the *Introduction and Fugue*, and his *Soliloquy.*

Thus, through its many varied activities, the St. Louis Symphony Orchestra distinguished itself as one of America's major orchestras, and enriched the lives of many music lovers, both in St. Louis and in other parts of the United States.

During the Golschmann era the management of the St. Louis Symphony not only dealt with the task of assembling a group of fine musicians and planning significant programs, but also dealt with the serious problems of finance. [46] The Symphony never took in enough money through ticket sales, recording royalties, and similar sources to cover actual operating expenses for a given season. The Golschmann period occurred before the days of generous government and foundation grants. Therefore, as in the past, the Symphony relied on the generosity of private donors to continue its activities. As Vladimir Golschmann once said,

The answer to maximum effectiveness for the St. Louis orchestra rests in the drumming into people's minds that when they die, they must leave some of their money to us. After all, they can't take it with them, and--since they must leave it--where will they find a worthier object than the orchestra? [47]

The Symphony had an extremely modest endowment fund. By 1949 it consisted of only $20,000. In that year the Symphony received $85,000 from the estate of Mrs. Leticia Parker Williams, a former St. Louisan, and daughter of Mrs. George Parker, who had left the organization a substantial gift of money in 1916. [48] But usually the funds intended as an endowment fund went to pay the operating expenses of the orchestra at the end of the season, and the organization still faced a deficit. Periodic financial crises arose, and at various times the St. Louis community faced the prospect of not having an orchestra.

After the Symphony passed a particularly threatening financial crisis in 1933, Walter Damrosch, conductor of the Boston Symphony, said,

> I could not imagine the great city of St. Louis without a symphony orchestra...I was confident that no matter what else might be sacrificed because of economic conditions, St. Louis would not give up its splendid orchestra. [49]

In 1942 Thomas Sherman wrote,

> The symphony is in immediate danger of dying an inglorious death...If this civic disaster should occur, it will have more money to spend and fewer things to spend it for than at any time in the last 20 years. [50]

And in 1954 St. Louis Mayor Raymond R. Tucker said, "The loss of the St. Louis Symphony Orchestra would signify a kind of bankruptcy and decadence that this community cannot afford." [51]

The principal means of paying for the operations of

Walter Damrosch, former conductor of the Boston Symphony. (Missouri Historical Society)

the organization was the annual maintenance fund drive, wherein the Symphony Society staged a campaign to solicit contributions to pay the expenses of the next season. It was difficult to plan the events for the next season without having sufficient money in hand. In 1936 the goal of the drive was $135,000, of which the Society succeeded in raising $118,102. [52] In 1951 the goal was $175,000; [53] in 1954 $200,000; [54] and in 1958 $250,000. [55] The orchestra did not usually achieve the total goal, but enough money was always raised so that the Symphony could continue operations. Frequently some of the money raised for the coming season was used to pay the expenses of the current season.

Among the citizens of St. Louis who helped the Symphony surmount these many financial difficulties was Oscar Johnson, Jr., the heir to a shoe manufacturing fortune. Johnson frequently contributed enough money to carry the orchestra over

54

Assistant Conductor Edward Murphy at the podium sometime in the sixties. (Edward Murphy)

particularly severe crises. He served as president of the Symphony Society from the 1933-1934 season through the 1954-1955 season. [56] Only twenty-seven years of age when he assumed the duties of president of the Society, Johnson involved himself with every facet of the Symphony's affairs. Arthur Gaines said of him,

> Oscar Johnson is the first symphony president I have ever known who would go to all the concerts, to the rehearsals, to radio broadcasts and gramophone recordings, who would go on tour with the orchestra and get up at six in the morning to catch a day coach to the next town.
>
> The most important thing about him is that he has an honest, genuine, deep love of music. He didn't take the job for prominence or publicity, or anything else. It is that sincere love of the thing that makes his influence so important. [57]

Johnson faced great difficulties when he became president. The Great Depression inhibited monetary contributions, and the orchestra had a new conductor. The Board of Directors of the Society hesitated to pay great sums of money to attract the leading soloist performers, so Johnson gave his own money to maintain the high standards of the orchestra. [58] Without the unselfish contributions of Oscar Johnson, it is doubtful that the Symphony could have survived.

Of course, the success of a major orchestra depends on the tireless efforts of many individuals. Mrs. Max Goldstein assumed a prominent role in the fund-raising activities of the Symphony. The wife of a prominent St. Louis physician (and founder of the Central Institute for the Deaf), Mrs. Goldstein called on many individuals to give money during the annual maintenance drives. She and other women interested in the survival of the orchestra approached local businessmen and pleaded with them to support the cause of music in St. Louis. Known as the "Mother of the Symphony," Mrs. Goldstein was a very charming and unassuming lady, and she served on the Board of

The orchestra and conductor just after the United States entered World War II. The banner in the background indicates the number of orchestra members who were serving in the armed forces. (Charles Trefts Photograph Collection, State Historical Society of Missouri)

Directors of the Symphony Society for sixty years beginning in 1903, including the entire Golschmann era.

Spokesmen for the Symphony turned to every available source for funds. In an effort to persuade the business community of St. Louis to give more money to the orchestra, Vladimir Golschmann told a Chamber of Commerce luncheon in 1941,

> In the city or around it, I have seen many signs welcoming visitors praising the many attractions they would find here, but never a mention of the St. Louis Symphony Orchestra. At the airport, visitors can read about Muny Opera, the factories, the old houses, the Museum, the park, et cetera....but what about the Symphony? Why have we been forgotten?
>
> All the members of our orchestra show a lot of interest in you. They patronize your stores, your offices and your banks. What about some reciprocity on your part? I know the answer some of you will give, "My wife goes to the Symphony." I am not talking about your wife. I am talking about you. [59]

The conductor himself made contributions to the maintenance fund campaign, [60] and musicians in the orchestra sometimes took pay cuts in order to insure the continuation of the organization. [61]

The Symphony Society sponsored various kinds of fund-raising events. One such event in 1950 involved a fashion show at Kiel Auditorium at which patrons paid from $7.50 to $100 per ticket to see fashion creations modeled by debutantes and professional models. The orchestra played under the direction of Golschmann and Farbman as the models walked across the stage, and the conductor's wife, Odette, narrated part of the show. Another event which benefited the maintenance fund was a special concert by the Symphony in 1953 under the direction of Richard Rodgers. A chorus of thirty singers from the Municipal Opera joined in the program, along with soloists Marguerite Piazza, Claramae Turner, Thomas Hayward, and Robert Weede. The audience, in the Convention Hall of Kiel Auditorium, numbering 10,571, was the largest ever assembled indoors in St. Louis for an orchestral event. [62] Rodgers contributed his services. Other musical personalities also made contributions. In 1954 Helen Traubel donated the proceeds of one of her nightclub appearances at the Hotel Chase to the maintenance fund. And Charles Goren appeared in 1958 for a series of lectures on playing bridge. This was sponsored by Famous-Barr Company, the Women's Association of the Symphony Society, and the *St. Louis Globe-Democrat.*

Despite these various sources of revenue, the orchestra still needed more money to overcome the expense of producing serious music. [63] Interested observers throughout the Golschmann period suggested new tax sources. The most serious proposal reached a climax in 1949 when the city administration drafted a property tax bill for submission to the Missouri legislature. The one-cent increase in taxes would have been used to support the Symphony and other musical events. This would have been similar to the tax used for the support of the city's art museum, zoo, and library system. But the proposal did not reach fruition. A form of city tax aid went to the orchestra for a time, beginning with the 1940s, when the city reduced the rent charged the Symphony for its use of Kiel Auditorium. In return, the orchestra performed four free public concerts per season. [64]

In addition, the Symphony organized annual season ticket drives. During a given campaign, hundreds of women spread the news about the benefits of season tickets. Frequently the drives were made more interesting by offers of a free season ticket to the person who succeeded in selling a given number of season tickets during the campaign period. During the 1954 season ticket drive Mayor Tucker stated, "The price of season tickets is a small investment in our City, in good music and personal enjoyment. Your purchase of season tickets now will help to insure the future of the Symphony." [65]

When Vladimir Golschmann assumed his position there were seventy-eight players in the orchestra, rising to eighty-four in his last season. Throughout his tenure the number of musicians fluctuated from season to season, sometimes increasing by several above eighty-four, and sometimes dropping by a few below seventy-eight. The number of musicians that the Symphony hired for a season depended on the amount of money it could acquire through the means previously outlined. This rather unstable condition, plus other factors such as low pay, lack of an adequate pension fund, [66] and a rather short season (usually between twenty and twenty-three weeks), caused a number of good musicians to seek positions with other orchestras. [67] St. Louis was like a "farm team" to the orchestras of Cleveland, New York, Boston, and Philadelphia. George Szell, conductor of the Cleveland Orchestra, frequently asked his musicians at their first rehearsal of the season, "Well, how did we rob St. Louis this season?" [68] The improvement of these conditions would have made for a better orchestra, but the solutions to the problems came during more recent years.

In the spring of 1955 the Board of Directors of the Symphony decided that the following season was to be the last in which Vladimir Golschmann would be the permanent conductor of the orchestra. They thought it appropriate that after twenty-five years as conductor Golschmann should become conductor emeritus, and that several guest conductors should share the duties with him during the 1956-1957 season, whereupon a new permanent conductor would take over the following season. As events developed, Golschmann stayed as conductor emeritus through the 1957-1958 season because it took longer than expected to find a new permanent man. Apparently a number of the members of the Board believed that Golschmann had simply been with the orchestra too long. They believed that he had fallen into a pattern of complacency and was accepting less quality music from the orchestra due to his distress over the fact that the orchestra was under-financed and that musicians were going to other cities. [69]

And Golschmann himself was tired of coping with the many administrative duties which the permanent conductor of a major orchestra must constantly face. He was discouraged by the lack of first-rate musicians available to the orchestra. During his last season he said,

> It is impossible to maintain the first-rate standing of this orchestra with the loss in the past three years of about forty per cent of the personnel. The time has come to let someone else assume the musical responsibilities of the St. Louis Symphony.

To all my friends in the audience, to my friends in the orchestra, to all those who have made these years happy ones for my wife and me, I want to express my deepest gratitude. [70]

The St. Louis Symphony played its last concert with Vladimir Golschmann as music director on Easter Sunday, April 6, 1958. An audience of 2,500 patrons watched Golschmann direct the orchestra in Paul Ben-Haim's *Fanfare to Israel*, Kabalevsky's *Symphony No. 2*, Mozart's *Symphony No. 40*, Satie's *Deux Gymnopedies*, and Ravel's *La Valse*. At the conclusion of this locally televised concert, Golschmann said to the audience, "We're a little short on music, so we're going to give the first bonus in twenty-seven years, the Polka and Fugue from *Schwanda* by Weinberger." [71] After the encore, the members of the orchestra who were with Golschmann during his entire tenure in St. Louis joined him on stage to acknowledge the applause of the audience. Later backstage, many of the musicians had tears in their eyes. The conductor said, "I cannot leave St. Louis altogether because St. Louis is a big part of my life." [72] He returned to St. Louis to guest-conduct the Symphony on several occasions

A capacity audience filled the Kiel Auditorium Opera House in 1945. (Charles Trefts Photograph Collection, State Historical Society of Missouri)

Maestro Golschmann chatting with Morton D. May, a vice president of the Symphony Society, in the fifties. (St. Louis Symphony)

after 1958, but the Golschmann era in the story of the orchestra was a part of history.

Mention has been made of the improvement in the quality of the Symphony after Golschmann took control. Throughout his tenure the orchestra remained at least very good, and at times it rose to outstanding heights. In 1933 Olin Downes of the *New York Times* described the orchestra as "homogenous in tone and effect, alive to the best standards of symphonic music and observant of these." He continued, "The net achievement of orchestra and conductor is a stirring and contagious projection of great music, one of which the City of St. Louis should be, and doubtless is, proud."[73] After pianist Josef Hofmann played an encore with the orchestra (his first in twenty years), he said, "I did it because the orchestra pleased me so much....I consider the St. Louis Symphony Orchestra one of the finest I have ever heard anywhere in the world."[74] In 1939 Thomas Sherman said that at that time there were only four orchestras in America, and perhaps five in the world, which were better than the St. Louis Symphony.[75] It was quite obvious that the

decade of the 1930s saw much improvement in the orchestra, after the lack of stability during the guest conductor period in the late twenties.

But most observers agree that the zenith of the Golschmann period came sometime during the 1940s. In 1949 Howard Taubman of the *New York Times* wrote, "Save for three or four of the finest orchestras in the East, the St. Louis Symphony is as good an ensemble as there is in the country."[76] In that same year Thomas Sherman said that the orchestra could not be considered the best or even the second best orchestra in the nation because of economic reasons. It was just not as large an ensemble as some of the others in the country. But he said that "it is fully capable of performing the greater part of the available literature in a way that correctly expresses its nobility, its delicacy, strength or whatever its special qualities may be."[77] Two of the finest musicians in the orchestra during that time say that it was at its best sometime during the early forties.[78]

In 1951 Deems Taylor ranked the Symphony in a group of orchestras somewhere behind those of Boston, New York, and Philadelphia. He put it in a class with the orchestras of Chicago, Cincinnati, Cleveland, San Francisco, Minneapolis, and Indianapolis.[79] But it was apparent to many observers that during the last few years of the Golschmann period the orchestra slipped in quality from its position of a few years before. Still, in 1956 Leopold Stokowski could write of the Symphony, "After conducting your orchestra several times I realize what Golschmann has done to build it to its present musical heights, making the Saint Louis Orchestra one of the greatest in the world."[80]

GUEST SOLOISTS
With the Orchestra
During the Golschmann Years

(NOT INCLUDING SOLO PERFORMANCES BY MEMBERS OF THE ORCHESTRA)

A Cappella Choir
1955-1956: December 11; Special Concert;
William Heyne, Conductor
Bach: *Cantata #63*
Cantata #65 (Excerpts)
Berlioz: *L'Enfance* (Excerpts)

Adler, Larry (Harmonica)
1941-1942: March 10; Special Concert
Berger: *Concerto*

Althouse, Paul (Tenor)
1931-1932: January 1-2
Wagner: *Lohengrin*
Walküre
1933-1934: November 24-25
Beethoven: *Fidelio*
Wagner: *Meistersinger*
1936-1937: November 20-21
Berlioz: *Damnation of Faust*

Anda, Geza (Piano)
1956-1957: November 2-3; Jascha Horenstein,
Conductor
Tchaikovsky: *Concerto #1*
1957-1958: February 22-23
Brahms: *Concerto #2*

Anderson, Leroy (Conductor)
1953-1954: January 24; Special Concert
Berlioz, Tchaikovsky, Strauss, Debussy,
Wagner, Anderson

"Argentinita" (Dancers)
1944-1945: January 31; Special Concert; Jean
Morel; Conductor
Program of Spanish dances

Arrau, Claudio (Piano)
1942-1943: November 6-7
Schumann: *Concerto A minor*
1946-1947: March 1-2
Brahms: *Concerto #2*
1950-1951: January 12-13
Beethoven: *Concerto #4*
1954-1955: March 4-5
Chopin: *Concerto #1*
1957-1958: January 18-19
Beethoven: *Concerto #5*
Georg Solti, Conductor

Babai, Bela (Violin)
1952-1953: February 19; Pop Concert;
Harry Farbman, Conductor
Romanian Dance, Gypsy Dance

Bachauer, Gina (Piano)
1953-1954: March 19-20
Rachmaninoff: *Concerto #2*

Baer, Frederic (Baritone)
1937-1938: March 18-19
Wagner: *Lohengrin* (concert version)

Bampton, Rose (Soprano)
1935-1936: April 3-4
Verdi: *Requiem*
1936-1937: November 20-21
Berlioz: *Damnation of Faust*

Barer, Simon (Piano)
1939-1940: November 17-18
Tchaikovsky: *Concerto #1*

One of the great favorites of St. Louis audiences, pianist Gina Bachauer appeared with the orchestra over a more than twenty-year period. (St. Louis Symphony)

Conductor Leroy Anderson first appeared with the Symphony in 1954. (St. Louis Symphony)

Pianist Geza Anda first appeared with the Symphony under the direction of Jascha Horenstein in 1956. (St. Louis Symphony)

Chilean pianist Claudio Arrau first played with the orchestra in St. Louis in 1942. (St. Louis Symphony)

Barnhart, Edward (Tenor)
1952-1953: February 8; Pop Concert;
Harry Farbman, Conductor
Verdi: *La Traviata*

Baromeo, Chase (Bass-Baritone)
1934-1935: March 15-16
Beethoven: *Symphony #9*
1936-1937: November 20-21
Berlioz: *Damnation of Faust*

Barzin, Leon (Conductor)
1944-1945: January 20-21
Bach, Beethoven, Kessler, Berezowsky
January 27-28
Schumann, Mozart, Liszt, Borodin
Ida Krehm, Piano

Bassage, Harold (Narrator)
1939-1940: February 9-10
Rosenthal: *Jeanne d'Arc*

Bauer, Harold (Piano)
1933-1934: February 16-17
Beethoven: *Concerto #5*

Baume, Emile (Piano)
1944-1945: January 13-14
Saint-Saëns: *Concerto #2*
Erich Leinsdorf, Conductor

Beasley, Beverly Anne (Soprano)
1957-1958: December 15; Pop Concert
Song: "T'was the Night Before Christmas"
Harry Farbman, Conductor

Beattie, Douglas (Bass-Baritone)
1937-1938: December 17-18
Bach: *Cantata #106*
Beethoven: *Symphony #9*

Beecham, Judy (Piano)
1945-1946: February 21; Pension Fund Concert
Delius: *Piano Concerto*
Thomas Beecham, Conductor

Beecham, Thomas (Conductor)
1940-1941: December 13-14
Handel, Delius, Mozart, Sibelius
1945-1946: February 21; Pension Fund Concert
Mozart, Handel, Delius, Sibelius
Judy Beecham, Piano

Berglund, Joel (Baritone)
1946-1947: February 1-2; Harry Farbman,
Conductor
Mozart: *Don Giovanni, Marriage of Figaro*
Wagner: *Walküre*

Berini, Mario (Tenor)
1943-1944: February 4; Special Concert;
Robert Stolz, Conductor
Robert Stolz: "The Woods of Vienna Are
Calling"
Lehar: "Yours Is My Heart Alone"
Rudolph Sieczynski: "Vienna, City of My
Dreams"
Strauss: *The Gypsy Baron*
Ralph Benatzky: "To You, To You"

Berkova, Saundra (Violin)
1947-1948: December 13-14
Weiniawski: *Concert #2*

Bernstein, Leonard (Conductor-Piano)
1944-1945: February 10-11
C.P.E. Bach, Haydn, Mozart, Tchaikovsky,
Rimsky-Korsakov, Bernstein, Stravinsky
Jennie Tourel, Mezzo-Soprano
February 17-18
Beethoven, Harris, Shostakovich
Ravel: *Concerto G* (Bernstein)
1945-1946: November 30-December 1
Beethoven, Chavez, Copland, Schumann
December 8-9
Bach: *Concerto #5* (Bernstein)
Debussy, Brahms

Betts, Robert (Tenor)
1934-1935: March 15-16
Beethoven: *Symphony #9*

Bible, Francis (Mezzo-Soprano)
  1955-1956: December 11; Special Concert
    Bach: *Cantata #63*
    Berlioz: *L'Enfance* (Excerpts)

Boguslawski, Moissaya (Piano)
  1941-1942: February 1; Pop Concert
    Tchaikovsky: *Concerto #1*

Border, Jean (Soprano)
  1954-1955: January 2; Pop Concert;
    Harry Farbman, Conductor
    Wagner: *Tannhäuser*

Brailowsky, Alexander (Piano)
  1947-1948: January 24-25
    Tchaikovsky: *Concerto #1*
  1948-1949: November 20-21
    Chopin: *Concerto #1*
  1950-1951: November 3-4
    Chopin: *Concerto #1*
  1953-1954: November 13-14
    Beethoven: *Concerto #5*

Brandes, Allan (Piano)
  1954-1955: November 28; Pop Concert;
    Harry Farbman, Conductor
    Tchaikovsky: *Concerto #1* (first movement)

Browning, Jean (Contralto)
  1947-1948: January 10-11
    de Falla: *El Amor Brujo*

Busch, Adolf (Violin)
  1931-1932: December 18-19
    Brahms: *Concerto D*

Buxton, Trudy (Piano)
  1955-1956: January 22; Pop Concert;
    Harry Farbman, Conductor
    Beethoven: *Concerto #1* (first movement)
  1956-1957: January 13; Pop Concert;
    Harry Farbman, Conductor
    Beethoven: *Concerto #2* (first movement)

Casadesus, Gaby (Piano)
  1943-1944: November 13-14; Robert Casadesus,
    Piano
    Mozart: *Concerto for Two Pianos*
  1950-1951: March 9-10; Robert and Jean
    Casadesus, Piano
    Bach: *Concerto for Three Pianos*

Casadesus, Jean (Piano)
  1950-1951: March 9-10; Robert and Gaby
    Casadesus, Piano
    Bach: *Concerto for Three Pianos*

Casadesus, Robert (Piano)
  1935-1936: January 24-25
    Mozart: *Concerto #26*
  1937-1938: January 28-29
    D'Indy: *French Mountain Air*
    Weber: *Concertstück F minor*
  1942-1943: December 11-12
    Mozart: *Concerto #21*
    Ravel: *Concerto for Left Hand*
  1943-1944: November 13-14; Gaby Casadesus,
    Piano
    Franck: *Symphonic Variation*
    Mozart: *Concerto for Two Pianos*
    Gaby Casadesus, Piano
  1945-1946: February 8-9
    Beethoven: *Concerto #4*
  1946-1947: December 21-22
    Beethoven: *Concerto for Pianoforte #5*
  1947-1948: January 2-3
    Mozart: *Concerto A minor*
    Casadesus: *Concerto E*
  1950-1951: March 9-10
    Mozart: *Concerto C minor*
    Bach: *Concerto for Three Pianos*
    Gaby and Jean Casadesus, Piano
  1954-1955: December 18-19
    Brahms: *Concerto #2*
  1956-1957: November 24-25;
    Georg Solti, Conductor
    Franck: *Symphonic Variations*
    Mozart: *Concerto D*

Henri Deering played two pairs of concerts with the orchestra while Golschmann was on the podium. (Missouri Historical Society)

Pianist Robert Casadesus played with the Symphony regularly for twenty years during the Golschmann era. He last played in St. Louis in 1971 when he performed Saint-Saens' **Concerto No. 4.** (St. Louis Symphony)

Tenor Giuseppe Di Stefano sang with the orchestra in a special concert in 1949. (Missouri Historical Society)

Jean Browning, later Jean Madeira, sang in the orchestra's presentation of de Falla's **El Amor Brujo** in 1948. (Missouri Historical Society)

Cassado, Gaspar (Cello)
    1937-1938: February 25-26
        Schubert: *Concerto A minor*

Cecil, Winifred (Soprano)
    1937-1938: December 17-18
        Bach: *Cantata # 106*
        Beethoven: *Symphony #9*

Chabbay, Leslie (Tenor)
    1955-1956: December 11
        Bach: *Cantata #63*
        Berlioz: *L'Enfance* (Excerpts)
    1957-1958: January 23-24;
        Georg Solti, Conductor
        Beethoven: *Symphony #9*

Chapple, Stanley (Conductor)
    1944-1945: February 3-4
        Brahms, Elgar, Barber, Sibelius

Chase, Gene (Narrator)
    1954-1955: November 24; Special Concert
        Copland: *Lincoln Portrait*

Chasins, Abram (Piano)
    1948-1949: February 9; Benefit Concert
        Gershwin: *Concerto in F*

Chavez, Carlos (Composer-Conductor)
    1938-1939: March 3-4
        Haydn, Buxtehude, Shostakovich, Chavez
    1939-1940: January 26-27
        Beethoven, Debussy, de Falla

Choral Union of the University of Missouri
    1949-1950: December 3-4;
        Jennie Tourel, Mezzo-Soprano
        Prokofiev: *Alexander Nevsky*
    1954-1955: March 12-13
        Beethoven: *Symphony #9*

Ciccolini, Aldo (Piano)
    1951-1952: November 16-17
        Beethoven: *Concerto #4*
    1952-1953: November 22-23

Honegger: *Concertino*
de Falla: *Nights in the Gardens of Spain*

Claes, Raymond (Boy Soprano)
    1954-1955: December 23-26
        Traditional Song: "Here, a Torch, Jeannette,
    Isabella"

Comfort, Jean (Mezzo-Soprano)
    1952-1953: February 8; Pop Concert;
        Harry Farbman, Conductor
        Bizet: *Carmen*
        Verdi: *Il Trovatore*
        Kern: *Showboat*
    1954-1955: February 18-19
        Mahler: *Symphony #2*

Concordia Seminary Chorus
    1955-1956: December 11; Special Concert;
        William Heyne, Conductor
        Bach: *Cantata #63* (Excerpts)
            Cantata #65
        Berlioz: *L'Enfance* (Excerpts)

Coombs, Carolee (Soprano)
    1957-1958: December 21-22
        Menotti: *The Telephone*

Curtin, Phyllis (Soprano)
    1955-1956: December 31-January 1
        Cosi Fan Tutte (concert version)
    1956-1957: January 19-20
        Mozart: *Don Giovanni* (concert version)

Curzon, Clifford (Piano)
    1950-1951: March 3-4
        Beethoven: *Concerto #5*

Daniels, Danny (Dancer)
    1954-1955: October 31; Special Concert;
        Morton Gould, Conductor

David, Russ (Piano)
    1942-1943: January 28; Special Concert;
        Andre Kostelanetz, Conductor
        Gershwin: *Rhapsody in Blue*

1956-1957: December 2; Special Concert;
 Harry Farbman, Conductor
 Gershwin: *Concerto in F* (finale)

De Carvalho, Eleazar (Conductor)
 1950-1951: January 6-7
 Weber, Haydn, Ibert, Tchaikovsky
 1952-1953: January 23-24
 Haydn, Schumann, Sibelius
 January 31-February 1
 Mozart, Beethoven, Guarnieri, de Falla, Albeniz

Deering, Henri (Piano)
 1934-1935: March 1-2
 Brahms: *Concerto #1*
 1956-1957: December 21-22
 Beethoven: *Concerto #3*

Della Chiesa, Vivian (Soprano)
 1945-1946: January 5-6
 Bizet: *Carmen*
 Verdi: *Forza del Destino*
 Mozart: *Marriage of Figaro*
 Debussy: *Beau Soir*
 1954-1955: February; Washington University
 Second Century Convocation Concert;
 Gustave Haenschen, Conductor
 Mascagni: *Cavalleria Rusticana*

De Sabata, Victor (Conductor)
 1951-1952: March 1-2
 Rossini, Schumann, Ghedini, Ravel, R. Strauss

Di Stefano, Giuseppe (Tenor)
 1949-1950: November 6; Fontbonne College Fund
 Concert
 Mozart: *Don Giovanni*
 Puccini: *La Bohème*
 Gounod: *Faust*

Doniger, Judith (Soprano)
 1948-1949: January 7-8
 Berg: *Wozzeck* (three excerpts)
 1950-1951: October 28-29
 Weber: *Freischütz*
 Barber: *Knoxville, Summer of 1915*

Dorfmann, Ania (Piano)
 1946-1947: February 21-22
 Beethoven: *Concerto #1*

Dorn, William (Piano)
 1948-1949: February 6; Pop Concert;
 Harry Farbman, Conductor
 Rachmaninoff: *Concerto #2*

Druary, John (Tenor)
 1953-1954: December 5-6;
 William Heyne, Conductor
 Bach: *Magnificat*

Dushkin, Samuel (Violin)
 1931-1932; February 5-6
 Stravinsky: *Concerto D*
 1934-1935: February 10; Pension Fund Concert;
 Igor Stravinsky, Conductor
 Stravinsky: *Selections for Piano and Violin*
 Igor Stravinsky, Piano
 1937-1938: January 14-15
 Mendelssohn: *Concerto E minor*
 1945-1946: December 28-29
 Martinu: *Suite Concertante*

Eastham, Bill (Narrator)
 1956-1957: March 24; Pop Concert;
 Harry Farbman, Conductor
 Wright-Forrest: *Kismet*

Echaniz, Jose (Piano)
 1937-1938: January 2
 de Falla: *Nights in the Gardens of Spain*
 Listz: *Concerto #2*

Elman, Mischa (Violin)
 1932-1933: December 29-30
 Mendelssohn: *Concerto E minor*
 1944-1945: December 30-31
 Brahms: *Concerto D*
 1946-1947: November 9-10
 Beethoven: *Concerto D*

English, Gay (Soprano)
 1953-1954: November 1; Pop Concert;
 Harry Farbman, Conductor

Romberg: *Maytime*
Caryll: *The Pink Lady*
Herbert: *Naughty Marietta*
Friml: "Donkey Serenade;" "A Tribute to Rom-
berg"

Erhart, Rita (Guitarist-Songstress)
1954-1955: March 20; Pop Concert;
Max Steindel, Conductor
Gomez: *Panamericana*

Eschen, Frank (Narrator)
1954-1955: January 2; Pop Concert;
Harry Farbman, Conductor
Kliensinger: *Tubby the Tuba*
Karl Toenjes, Tuba
1956-1957: December 2; Special Concert;
Harry Farbman, Conductor
Prokofiev: *Peter and the Wolf*

Eto, Toshiya (Violin)
1952-1953: November 8-9
Glazounov: *Concerto A minor*

Eustis, Dorothy (Piano)
1948-1949: December 12; Pop Concert;
Harry Farbman, Conductor
Grieg: *Concerto A minor*

Falkner, Keith (Bass-Baritone)
1935-1936: April 3-4
Verdi: *Requiem*

Fear, Arthur (Baritone)
1936-1937: March 5-6
Wagner: *Meistersinger*
Walton: *Belshazzar's Feast*

Fender, Harry (Commentator-Radio Personality)
1954-1955: March 20; Pop Concert;
Max Steindel, Conductor
Commentator for the concert

Ferguson, Bernard (Baritone)
1932-1933: January 21; Pop Concert;
Scipione Guidi, Conductor
Massenet: *Le Roi de Lahore*

Ferrer, Jose (Narrator)
1951-1952: December 10; United Nations Human
Rights Day Concert
Copland: *Preamble*

Fiedler, Arthur (Conductor)
1957-1958: February 11, 12, 14, 15; New Year's
Eve Gala Pop Concerts

Firkusny, Rudolf (Piano)
1950-1951: December 29-30
Brahms: *Concerto #1*
1951-1952: January 5-6
Beethoven: *Concerto #3*

Fleisher, Leon (Piano)
1949-1950: November 4-5
Brahms: *Concerto #1*
1953-1954: January 22-23
Beethoven: *Concerto #2*
1955-1956: November 5-6
Beethoven: *Concerto #4*

Foote, Bruce (Bass)
1950-1951: March 23; Bach Festival Concert;
William Heyne, Conductor
Bach: *St. John Passion*
1953-1954: March 28; Bach Festival Concert;
William Heyne, Conductor
Bach: *St. John Passion*

Foss, Lukas (Conductor)
1954-1955: December 31-January 1
Bach, Monteverdi, Stravinsky, Gershwin,
Schubert
1955-1956: February 17-18
Foss: *Concerto #2*

Foster, Patrice (Piano)
1952-1953: November 2; Pop Concert;
Harry Farbman, Conductor
Gershwin: *Rhapsody in Blue*

Foster, Sidney (Piano)
1948-1949: October 31; Pop Concert;
Harry Farbman, Conductor
Tchaikovsky: *Concerto #1*

Francescatti, Zino (Violin)
  1946-1947: January 4-5
    Paganini: *Concerto #1*
  1947-1948: February 7-8
    Beethoven: *Concerto D*
  1948-1949: February 12-13
    Bach: *Concerto A minor*
    Prokofiev: *Concerto #2*
  1952-1953: November 14-15
    Brahms: *Concerto D*
  1953-1954: March 6-7
    Beethoven: *Concerto D*
  1954-1955: March 18-19
    Tchaikovsky: *Concerto D*
  1955-1956: January 28-29
    Beethoven: *Concerto D*
  1957-1958: January 9-10
    Beethoven: *Concerto D*

Frantz, Dalies (Piano)
  1936-1937: January 8-9;
    Scipione Guidi, Conductor
    Brahms: *Concerto #1*

Gabrilowitsch, Ossip (Piano)
  1931-1932: February 12-13
    Schumann: *Concerto A*
  1933-1934: March 9-10
    Brahms: *Concerto #2*

Galloway, Charles, Jr. (Narrator- Conductor)
  1939-1940: November 10-11
    Prokofiev: *Peter and the Wolf*
  1946-1947: February 7-8
    Copland: *Lincoln Portrait*
  1948-1949: December 23-25
    Copland: *Lincoln Portrait*;
    Harry Farbman, Conductor
  1949-1950: March 26-27
    Thompson: *Testament of Freedom*

Ganz, Rudolph (Composer-Conductor-Piano)
  1935-1936: March 27-28
    Tchaikovsky: *Concerto #1*
  1942-1943: November 27-28
    Tchaikovsky: *Concerto #1*
  1951-1952: December 28-29
    Ganz: *Symphonic Overture*

Garbousova, Raya (Cello)
  1935-1936: January 3-4
    Boccherini: *Concert B*
    Tchaikovsky: *Roccoco Theme*
  1939-1940: January 12-13
    Haydn: *Concerto D*
  1943-1944: January 22-23
    Saint-Saëns: *Concerto A minor*
    Andre Kostelanetz, Conductor
  1947-1948: November 7-8
    Barber: *Concerto for Violin and Orchestra*
  1954-1955: January 14-15
    Couperin: *Pieces en Concert*
    Pieti: *Concerto #2*
    Harry Farbman, Conductor

George, Helen (Soprano)
  1955-1956: December 31-January 1
    Mozart: *Cosi Fan Tutte* (concert version)
  1956-1957: January 19-20
    Mozart: *Don Giovanni* (concert version)

Gershwin, George (Conductor-Piano)
  1935-1936: March 1; Pension Fund Concert
    Gershwin: *Concerto in F; Porgy and Bess*

Glaz, Herta (Contralto)
  1943-1944: February 4; Special Concert;
    Robert Stolz, Conductor
    Robert Stolz: *White Horse Inn*
    Oscar Straus: *The Chocolate Soldier*
    Strauss: *The Gypsy Baron*
    Ralph Benatzky: "To You, To You"

Glenn, Carroll (Violin)
  1942-1943: February 12-13
    Beethoven: *Concerto D*
  1948-1949: January 1-2
    Khatchaturian: *Concerto*

Goldberg, Szymon (Violin)
  1950-1951: November 17-18
    Mendelssohn: *Concerto E minor*
  1951-1952: November 30-December 1
    Beethoven: *Concerto D*
  1953-1954: February 5-6
    Brahms: *Concerto D*

Golschmann, Boris (Piano)
1938-1939: February 3-4
Mozart: *Concerto #20*
Franck: *Symphonic Variations*

Goltzer, Albert (Oboe)
1947-1948: November 29-30
Cimarosa: *Concerto*

Gooch, David (Boy Soprano)
1954-1955: December 23-26
Traditional song: "Here a Torch, Jeannette, Isabella"

Gorin, Igor (Baritone)
1940-1941: March 7-8
Goldmark: *Queen of Sheba*
Bellini: *I Puritani*
Verdi: *Don Carlos*
Songs: Gretchaninov, Gorin, Tchaikovsky, Moussorgsky

Gould, Glenn (Piano)
1956-1957: December 29-30
Beethoven: *Concerto #4*
1957-1958: November 23-24
Bach: *Concerto #5*

Gould, Herbert (Bass)
1937-1938: March 18-19
Wagner: *Lohengrin* (concert version)

Gould, Morton (Composer-Conductor)
1943-1944: March 18; Special Concert
Gould (orchestration): "American Songs Set for Strings;" "American Salute;" "Red Cavalry March;" "St. Louis Blues"
1944-1945: March 18; Special Concert
Gould, Schumann, Harris, Copland
1954-1955: October 31; Special Concert
Mendelssohn, Gould, Tchaikovsky, Lehar-Gould, Gershwin

Grace Methodist Church Choir
1957-1958: January 23-24
Beethoven: *Symphony #9*

Graf, Uta (Soprano)
1951-1952: December 10; United Nations Human Rights Day Concert
Beethoven: *Symphony #9* (finale)
1957-1958: January 23-24; Georg Solti, Conductor
Beethoven: *Symphony #9*

Graffman, Gary (Piano)
1956-1957: January 11-12
Prokofiev: *Concerto #3*

Grandjany, Marcel (Harp)
1947-1948: January 30-31
Handel: *Concerto B-flat*
Ravel: *Introduction and Allegro*

Greiner, Seth (Piano)
1941-1942: March 1; Pop Concert
Franck: *Symphonic Variations*
1950-1951: March 13
Rachmaninoff: *Concert #2*
Addinsell: *Warsaw Concerto*

Gridley, Dan (Tenor)
1935-1936: April 3-4
Verdi: *Requiem*

Grumiaux, Arthur (Violin)
1951-1952: January 25-26
Chausson: *Poème*
Ravel: *Tzigane*

Gulda, Friedrich (Piano)
1951-1952: October 27-28
Schumann: *Concerto A minor*
1952-1953: October 30-31
Mozart: *Concerto #23*

Hackman, Carolyn (Contralto)
1957-1958: January 23-24; Georg Solti, Conductor
Beethoven: *Symphony #9*

Haenschen, Gustave (Conductor)
1954-1955: February 20; Washington University Second Century Convocation Concert
Strauss, Tchaikovsky, Kern, Berlin, Rodgers, Gershwin

Rudolf Firkusny has recorded the Dvořák **Piano Concerto in G minor** with the orchestra. (St. Louis Symphony)

Conductor Arthur Fiedler led the Symphony in a series of pop concerts in 1958. He has since returned to direct the orchestra at their permanent hall and at the Mississippi River Festival. (St. Louis Symphony)

Mischa Elman, one of the great violinists to appear with the orchestra during the Golschmann era. (The Cleveland Orchestra)

Handzlik, Jean (Contralto)
  1953-1954: December 5-6;
    William Heyne, Conductor
  Bach: *Magnificat*

Harder, William (Baritone)
  1955-1956: Rodgers-Hammerstein Festival

Harrell, Mack (Baritone)
  1946-1947: March 15; Special Concert;
    Edwin McArthur, Conductor
  Strauss: *Die Fledermaus*
  Lehar: *Merry Widow; Sari*
  Sieczynski: "Vienna, City of My Dreams"
  1950-1951: March 23; Bach Festival Concert;
    William Heyne, Conductor
  Bach: *St. John Passion*
  March 24; Bach Festival Concert;
    William Heyne, Conductor
  Bach: *Cantata #31; Easter Oratorio Cantata #4*

Havens, Gladys (Contralto)
  1934-1935: March 15-16
  Beethoven: *Symphony #9*

Hayes, Jim (Baritone)
  1951-1952: November 18; Pop Concert;
    Harry Farbman, Conductor
  Wagner: *Tannhäuser*
  Weill: *Knickerbocker Holiday*
  Herbert: *Eileen*
  Kleinsinger: *Tubby the Tuba*
  Jim Hayes, Narrator

Haynes, Eugene (Piano)
  1949-1950: December 27; Pop Concert;
    Harry Farbman, Conductor
  Chopin: *Concerto #1*

Hayward, Thomas (Tenor)
  1952-1953: February 22; Special Concert;
    Richard Rodgers, Conductor
  Rodgers: "My Heart Stood Still;" "If I Loved
  You;" "Younger Than Springtime;" "There's A
  Small Hotel;" "People Will Say We're In Love;"
  "Oklahoma"

Heckman, Winifred (Contralto)
  1955-1956: Rodgers-Hammerstein Festival

Heifetz, Jascha (Violin)
  1934-1935: January 11-12
  Beethoven: *Concerto D*
  1936-1937: November 6-7
  Brahms: *Concerto D*
  1938-1939: January 27-28
  Mozart: *Concerto #4*
  Prokofiev: *Concerto #2*
  1940-1941: November 15-16
  Walton: *Concerto*
  1946-1947: February 15-16
  Korngold: *Concerto D*
  Waxman: *Carmen Fantasy*
  1948-1949: January 15-16
  Beethoven: *Concerto D*
  1955-1956: December 3-4
  Brahms: *Concerto D*

Henriot, Nicole (Piano)
  1950-1951: January 26-27
  Ravel: *Concerto G*
  1951-1952: December 10; Special Concert
  Tchaikovsky: *Concerto #1*
  1952-1953: January 8-9
  Bach: *Brandenburg Concerto*
  Ravel: *Concerto G*

Hess, Myra (Piano)
  1931-1932: January 22-23
  Beethoven: *Concerto #3*
  1938-1939: December 22-23
  Beethoven: *Concerto #4*
  1952-1953: March 6-7
  Schumann: *Concerto A minor*

Heyne, William (Conductor)
  1950-1951: March 23; Bach Festival Concert
  Bach: *St. John Passion*
  March 24; Bach Festival Concert
  Bach: *Cantata #4; Cantata # 31; Easter Oratorio*
  1951-1952: December 13; Special Concert
  Bach: *Christmas Oratorio*
  March 18; Bach Festival Concert
  Bach: *Mass B minor*

Rudolph Ganz returned several times to St. Louis to conduct the orchestra which he had earlier headed. (St. Louis Symphony)

Cellist Raya Garbousova appeared with the orchestra several times during the Golschmann era; once under the direction of Andre Kostelanetz. (St. Louis Symphony)

In 1976 Lukas Foss directed the Symphony in performances of his **Folk Song for Orchestra**. (St. Louis Symphony)

Violinist Zino Francescatti played the Saint-Saens **Concerto No. 3** with the orchestra in 1974. (St. Louis Symphony)

Pianist Ossip Gabrilowitsch as he appeared when he played with the orchestra in the early thirties. (St. Louis Symphony)

Morton Gould has served as guest conductor with the orchestra in a series of special concerts featuring his own compositions. (St. Louis Symphony)

1953-1954: December 5-6
  Bach: *Magnificat D*
  March 28; Bach Festival Concert
  Bach: *St. John Passion*
1955-1956: December 11; Special Concert
  Bach: *Cantata #63;*
    Cantata #65 (Excerpts)
  Berlioz: *L'Enfance* (Excerpts)

Hiller, Jean (Soprano)
  1952-1953: February 8; Pop Concert;
    Harry Farbman, Conductor
  Verdi: *La Traviata*
  Strauss: *Die Fledermaus*

Hilsberg, Alexander (Conductor)
  1957-1958: November 9-10
  Bach, Debussy, Brahms, R. Strauss

Hobson, Jane (Mezzo-Soprano)
  1955-1956: December 31-January 1
  Mozart: *Cosi Fan Tutte* (concert version)

Hofmann, Josef (Piano)
  1933-1934: December 29-30
  Rubinstein: *Concerto #4*
  1935-1936: March 6-7
  Schumann: *Concerto A minor*
  1937-1938: November 19-20
  Beethoven: *Concerto #4*

Horenstein, Jascha (Conductor)
  1956-1957: October 27-28
  Bach, Hindemith, Beethoven
  November 2-3
  Ravel, Tchaikovsky, Prokofiev
  Geza Anda, Piano

Horowitz, Vladimir (Piano)
  1931-1932: March 4-5
  Rachmaninoff: *Concerto #3*
  1933-1934: January 27-28
  Tchaikovsky: *Concerto #1*
  1939-1940: February 23-24
  Rachmaninoff: *Concerto #3*
  1941-1942: January 23-24

Brahms: *Concerto #2*
1952-1953: February 14-15
  Tchaikovsky: *Concerto #1*

Horszowski, Miecsyslav (Piano)
  1948-1949: October 29-30
  Beethoven: *Concerto #4*

House, Richard (Boy Soprano)
  1954-1955: December 23-26
  Traditional Song: "Here A Torch, Jeannette,
    Isabella"

Huberman, Bronislaw (Violin)
  1942-1943: November 20-21
  Brahms: *Concerto D*

International Ladies' Garment Workers Chorus
  1956-1957: December 2; Special Concert;
    Harry Farbman, Conductor

Iturbi, Jose (Piano)
  1932-1933: January 13-14
  Beethoven: *Concerto #4*
  Wiener: *Franco-American Concerto*
  1934-1935: February 15-16
  Haydn: *Concerto D*
  1940-1941: January 3-4
  Beethoven: *Concerto #3*

Janssen, Werner (Conductor)
  1935-1936: November 22-23
  Mozart, Sibelius, Fuleihan, Strauss

Jepson, Helen (Soprano)
  1942-1943: November 13-14
  Mozart: *Marriage of Figaro; Concert Aria*
  Songs: Duparc, Carpenter, Hageman

Johannesen, Grant (Piano)
  1954-1955: October 29-30
  Beethoven: *Concerto #3*

Johnson, Richard and Milliken, David (Duo-Piano)
  1948-1949: November 17; Special Concert;
    Andre Kostelanetz, Conductor
  Saint-Saëns: *Carnival of Animals*

Pianist Josef Hofmann appeared with the Symphony several times during the thirties. (Missouri Historical Society)

The legendary Vladimir Horowitz was accompanied by the orchestra on numerous occasions throughout the Golschmann era. (St. Louis Symphony)

Pianist Jose Iturbi appeared with the orchestra for **three pairs of concerts during the Golschmann era. (Missouri Historical Society)**

Pianist Gary Graffman's 1975 appearance with the orchestra featured the **Concerto No. 1** by Brahms. (St. Louis Symphony)

Kapell, William (Piano)
    1942-1943: January 29-30
      Rachmaninoff: *Concerto #2*
    1943-1944: November 27-28
      Khatchaturian *Piano Concerto*
    1944-1945: December 2-3
      Rachmaninoff: *Concerto #3*
    1945-1946: November 24-25
      Brahms: *Concerto #1*
    1946-1947: December 7-8
      Prokofiev: *Concerto #3*
    1948-1949: October 23-24
      Beethoven: *Concerto #2*
    1951-1952: November 24-25
      Rachmaninoff: *Rhapsody on a Theme of Paganini*

Kentner, Louis (Piano)
    1957-1958: December 26-27;
      Fernando Previtali, Conductor
    Tchaikovsky: *Concerto #1*

Kirkpatrick, John (Piano)
    1943-1944: February 5-6
      MacDowell: *Concerto #2*

Knowles, Lilian (Contralto)
    1937-1938: December 17-18
      Bach: *Cantata #106*
      Beethoven: *Symphony #9*

Kogan, Leonid (Violin)
    1957-1958: March 2; Special Concert
      Vivaldi: *Concerto G minor*
      Brahms: *Concerto D*

Kombrink, Llona (Soprano)
    1954-1955: February 18-19;
      Harry Farbman, Conductor
    Mahler: *Symphony #2*

Kostelanetz, Andre (Conductor)
    1942-1943: January 28; Special Concert
      Reznicek, Kern, Wagner, Gershwin, Copland, Ravel
      Carl Sandburg, Narrator
      Russ David, Piano

    1943-1944: January 22-23
      Kabalevsky, Franck, Stravinsky, Saint-Saëns
        Raya Garbousova, Cello
      March 8; Special Concert
      Gershwin, Kern, Grofé, and others
    1944-1945: November 23; Special Concert
      Prokofiev, Bishop, Fauré, Delibes, Ravel, Tchaikovsky, Donizetti
        Lily Pons, Soprano
    1945-1946: November 5; Special Concert
      Mozart, Kabalevsky, Addinsell, Grofé
      January 28; Special Concert
      Bach, Beethoven, Rimsky-Korsakov, Kern, Kostelanetz, Debussy, Tchaikovsky
    1946-1947: November 20; Special Concert
      Handel, Rimsky-Korsakov, Enesco, Grofé, Kern-Bennett
      January 20; Special Concert
      Grétry, Tchaikovsky, Addinsell, Scott, Debussy, Rodgers, Grofé
    1947-1948: November 10; Special Concert
      Berlioz, Tchaikovsky, Ravel, Chopin, Strauss, Porter
      January 21; Special Concert
      Rimsky-Korsakov, Verdi, Bishop, Ravel, Grofé, Ponce, Strauss, Kern, Rossini
        Lily Pons, Soprano
    1948-1949: November 17; Special Concert
      Mozart, Haydn, Saint-Saëns, Kern, Lecuona, Sieczynski, Strauss
        Richard Johnson and David Milliken, Duo-Piano
      January 10; Special Concert
      Khatchaturian, Verdi, Gounod, Rossini, Dell'Acqua, Gershwin, Bachelet, Strauss, Debussy, de Falla, Delibes
    1950-1951: January 14; Special Concert
      Tchaikovsky, Rodgers, Gershwin, Berlin
    1955-1956: November 27; Special Concert
      Kabalevsky, Grofé, Offenbach, Sihanouk, Gershwin, Kern

Krachmalinich, Jacob (Violin)
    1954-1955: November 24; Special Concert
      Bruch: *Concert #1*

Kraft, Marie Simmelink (Soprano)
    1953-1954: January 30-31;

Leopold Stokowski, Conductor
Elwell: "The Forever Young"

Krebs, Beatrice (Contralto)
  1953-1954: March 28; Bach Festival Concert;
    William Heyne, Conductor
  Bach: *St. John Passion*

Krehm, Ida (Piano)
  1941-1942: December 12-13
  Brahms: *Concerto #1*
  1944-1945: January 27-28
  Mozart: *Concerto #20*
  Listz: *Hungarian Fantasy*

Kreisler, Fritz (Violin)
  1934-1935: November 8-10
  Brahms: *Concerto D*
  1935-1936: November 29-30
  Mendelssohn: *Concerto E minor*
  1938-1939: November 18-19
  Brahms: *Concerto D*

Kueter, Paul (Piano)
  1948-1949: February 20; Pop Concert;
    Harry Farbman, Conductor
  Gershwin: *Concerto in F*

Kullman, Charles (Tenor)
  1937-1938: March 8-9
  Wagner: *Lohengrin* (concert version)

Labunsky, Wiktor (Piano)
  1940-1941: February 16; Pop Concert;
    Harry Farbman, Conductor
  Paderewski: *Polish Fantasy for Piano and Orchestra*

Lane, Gloria (Contralto)
  1953-1954: Rodgers-Hammerstein Festival

Lanza, Mario (Tenor)
  1946-1947: January 18-19
  Flotow: *Martha*
  Puccini: *La Bohème*

Lavin, Avram (Cello)
  1950-1951: December 15-16
  Boccherini: *Concerto #2*
  Malipiero: *Concerto*

Lawrence, Marjeorie (Soprano)
  1940-1941: January 17-18
  Gluck: *Iphigenie Tauride*
  Wagner: *Tannhäuser*
  R. Strauss: *Salome*

Legend Singers; Kenneth Billups, Director
  1949-1950: December 27; Pop Concert;
    Harry Farbman, Conductor
  Taylor: "Yule Tide"
  Dickinson: "The Shepherd's Story"
  Handel: *Messiah*
  Gershwin: *Porgy and Bess*
  1955-1956: February 5; Pop Concert;
    Harry Farbman, Conductor
  Kleinsinger: *Brooklyn Baseball Cantata*

Lehmann, Lotte (Soprano)
  1938-1939: December 9-10
  Beethoven: *Fidelio*
  Songs: *Strauss*
  Wagner: *Tristan und Isolde*

Leinsdorf, Erich (Conductor)
  1944-1945: January 13-14
  Beethoven, Saint-Saëns, Wagner
    Emile Baume, Piano
  1947-1948: December 27-28
  Mendelssohn, Mozart, Ravel, Wagner
    Isaac Stern, Violin
  1956-1957: November 30-December 1
  Berlioz, Dvořák, Beethoven, Wagner
    Leslie Parnas, Cello

Lev, Ray (Piano)
  1939-1940: December 22-23
  Beethoven: *Concerto #3; Triple Concerto*

Levant, Oscar (Piano-Conductor)
  1941-1942: November 16; Special Concert
  Gershwin: *Concerto in F; Rhapsody in Blue*

Levant: *Nocturne; Capriccio*
Levant, Piano
1949-1950: February 26; Special Concert
Khatchaturian: *Concerto*
Gershwin: *Rhapsody in Blue*
Levant, Piano
1951-1952: March 9; Special Concert;
Harry Farbman, Conductor
Gershwin: *Concerto in F; Rhapsody in Blue*
Levant, Piano

Levitski, Mischa (Piano)
1932-1933: November 4-5
Saint-Saëns: *Concerto #2*

Lewis, Richard (Tenor)
1957-1958: November 14-15
Mahler: *Das Lied Von der Erde*

Liberace (Piano)
1953-1954: March 21; Special Concert;
George Liberace, Conductor

Libove, Charles (Violin)
1948-1949: January 18; Pop Concert;
Harry Farbman, Conductor
Beethoven: *Romance in F for Violin*
Saint-Saëns: *Introduction and Rondo Capriccioso*

Lipkin, Seymour (Piano)
1948-1949: February 4-5
Rachmaninoff: *Rhapsody on A Theme of Paganini*

List, Eugene (Piano)
1935-1936: February 7-8
Shostakovitch: *Concerto #1*
1946-1947: November 1-2
Rachmaninoff: *Concerto #2*
1948-1949: January 1-2
Tchaikovsky: *Concerto #1*

Ljangberg, Goeta (Soprano)
1932-1933: March 17-18
Wagner: *Lohengrin, Tannhäuser, Tristan und Isolde*

Lloyd, David (Tenor)
1954-1955: March 12-13
Beethoven: *Symphony #9*
1955-1956: December 31-January 1
Mozart: *Cosi Fan Tutte* (concert version)

Lopez, Pilar (Dancer)
1944-1945: January 31; Special Concert;
Jean Morel, Conductor
Program of Spanish dances
"Argentinita" dancers

Lowe, Jack (Whittemore and Lowe, Duo-Piano)
1947-1948: November 15-16
K. P. E. Bach: *Concerto F for Two Pianos*
Poulenc: *Concerto D minor for Two Pianos*

Luboshutz, Pierre and Nemenoff, Genia (Duo-Piano)
1942-1943: January 15-16
Mozart: *Concerto E-flat Major for Two Pianos*
McDonald: *Concerto for Two Pianos*
1948-1949: January 21-22
Martinu: *Concerto for Two Pianos*
1951-1952: November 2-3
Bach: *Concerto C for Two Pianos*
Martinú: *Concerto for Two Pianos*

Lustgarten, Edgar (Cello)
1946-1947: December 27-28;
Harry Farbman, Conductor
Brahms: *Double Concerto*
1947-1948: December 6-7
Bloch: *Schelomo*
1948-1949: November 6-7
Boccherini: *Concerto B-flat Major*

Lutheran High School Chorus
1954-1955: February 18-19
Mahler: *Symphony #2*

MacGregor, Phillip (Bass)
1951-1952: March 8; Bach Festival Concert;
William Heyne, Conductor
Bach: *Mass B minor*

MacGregor, Willard (Piano)
1939-1940: December 1-2
Beethoven: *Concerto #1*

Andre Kostelanetz conducted the orchestra on many occasions. His wife, Lily Pons, appeared with him in two concerts. (St. Louis Symphony)

Luboshutz and Nemenoff, duo-pianists, played in three pairs of concerts with the Symphony during the Golscmann era. (Missouri Historical Society)

Pianist Mischa Levitski appeared with the Symphony at the old Odeon Theatre. (Missouri Historical Society)

Soprano Lotte Lehmann sang with the orchestra in 1938. (Missouri Historical Society)

Magalov, Nikita (Piano)
1949-1950: February 18-19
Tchaikovsky: *Concerto #1*

Makowski, Ray (Percussion)
1957-1958: December 15; Pop Concert;
William Farbman, Conductor
Schreiner: *The Worried Drummer*

Malcuzynski, Witold (Piano)
1944-1945: November 11-12
Chopin: *Concerto #2*

Marechal, Maurice (Cello)
1938-1939: February 24-25
Lalo: *Concerto D*

Markevitch, Igor (Conductor)
1956-1957: December 8-9
Bach, Tchaikovsky, Brahms, de Falla
December 14-15
Handel, Beethoven, Prokofiev, Roussel
Berl Senofsky, Violin

Marshall, Lois (Soprano)
1956-1957: January 19-20
Mozart: *Don Giovanni* (concert version)

Martini, Nino (Tenor)
1937-1938: April 10; Pension Fund Concert
Puccini: *La Bohème*
Meyerbeer: *L'Africana*
Songs: Pergolesi, Grever, Bemberg, Mattei,
Campbell-Tipton, Bridge, Calleja, Serrano

Mayes, Samuel (Cello)
1942-1943: December 18-20
Haydn: *Concerto D*

Maynor, Dorothy (Soprano)
1951-1952: December 13; Special Concert;
William Heyne, Conductor
Bach: *Christmas Oratorio*
Mozart: *Alleluia*
1953-1954: October 30-31
Handel: *Semele*
Mozart: *Cosi Fan Tutte*

Villa-Lobos: *Brasileiras #5*
Strauss: Songs

McCollum, John (Tenor)
1956-1957: January 19-20
Mozart: *Don Giovanni* (concert version)

McDonnell, Priscilla (Mezzo-Soprano)
1956-1957: Special Concert

Melchior, Lauritz (Tenor)
1934-1935: November 16-17
Wagner: *Walküre, Siegfried*
1947-1948: March 20; Pop Concert;
Edwin McArthur, Conductor
Grieg: "Eros"
Lange-Miller: "Kornmolasgladsen"
C. E. Sjoeberg: *"Tonera"*
Gounod: *"Ave Maria"*
Schubert: "Who Is Sylvia"
Schumann: "Two Grenadiers"
1949-1950: January 24; Special Concert
Wagner: *Tristan und Isolde* (concert version)
Helen Traubel, Soprano

Menuhin, Yehudi (Violin)
1933-1934: February 9-10
Beethoven: *Concerto D*
1937-1938: December 23-26
Schumann: *Concerto D minor*
Brahms: *Concerto D*
1941-1942: January 30-31
Chausson: *Poème*
Paganini: *Concerto #1*
1944-1945: March 3-4
Beethoven: *Concerto D*
1950-1951: November 25-26
Brahms: *Concerto D*
1953-1954: November 7-8
Mendelssohn: *Concerto D minor*
Bartók: *Rhapsody #2*

Meredith, Morley (Baritone)
1953-1954: December 5-6;
William Heyne, Conductor
Bach: *Magnificat D*

1957-1958: January 23-24;
    Georg Solti, Conductor
    Beethoven: *Symphony #9*

Michelangeli, Arturo (Piano)
    1948-1949: December 18-19;
        Harry Farbman, Conductor
        Schumann: *Concerto A minor*
    1949-1950: January 27-28;
        Harry Farbman, Conductor
        Beethoven: *Concerto #9*

Mildner, Jeanne (Piano)
    1957-1958: November 3; Pop Concert;
        Harry Farbman, Conductor
        Chopin: *Concerto #2* (second and third
        movements)

Milhaud, Darius (Composer-Conductor-Piano)
    1941-1942: January 9-10
        Milhaud: *Concerto #2*
        Symphony #1

Milliken, David (Johnson and Milliken, Duo-Piano)
    1948-1949: November 17; Special Concert;
        Andre Kostelanetz, Conductor
        Saint-Saëns: *Carnival of Animals*

Milstein, Nathan (Violin)
    1932-1933: February 10-11
        Goldmark: *Concerto #1*
    1934-1935: February 1-2
        Dvořák: *Concerto A minor*
    1935-1936: January 10-11
        Tchaikovsky: *Concerto D*
    1939-1940: March 8-9
        Brahms: *Concerto D*
    1940-1941: February 28-March 1
        Lalo: *Symphonie espagnole*
    1944-1945: November 4-5
        Tchaikovsky: *Concerto D*
    1945-1946: November 10-11
        Brahms: *Concerto D*
    1947-1948: November 29-30
        Brahms: *Concerto D*
    1949-1950: December 10-11;
        Harry Farbman, Conductor

Beethoven: *Concerto D*
1951-1952: January 19-20
    Brahms: *Concerto D*
1953-1954: January 2-3
    Bach: *Concerto E*
    Prokofiev: *Concerto #1*
1954-1955: December 10-11
    Lalo: *Symphonie espagnole*
1956-1957: January 5-6
    Brahms: *Concerto D*

Mitchell, Evelyn (Piano)
    1955-1956: October 30; Pop Concert;
        Harry Farbman, Conductor
        Grieg: *Concerto A minor* (first movement)

Mitchell, Jeanne (Violin)
    1950-1951: December 23-24
        Prokofiev: *Concerto #2*

Mitropoulos, Dimitri (Conductor)
    1951-1952: December 8-9
        Brahms, Beethoven, Krenek

Monath, Hortense (Piano)
    1943-1944: December 18-19
        Mozart: *Concerto #21*

Mondry, Janice (Contralto)
    1954-1955: March 12-13
        Beethoven: *Symphony #9*

Monteux, Pierre (Conductor)
    1957-1958: October 17-18
        Mendelssohn, Brahms, Creston, R. Strauss,
        Sibelius

Morales, Sergio (Bass)
    1955-1956: January 8; Pop Concert;
        Harry Farbman, Conductor
        Mozart: *Don Giovanni*
        Rossini: *The Barber of Seville*
        Kern: "Ol' Man River"

Morel, Jean (Conductor)
    1944-1945: January 31; Special Concert;
        "Argentinita" Dancers
        Program of Spanish dances

Morgan, Mac (Baritone)
   1955-1956: December 31-January 1
      Mozart: *Cosi Fan Tutte*
   1956-1957: January 19-20
      Mozart: *Don Giovanni* (concert version)

Morini, Erika (Violin)
   1945-1946: December 14-15;
      Harry Farbman, Conductor
      Bruch: *Concerto #1*
   1953-1954: November 27-28
      Tchaikovsky: *Concerto D*

Munch, Charles (Conductor)
   1948-1949: December 10-11
      Handel, Mendelssohn, Debussy, Dukas

Murray, Bonnie (Soprano)
   1955-1956: Rodgers-Hammerstein Festival

Nadien, David (Violin)
   1948-1949: November 28; Pop Concert;
      Harry Farbman, Conductor
      Lalo: *Symphonie espagnole*

Nemenoff, Genia (Luboshutz and Nemenoff,
      Duo-Piano)
   1942-1943: January 15-16
      Mozart: *Concerto E-flat Major for Two Pianos*
      McDonald: *Concerto for Two Pianos*
   1948-1949: January 21-22
      Martinu: *Concerto for Two Pianos*
   1951-1952: November 2-3
      Bach: *Concerto C for Two Pianos*
      Martinu: *Concerto for Two Pianos*

Neveu, Ginette (Violin)
   1948-1949: November 26-27
      Brahms: *Concerto D*

Newsome, Gil (Narrator)
   1953-1954: November 27-28
      Rosenthal: *Jeanne d'Arc*

Nicholas, Eden (Narrator)
   1957-1958: November 3
      Prokofiev: *Peter and the Wolf*

Nikolaidi, Elena (Contralto)
   1950-1951: February 3-4
      Gluck: *Alceste*
      Verdi: *Macbeth*
      Mahler: *Songs of a Wayfarer*
   1951-1952: December 10; United Nations Human
         Rights Day Concert
      Beethoven: *Symphony #9* (finale)
   1952-1953: November 28-29
      Wagner: Songs
      Gluck: *Alceste*
      Rossini: *Semiramide*

Nordoff, Paul (Narrator)
   1956-1957: November 4
      Nordoff: *The Frog Prince*

Norris, Mary (Piano)
   1949-1950: November 27; Special Concert
      Rachmaninoff: *Rhapsody on a Theme of
      Paganini*

Novaes, Guiomar (Piano)
   1952-1953: October 25-26
      Beethoven: *Concerto #4*

O'Connell, Charles (Conductor)
   1941-1942: December 7; Special Concert
      McDonald-Smith, Bach, Beethoven, Wagner

O'Keefe, Francis (Tenor)
   1954-1955: December 23-26
      Schubert: *"Ave Maria"*
         St. Louis Cathedral Men's Choir

Peerce, Jan (Tenor)
   1941-1942: March 13-14
      Handel: *Jeptha*
      Wagner: *Meistersinger*
      Bizet: *Pearl Fishers*
      Verdi: *Aida*
      Scott: "Jasmine Door"

Pellerito, Augustine (Soprano)
   1951-1952: March 16; Special Concert
      Verdi: *La Forza Del Destina*

Tenor Lauritz Melchior and his wife as they looked in the twenties. He sang with the Symphony for the last time in 1950 with Helen Traubel. (Missouri Historical Society)

The French conductor Pierre Monteux was on the Symphony podium for a pair of concerts in 1957. (Missouri Historical Society)

Charles Munch served as one of the guest conductors in 1948. (Missouri Historical Society)

1955-1956: October 30; Pop Concert;
　　Harry Farbman, Conductor
　　Romberg: *The New Moon*
　　Puccini: *Madame Butterfly*
　　Herbert: *Naughty Marietta*

Pennario, Leonard (Piano)
　　1953-1954: December 11-12
　　　Prokofiev: *Concerto #3*
　　　Bartók: *Concerto #3*
　　1954-1955: November 12-13
　　　Rachmaninoff: *Concerto #2*
　　1955-1956: February 3-4
　　　Bartók: *Concerto #3*

Phillips, Helen (Soprano)
　　1954-1955: March 12-13
　　　Beethoven: *Symphony #9*

Piatigorsky, Gregor (Cello)
　　1934-1935: March 8-9
　　　Haydn: *Concerto D*
　　1936-1937: January 15-16
　　　Schumann: *Concerto A minor*
　　1941-1942: November 21-22
　　　Dvořák: *Concerto B minor*
　　1945-1946: November 2-3
　　　Schumann: *Concerto A minor*
　　　R. Strauss: *Don Quixote*
　　1946-1947: January 10-11
　　　Haydn: *Concerto D*
　　　R. Strauss: *Don Quixote*
　　1948-1949: February 18-19
　　　Dvořák: *Concerto B minor*
　　1950-1951: February 17-18
　　　Saint-Saëns: *Concerto A minor*
　　　Milhaud: *Concerto #1*
　　1954-1955: February 12-13
　　　Schumann: *Concerto A*
　　　Brahms: *Double Concerto*
　　　Isaac Stern, Violin
　　1956-1957: February 16-17
　　　Saint-Saëns: *Concerto #1*

Piazza, Marguerite (Soprano)
　　1952-1953: February 22: Richard Rodgers Concert

Richard Rodgers, Conductor
Songs: "Hello, Young Lovers;" "When I Marry
Mr. Snow;" "A Wonderful Guy;" "With a Song in
My Heart;" "People Will Say We're in Love;"
"Oklahoma"

Pingel, James (Baritone)
　　1949-1950: January 29; Pop Concert;
　　　Harry Farbman, Conductor
　　　D'Hardelot: "Because"
　　　Handel: *Atalanta*

Pinza, Ezio (Bass)
　　1941-1942: February 6-7
　　　Mozart: *Don Giovanni*
　　　Moussorgsky: *Boris Godounov*
　　　Brahms: *"Vier Ernste Gesanga"*

Plank, Thomas (Bass)
　　1952-1953: February 8; Pop Concert;
　　　Harry Farbman, Conductor
　　　Bizet: *Carmen*
　　　Kern: *Showboat*

Polk, Eloise (Piano)
　　1947-1948: March 5-6
　　　Beethoven: *Concerto #1*
　　1949-1950: December 31-January 1
　　　Beethoven: *Concerto #4*
　　1951-1952: December 22-23
　　　Chopin: *Concerto #1*
　　1957-1958: April 1; Benefit Concert
　　　Beethoven: *Concerto #4*

Pons, Lily (Soprano)
　　1944-1945: November 23; Special Concert;
　　　Andre Kostelanetz, Conductor
　　　Bishop: "Gentle Lark"
　　　Fauré: *"Roses d'Isparhan"*
　　　Delibes: *Lakmé*
　　　Donezetti: *Lucia de Lammermoor*
　　1947-1948: January 21; Special Concert;
　　　Andre Kostelanetz, Conductor
　　　Verdi: *Rigoletto*
　　　Bishop: "Gentle Lark"
　　　Ponce: "Estrellita"
　　　Strauss: "On the Beautiful Blue Danube"

Famed tenor Jan Peerce has appeared with the orchestra on several occasions. (St. Louis Symphony)

Pianist Leonard Pennario recorded the Bartók and Prokofiev third concertos with the Symphony in 1953. (St. Louis Symphony)

Rossini: *Barber of Seville*
1948-1949: January 10; Special Concert;
  Andre Kostelanetz, Conductor
  Verdi: *Rigoletto*
  Gounod: *Mereille*
  Strauss: "Voices of Spring"
  Delibes: *Lakmé*
  Della'Acqua: *Villanella*
  Bachelet: *"Chere Nuit"*

Pontifical Boys' Choir
1954-1955: December 23-26
  Yon, Reger, Schubert

Posselt, Ruth (Violin)
1939-1940: February 9-10
  Dvořák: *Concerto A minor*

Previtali, Fernando (Conductor)
1956-1957: January 25-26
  Rossini, Brahms, Verdi, Busoni, Martucci
1957-1958: December 26-27
  Verdi, Tchaikovsky, Brahms
  Louis Kentner, Piano

Primrose, William (Viola)
1949-1950: February 24-25
  Handel-Barbirolli: Concerto
  Bartók: *Concerto*

Prokofiev, Sergei (Composer-Conductor-Piano)
1936-1937: January 29-30
  Prokofiev: *Concerto #3;* Suite from *Love for Three Oranges*
  Prokofiev, Conductor

Quartararo, Florence (Soprano)
1948-1949: December 4-5
  Boito: *Mefistofele*
  Mozart: *Marriage of Figaro; Don Giovanni*
  Verdi: *La Traviata*

Rabin, Michael (Violin)
1951-1952: November 10-11
  Paganini: *Concerto #1*
1952-1953: February 6-7
  Prokofiev: *Concerto #2*

Rabushka, Joseph (Violin)
1943-1944: December 26-27
  Paganini: *Concerto #1* (first movement)
1948-1949: November 12-13
  Mozart: *Concerto #4*

Rachmaninoff, Sergei (Composer-Piano)
1932-1933: March 10-11
  Rachmaninoff: *Concerto #2*
1934-1935: December 14-15
  Rachmaninoff: *Rhapsody on a Theme of Paganini*
1935-1936: November 15-16
  Rachmaninoff: *Concerto #3*
1936-1937: November 27-28
  Rachmaninoff: *Concerto #2*
1938-1939: November 4
  Rachmaninoff: *Concerto #1*
November 5
  Beethoven: *Concerto #1*

Rasely, George (Tenor)
1937-1938: December 17-18
  Bach: *Cantata #106*
  Beethoven: *Symphony #9*

Reening, Maria (Soprano)
1938-1939: November 25-26
  Weber: *Euryanthe*
  R. Strauss: *Arabella*

Reiner, Fritz (Conductor)
1935-1936: January 31-February 1
  Handel, Brahms, Debussy, Berlioz, Grétry-Mottl

Renardy, Ossy (Violin)
1950-1951: February 23-24
  Paganini: *Concerto #1*

Rethberg, Elisabeth (Soprano)
1933-1934: December 8-9
  Weber: *Freischütz*
  Schubert: Songs

Ricci, Ruggiero (Violin)
1933-1934: December 1-2
  Lalo: *Symphonie espagnole*

The celebrated bass singer Ezio Pinza appeared with the Symphony in 1942. (Missouri Historical Society)

Lily Pons sang with the Symphony during the forties and her husband Andre Kostelanetz guest-conducted. (Missouri Historical Society)

Conductor Fritz Reiner was on the podium with the Symphony in 1936. (Missouri Historical Society)

Violinist Ruggiero Ricci first appeared with the orchestra in 1933. He recently made the Dvořák recording with the orchestra. (St. Louis Symphony)

Cellist Leonard Rose has been appearing with the orchestra for over twenty years. (St. Louis Symphony)

The outstanding cellist Gregor Piatigorsky appeared with the orchestra on numerous occasions, including a pair of concerts featuring him and Isaac Stern in the Brahms **Double Concerto** in 1955. (Missouri Historical Society)

Riverton Dancers; Elizabeth Schneider, Director
  1952-1953: March 8; Pop Concert;
    Harry Farbman, Conductor
    Copland: *Rodeo*
    Grofe: *Mississippi Suite*
  1957-1958: December 15; Pop Concert;
    Harry Farbman, Conductor
    "T'was the Night Before Christmas"

Robinson, Wilson (Piano)
  1949-1950: February 4-5
    Hindemith: *Theme and Four Variations*

Rodgers, Richard (Composer-Conductor)
  1952-1953: February 22; Special Concert
    Program of Rodgers music

Roecker, Edward (Baritone)
  1946-1947: March 23; Special Concert;
    Edwin McArthur, Conductor
    Friml: "Song of the Vagabonds;" "Rose Marie"
    Romberg: *The Desert Song*

Romberg, Sigmund (Composer-Conductor)
  1946-1947: October 20; Maintenance Fund Concert
    Offenbach, Strauss, Sousa, Kern, Rodgers,
    Schubert-Romberg, Romberg, Lehar

Rose, Leonard (Cello)
  1955-1956: October 28-29
    Saint-Saëns: *Concerto A minor*

Rosenthal, Manuel (Composer-Conductor)
  1946-1947: November 23-24
    Rosenthal: *Musique de Table*

Rosenthal, Moriz (Piano)
  1936-1937: February 14; Pension Fund Concert
    Chopin: *Concerto #1*
    Listz: *Hungarian Fantasy*

Rounseville, Robert (Tenor)
  1951-1952: December 10; United Nations Human
    Rights Day Concert
    Beethoven: *Symphony #9* (finale)

Rubinstein, Arthur (Piano)
  1937-1938: December 10-11
    Brahms: *Concerto #2*
  1938-1939: March 10-11
    Tchaikovsky: *Concerto #1*
  1940-1941: November 8-9
    Beethoven: *Concerto #4*
    de Falla: *Nights in the Gardens of Spain*
  1941-1942: November 28-29
    Chopin: *Concerto #1*
  1942-1943: March 5-6
    Beethoven: *Concerto #4*
  1943-1944: January 15-16
    Rachmaninoff: *Rhapsody on a Theme of Paganini; Concerto #2*
  1944-1945: February 24-25;
    Harry Farbman, Conductor
    Tchaikovsky: *Concerto #1*
  1945-1946: January 19-20
    Schumann: *Concerto A minor*
    de Falla: *Nights in the Gardens of Spain*
  1946-1947: November 23-24
    Mozart: *Concerto #23*
    Chopin: *Concerto #2*
  1947-1948: February 21-22
    Brahms: *Concerto #2*
  1949-1950: November 12-13
    Mozart: *Concerto #23*
    de Falla: *Nights in the Gardens of Spain*
  1951-1952: March 22-23
    Brahms: *Concerto #2*
    Chopin: *Concerto #2*
    Rachmaninoff: *Rhapsody on a Theme of Paganini*
  1954-1955: March 26
    Beethoven: *Concerto #4*
    March 27
    Tchaikovsky: *Concerto #1*
  1955-1956: March 17
    Schumann: *Concerto A minor*
    March 18
    Chopin: *Concerto #1*
  1956-1957: March 16
    Chopin: *Concerto #2*
    March 17
    Rachmaninoff: *Concerto #2*
  1957-1958: February 8; Special Concert

Brahms: *Concert #1*
Rachmaninoff: *Concerto #2*
February 9; Special Concert
Chopin: *Concerto #1*
Schumann: *Concerto A minor*

Rudnitsky, Alvin (Violin)
  1950-1951: December 31; Pop Concert;
    Harry Farbman, Conductor
  Lalo: *Symphonie espagnole* (andante, rondo)

Russell, Shirley (Soprano)
  1954-1955: December 4-5
  Fauré: *Requiem*

Russo, Maria (Soprano)
  1948-1949: February 20; Pop Concert;
    Harry Farbman, Conductor
  Mozart: *Marriage of Figaro*
  Kreisler: "Stars in My Eyes"
  Oscar Straus: "My Hero"
  1955-1956: November 13; Pop Concert;
    Harry Farbman, Conductor
  Bizet: *Carmen*
  Sieczynski: "Vienna, City of My Dreams"
  Lara: "Granada"

St. Anthony Choristers
  1935-1936: December 20-21
    Bach: *St. Matthew Passion*
    Borodin: *Prince Igor*

St. Louis Bach Festival Chorus:
  William Heyne, Director
  1950-1951: March 23; Bach Festival Concert
    Bach: *St. John Passion*
    March 24; Bach Festival Concert
    Bach: *Cantata #31*
  1951-1952: December 13; Special Concert
    Bach: *Christmas Oratorio*
    March 8; Bach Festival Concert
    Bach: *Mass B minor*
  1953-1954: December 5-6
    Bach: *Magnificat D*
    March 28; Bach Festival Concert
    Bach: *St. John Passion*

1955-1956: December 11; Special Concert
  Bach: *Cantata #65* (Excerpts)
    Cantata #63
  Berlioz: *L'Enfance* (Excerpts)

St. Louis Cathedral Men's Choir
  1954-1955: December 23-26
    Yon: "Gesu Bambino"
    Reger: "Virgin's Slumber Song"
    Schubert: "Ave Maria"
      Francis O'Keefe, Tenor

St. Louis Civic Ballet; Stanley Herbertt, Director
  1956-1957: March 24; Pop Concert;
    Harry Farbman, Conductor
    Wright-Forrest: *Kismet*
  1957-1958: January 26; Pop Concert;
    Harry Farbman, Conductor
    Tchaikovsky: *The Nutcracker*

St. Louis Institute of Music Chorus
  1952-1953: February 8; Pop Concert;
    Harry Farbman, Conductor
    Bizet: *Carmen*
    Verdi: *La Traviata*
    Romberg: *The Desert Song*
    Strauss: *Die Fledermaus*
    Kern: *Showboat*

Salvador, Mario (Organ)
  1954-1955: December 23-26
    Fischer: *Choral Fantasy*
    Widor: *Toccata*
    Purvis: *Carol Rhapsody*

Sandburg, Carl (Narrator)
  1942-1943: January 28: Special Concert;
    Andre Kostelanetz, Conductor
    Copland: *Lincoln Portrait*

Sanjuan, Pedro (Composer-Conductor)
  1951-1952: December 14-15
    Sanjuan: *La Macumba*

Sanroma, Jesus Maria (Piano)
  1945-1946: February 2-3
    Gershwin: *Concerto in F; Rhapsody in Blue*

1946-1947: October 26-27
  Grieg: *Concerto A minor*
  Gershwin: *Rhapsody in Blue*
1947-1948: January 10-11
  Rachmaninoff: *Concerto #2*
1949-1950: January 7-8
  Ravel: *Concerto G*

Schatzkamer, William (Piano)
  1955-1956: January 14-15
    Khatchaturian: *Concerto D-flat*

Schiller, Edith (Piano)
  1944-1945: November 18-19;
    Harry Farbman, Conductor
    Schumann: *Concerto A minor*
  1946-1947: March 22; Special Concert;
    Edwin McArthur, Conductor
    Gershwin: *Rhapsody in Blue*
  1947-1948: December 19-20;
    Harry Farbman, Conductor
    Beethoven: *Concerto #3*
  1948-1949: January 10; Special Concert;
    Andre Kostelanetz, Conductor
    Gershwin: *Rhapsody in Blue*
  1949-1950: December 16-17;
    Harry Farbman, Conductor
    Rachmaninoff: *Concerto #2*
  1954-1955: November 6-7
    Beethoven: *Triple Concerto*

Schippers, Thomas (Conductor-Piano)
  1955-1956: November 19-20
    Schubert, Bizet, Menotti, Hindemith, Wagner
  1957-1958: January 30-31
    Strauss, Mendelssohn, Sibelius

Schmitz, E. Robert (Piano)
  1934-1935: November 23-24
    Mozart: *Concerto #20*
    de Falla: *Nights in the Gardens of Spain*
  1940-1941: December 6-7
    Prokofiev: *Concerto #3*

Schnabel, Arthur (Piano)
  1933-1934: November 17-18
    Beethoven: *Concerto #3*
  1934-1935: January 25-26
    Beethoven: *Concerto #5*
  1937-1938: March 11-12
    Schumann: *Concerto A minor*

Schnittke, Glenn (Tenor)
  1950-1951: March 23; Bach Festival Concert;
    William Heyne, Conductor
    Bach: *St. John Passion*
    March 24; Bach Festival Concert;
    William Heyne, Conductor
    Bach: *Cantata #31; Easter Oratorio; Cantata #4*
  1951-1952: December 13; Special Concert;
    William Heyne, Conductor
    Bach: Christmas Oratorio
    March 8; Bach Festival Concert;
    William Heyne, Conductor
    Bach: *Mass B minor*
  1953-1954: March 28; Bach Festival Concert;
    William Heyne, Conductor
    Bach: *St. John Passion*

Schorr, Friedrich (Baritone)
  1931-1932: March 11-12
    Wagner: *Meistersinger; Walküre*

Scott, Ann (Soprano)
  1957-1958: January 12; Pop Concert;
    Harry Farbman, Conductor
    Rossini: *Barber of Seville*
    Strauss: *Die Fledermaus*
    Rodgers: *The King and I*

Scottish Rite Choir; Charles Galloway, Director
  1952-1953: January 25; Pop Concert;
    Harry Farbman, Conductor
    Gounod: *Sanctus (Messe Solennelle)*
    Warren: "God of Our Fathers"
    Sullivan: "Onward Christian Soldiers"; *Iolanthe*

Segovia, Andres (Guitar)
  1954-1955: November 20-21
    Castelinuovo-Tedesco: *Concerto D*

Pianist Rudolf Serkin first appeared with the Symphony in 1937. In 1974 they played the Brahms **Concerto No. 2**. (St. Louis Symphony)

Beginning in 1937 pianist Artur Rubinstein appeared with the orchestra almost every season throughout the Golschmann era. (St. Louis Symphony)

Beverly Sills, New York City and Metropolitan Opera soprano, appeared with the orchestra in a 1953 pair of Bach concerts. (Photo Courtesy, New York Philharmonic; Photo Division, CBS Television Network)

Violinist Albert Spalding was one of the great artists who appeared with the orchestra during Golschmann's first season. (Missouri Historical Society)

Senofsky, Berl (Violin)
  1956-1957: December 14-15;
    Igor Markevitch, Conductor
  Prokofiev: *Concerto #1*

Serkin, Rudolf (Piano)
  1936-1937: February 26-27
    Beethoven: *Concerto #5*
  1941-1942: February 27-28
    Schumann: *Concerto A minor*
  1948-1949: January 29-30
    Beethoven: *Concerto #5*
  1952-1953: January 17-18;
    Harry Farbman, Conductor
    Brahms: *Concerto #2*
  1955-1956: December 9-10
    Beethoven: *Concerto #5*
  1956-1957: February 9-10
    Schumann: *Concerto A minor*

Shelton, Edgar (Piano)
  1932-1933: December 2-3
    Tchaikovsky: *Concerto #1*

Shumsky, Oscar (Violin)
  1954-1955: November 26-27
    Brahms: *Concerto D*

Sienczynski, Ruth (Piano)
  1936-1937: December 26-27
    Saint-Saëns: *Concerto #2*

Sills, Beverly (Soprano)
  1953-1954: December 5-6;
    William Heyne, Conductor
    Bach: *Magnificat D*

Simmons, Mary (Soprano)
  1953-1954: March 28; Bach Festival Concert;
    William Heyne, Conductor
    Bach: *St. John Passion*

Singher, Martial (Baritone)
  1948-1949: December 4-5
    Rameau: *Les Indes galantes*
    Berlioz: *Damnation of Faust*
    Mozart: *Don Giovanni*

Verdi: *La Traviata*
  1949-1950: December 22-23
    Rameau: *Les Indes galantes*
    Berlioz: *Damnation of Faust*
    Ravel: *Don Quixote*
    Duparc: *Phidyle*
  1954-1955: December 4-5
    Fauré: *Requiem*

Sirota, Leo (Piano)
  1953-1954: November 21-22
    Strauss: *Burleske*

Skolovsky, Zadel (Piano)
  1950-1951: November 11-12
    Bach: *Concerto D minor*
    Milhaud: *Concerto #4*
  1954-1955: December 31-January 1;
    Lukas Foss, Conductor
    Gershwin: *Concerto in F*

Skorodin, Elaine (Violin)
  1957-1958: January 26; Pop Concert;
    Harry Farbman, Conductor
    Paganini: *Concerto*

Slater, Ruth (Contralto)
  1950-1951: March 23; Bach Festival Concert;
    William Heyne, Conductor
    Bach: *St. John Passion*
    March 24: Bach Festival Concert;
    William Heyne, Conductor
    Bach: *Easter Oratorio; Cantata #4*

Smith, Ethel (Organ)
  1952-1953: November 16; Special Concert
    Debussy: *Clair de Lune*
    de Falla: *Ritual Fire Dance*
    Kabalevsky: *Comedian's Galop*
    Bach: *"Little" Fugue*
    Lecuona: *Andalucia*

Smith, Kenneth (Bass)
  1955-1956: December 31-January 1
    Mozart: *Cosi Fan Tutte* (concert version)
  1956-1957: January 19-20
    Mozart: *Don Giovanni* (concert version)

Leopold Stokowski guest-conducted the St. Louis Symphony in the fifties. (Photo courtesy New York Philharmonic; Whitestone)

Soprano Eleanor Steber sang the vocal part in Mahler's **Symphony No. 4** with the Symphony during the 1968-1969 season. (Missouri Historical Society)

Igor Stravinsky was one of the great composers to guest-conduct the Symphony. (Photo courtesy New York Philharmonic)

Joseph Szigeti played with the Symphony many times throughout the forties. (Missouri Historical Society)

Albert Stoessel was a native of St. Louis. The suite from his opera, **Garrick**, was first performed by the Symphony in 1938. (Ernst C. Krohn Special Collections, Gaylord Music Library, Washington University, St. Louis, Missouri)

Gladys Swarthout, here dressed in her Carmen costume, sang with the orchestra in 1939. (Missouri Historical Sociey)

Smutz, Dorothy Dring (Piano)
  1953-1954: November 15; Pop Concert;
    Harry Farbman, Conductor
    Listz: *Concerto #1*

Solti, Georg (Conductor)
  1955-1956: December 22-23
    Wagner, Mozart, Bartók, Beethoven
  1956-1957: November 16-17
    Mozart, Stravinsky, Brahms
    November 24-25
    Haydn, Franck, Mozart, Kodály
      Robert Casadesus, Piano
  1957-1958: October 30-November 1
    Beethoven
    January 4-5
    Beethoven
    January 9-10
    Beethoven
    Zino Francescatti, Violin
    January 18-19
    Beethoven
      Claudio Arrau, Piano
    January 23-24
    Beethoven

Southwestern Singers
  1952-1953: March 14-15
    Mozart: "Ave Verum"
    Borodin: *Polovtsian Dances*
  1954-1955: December 4-5
    Fauré: *Requiem*

Spalding, Albert (Violin)
  1931-1932: November 13-14
    Respighi: *Concerto Gregoriano*
  1933-1934: March 2-3
    Bach: *Concerto E*
    Chausson: *Poème*
  1936-1937: March 12-13
    Bruch: *Concerto #1*
  1945-1946: February 16-17
    Sibelius: *Concerto D minor*

Spencer, Margaret (Soprano)
  1946-1947: March 15; Special Concert;
    Edwin McArthur, Conductor

Strauss: *Die Fledermaus*
Kreisler: "Midnight Bells"

Spivakovsky, Tossy (Violin)
  1949-1950: November 18-19
    Bartók: *Concerto*
  1955-1956: November 25-26;
    Harry Farbman, Conductor
    Mendelssohn: *Concerto E minor*
  1957-1958: March 15-16
    Mozart: *Adagio E minor*
    Menotti: *Concerto A minor*

Steber, Eleanor (Soprano)
  1947-1948: November 1-2
    Weber: *Freischütz*
    Mozart: *Marriage of Figaro*
    Verdi: *Otello*
    Puccini: *Madama Butterfly; La Bohème*

Steffe, Edwin (Baritone)
  1956-1957: January 19-20
    Mozart: *Don Giovanni* (concert version)

Stein, Ronald (Piano)
  1954-1955: February 20; Washington University
    Second Century Convocation Concert;
    Gustave Haenschen, Conductor
    Addinsell: *Warsaw Concerto*

Stern, Isaac (Violin)
  1943-1944: January 29-30;
    Harry Farbman, Conductor
    Brahms: *Concerto D*
  1944-1945: December 16-17
    Mendelssohn: *Concerto E minor*
  1946-1947: November 29-30
    Bach: *Concerto #2*
    Lalo: *Symphonie espagnol*
  1947-1948: December 27-28;
    Erich Leinsdorf, Conductor
    Mozart: *Concerto #3*
    Ravel: *Tzigane*
  1949-1950: January 21-22
    Tchaikovsky: *Concerto D*
  1951-1952: December 28-29
    Lalo: *Symphonie espagnol*

Baritone John Charles Thomas sang with the Symphony in 1931. (Missouri Historical Society)

St. Louis-born contralto Marion Telva, here shown in operatic costume, made several guest appearances with the orchestra. (Ernst C. Krohn Special Collections, Gaylord Music Library, Washington University, St. Louis, Missouri)

Four members of the orchestra joined composer Alexander Tansman at the piano: Corinne Frederick, and standing left to right, are Herbert Van den Burg, Max Steindel, and Scipione Guidi. (Missouri Historical Society)

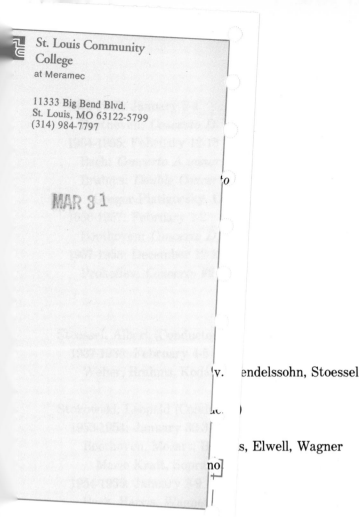

Stolz, Robert (Conductor)
1943-1944: February 4; Special Concert
All-Viennese program
Herta Glaz, Contralto
Mario Berini, Tenor

Strauss, Paul (Conductor)
1957-1958: October 26-27
Britten, Schumann, Brahms
Andre Tchaikovsky, Piano

Stravinsky, Igor (Composer-Conductor-Piano)
1934-1935: February 10; Pension Fund Concert
Stravinsky program
1941-1942: December 19-20
Cherubini, Stravinsky, Tchaikovsky

Summers, Lydia (Contralto)
1951-1952: March 8; Bach Festival Concert;
William Heyne, Conductor
Bach: *Mass B minor*

Sumner High School A Capella Choir and Alumni
Choir; Kenneth Billups, Director
1953-1954: November 29; Pop Concert;
Harry Farbman, Conductor
Spirituals: "My Soul Is a Witness;" "I Been
'Busked;" "Ole Moses Put Pharoah in His Place"
1954-1955: February 18-19;
Harry Farbman, Conductor
Mahler: *Symphony #2*
1955-1956: January 20-21
Stravinsky: *Symphony of Psalms*

Swarthout, Gladys (Mezzo-Soprano)
1939-1940: December 8-9
Bach: *Recitative and Rondo*
Purcell: *Dido and Aeneas*; "Nymphs and
Shepherds"
Canteloube: *"Chants d'Auvergne*

Szigeti, Joseph (Violin)
1940-1941: February 14-15
Beethoven: *Concerto D*
1941-1942: November 7-8
Brahms: *Concerto D*
1943-1944: November 6-7
Mendelssohn: *Concerto E minor*
1945-1946: January 25-26
Prokofiev: *Concerto #1*
1950-1951: March 17-18
Corelli: *La Folia*
Mozart: *Concerto #3*

Tansman, Alexander (Composer-Piano)
1932-1933: January 6-7
Tansman: *Concerto #2*
1936-1937: December 18-19
Tansman: *Concertino for Piano*

Tauber, Richard (Tenor)
1938-1939: March 19; Pension Fund Concert
Schumann: *"Dichterliebe"*
Bizet: *Carmen*
Strauss-Korngold: *"Lieder Liebe"*

Tchaikovsky, Andre (Piano)
1957-1958: October 26-27; Paul Strauss, Conductor
Schumann: *Concerto A minor*

Pianist Alexander Uninsky appeared as soloist with the orchestra on numerous occasions during the forties and fifties. (Missouri Historical Society)

Baritone Lawrence Tibbett sang operatic selections with the orchestra in the thirties. (St. Louis Symphony)

Sopranos Helen Traubel and Margaret Truman both appeared separately with the orchestra during the 1949-1950 season. (St. Louis Post-Dispatch)

Telva, Marion (Contralto)
1932-1933: November 18-19
Tchaikovsky: *Jeanne d'Arc*
Songs: Schubert, Strauss
1937-1938: March 18-19
Wagner: *Lohengrin* (concert version)

Templeton, Alec (Piano)
1940-1941: February 25; Pension Fund Concert
Schumann: *Concerto A minor*
1945-1946: October 27-28
Grieg: *Concerto A minor*

Thomas, John Charles (Baritone)
1931-1932: December 4-5
Verdi: *Otello*
Songs: Strauss, Brahms, Marx

Thomas, Thomas L. (Baritone)
1954-1955: February 20; Washington University
Second Century Convocation Concert
Kern: *Showboat*

Thomson, Virgil (Composer-Conductor)
1942-1943: February 5-6
Thomson: *Fanfare for France; Symphony #2*

Tibbett, Lawrence (Baritone)
1935-1936: December 13-14
Handel: *Semele*
Verdi: *Otello*
Rossini: *Barber of Seville*
Wagner: *Walküre*
1938-1939: February 10-11
Mozart: *Don Giovanni*
Verdi: *Masked Ball*
Wagner: Tannhäuser; Traume; Meistersinger

Tipo, Maria (Piano)
1954-1955: February 25-26
Mozart: *Concerto #21*

Torres, Carmen (Soprano)
1946-1947: November 15-16
Gluck: *Poride Elena*
Mozart: *Magic Flute*

Donizetti: *Lucia de Lammermoor*
Songs: Bachelet, Delibes, Calleja, de Falla

Tourel, Jennie (Mezzo-Soprano)
1944-1945: February 10-11;
Leonard Bernstein, Conductor
Stradella: *"Pieta, Signore"*
Tchaikovsky: *Jeanne d'Arc*
Bernstein: *Jeremiah Symphony*
Duparc: *"Invitation au Voyage"*
1949-1950: December 3-4
Duparc: *Invitation au Voyage*
Ravel: "Kaddish"
Prokofiev: *Alexander Nevsky*
Rossini: *Barber of Seville*
1957-1958: November 14-15
Mahler: *Das Lied von der Erde*

Traubel, Helen (Soprano)
1932-1933: January 28; Pop Concert;
Scipione Guidi, Conductor
Verdi: *Aida*
Wagner: *Lohengrin*
1934-1935: February 15-16
de Falla: *El Amor Brujo*
1935-1936: December 20-21
Bach: *St. Matthew Passion*
Ravel: *Shéhérazade*
1937-1938: March 18-19
Wagner: *Lohengrin* (concert version)
1940-1941: January 31-February 1
Wagner: *Tristan und Isolde; Götterdämmerung*
1945-1946: February 23-24
Beethoven: *Die Ehre Gottes Aus der Natur;*
Egmont
Wagner: *Tristan und Isolde*
1949-1950: January 24; Special Concert
Wagner: *Tristan und Isolde* (concert version)

Travers, Patricia (Violin)
1943-1944: March 4-5
Tchaikovsky: *Concerto D*
1947-1948: January 16-17
Saint-Saëns: *Concerto #3*

Truman, Margaret (Soprano)
  1949-1950: October 29-30
    Mozart: *Marriage of Figaro*
    Glazounov: *La Primavera*
  1950-1951: March 11; Special Concert
    Mozart: *Marriage of Figaro*
    Delibes: *Coppélia*

Turner, Claramae (Contralto)
  1952-1953: February 22; Special Concert;
    Richard Rodgers, Conductor
    Rodgers: "It's a Grand Night for Singing;" "Bali
    Ha'i;" "Where or When;" "Out of My Dreams;"
    "Oklahoma"

Ukena, Paul (Bass)
  1953-1954: March 28; Bach Festival Concert;
    William Heyne, Conductor
    Bach: *St. John Passion*
  1955-1956: December 11; Special Concert;
    William Heyne, Conductor
    Bach: *Cantata #63*
    Berlioz: *L'Enfance* (Excerpts)

Uninsky, Alexander (piano)
  1944-1945: November 25-26
    Prokofiev: *Concerto #3*
  1945-1946: November 16-17
    Tchaikovsky: *Concerto #1*
  1946-1947: January 24-25
    Chopin: *Concerto #1*
  1947-1948: November 21-22
    Beethoven: *Concerto #5*
  1949-1950: November 25-26
    Chopin: *Concerto #1*
  1951-1952: February 22-23
    Prokofiev: *Concerto #3*
  1955-1956: January 6-7
    Tchaikovsky: *Concerto #1*
  1957-1958: November 27-29
    Chopin: *Concerto #1*

University of Missouri Choral Union
  R. Oscar Clymer, Director
  1949-1950: December 3-4
    Prokofiev: *Alexander Nevsky*

1954-1955: March 12-13
  Beethoven: *Symphony #9*

Van Remoortel, Edouard (Conductor)
  1957-1958: December 7-8
    Wagner, Brahms, Sibelius
    Melvin Ritter, Violin
    Leslie Parnas, Cello
  December 12-13
    Bartók, Prokofiev, Schumann, Dukas
    Isaac Stern, Violin

Versaci, Frank (Flute)
  1947-1948: Special Concert
  1948-1949: Special Concert

Villa-Lobos, Heitor (Composer-Conductor)
  1955-1956: December 17-18
    Handel, Honegger, Strauss, Villa-Lobos

Vlashek, Helen (Soprano)
  1950-1951: December 31; Pop Concert;
    Harry Farbman, Conductor
    Puccini: *La Bohème; Madama Butterfly*

Vreeland, Jeannette (Soprano)
  1931-1932: October 30-31
    Mozart: *"Il Re Pastore"*
    Songs: Thuille, Marx, Dvořák
  1934-1935: March 15-16
    Beethoven: *Symphony #9*
  1935-1936: April 3-4
    Verdi: *Requiem*

Wagner, Josef (Piano)
  1938-1939: December 29-30;
    Scipione Guidi, Conductor
    Chopin: *Concerto #2*

Warfield, William (Bass-Baritone)
  1951-1952: December 10; United Nations Human
    Rights Day Concert
    Beethoven: *Symphony #9* (Finale)

Warren, Leonard (Baritone)
  1955-1956: February 11-12

Donaudy: *"O Del Mio Amato Ben"*
Handel: *Xerxes*
Verdi: *Otello*
Gounod: *Faust*
Giordano: *Andrea Chenier*

Washington University Chorus
1954-1955: Washington University Second
Century Convocation Concert;
Gustave Haenschen, Conductor
February 20
Mascagni: *Cavalleria Rusticana*
Kern: *Showboat*

Weber, Harry (Baritone)
1953-1954: November 1; Pop Concert;
Harry Farbman, Conductor
Romberg: *Maytime*
Rodgers: *South Pacific, Carousel*
Friml: "Donkey Serenade"
A Tribute to Romberg
1954-1955: Public School Administration Concert
1955-1956: Rodgers-Hammerstein Festival

Webster, Beveridge (Piano)
1934-1935: December 28-29
Schumann: *Concerto A minor*
1939-1940: March 15-16
Mendelssohn: *Concerto G minor*
Stravinsky: *Capriccio*

Weede, Robert (Baritone)
1952-1953: February 22; Special Concert;
Richard Rodgers, Conductor
Rodgers: "It's a Grand Night for Singing;" "Blue
Room;" "Soliloquy;" (*Carousel*) "Some Enchan-
ted Evening;" "With a Song in My Heart;" "The
Surrey with a Fringe on Top;" "Oklahoma"

Welitch, Ljuba (Soprano)
1951-1952: February 16-17
R. Strauss: *"Im Abendrot"* from "Four Last
Songs;" *Salome* (final scene)

Whittemore and Lowe (Duo-Piano)
1946-1947: November 15-16
K.P.E. Bach: *Concerto for Two Pianos*
Poulenc: *Concerto D minor for Two Pianos*

Willoughby, Jay (Baritone)
1957-1958: December 21-22
Menotti: *The Telephone*

Wittgenstein, Paul (Piano)
1943-1944: February 19-20
Ravel: *Concerto for the Left Hand*

Yeend, Francis (Soprano)
1946-1947: January 18-19
Gounod: *Faust*
Puccini: *La Bohème*

Zimbalist, Efrem (Violin)
1937-1938: December 3-4
Tchaikovsky: *Concerto D*

CHAPTER IV

INTO A NEW ERA

The legacy of the Golschmann years to the history of the St. Louis Symphony Orchestra was indeed great. Everyone associated with the institution during those years helped contribute to something very special in the minds of many music-loving St. Louisans.

As time elapses, new audiences emerge. And the events of the orchestra over the past twenty years are more familiar to a growing number of music patrons. Since 1958 the St. Louis Symphony Orchestra has reached new heights, and a proud history is constantly being enhanced.

The Symphony Society hired a young Belgian conductor, Edouard Van Remoortel, to replace Vladimir Golschmann. Thomas Sherman called him a "musician of intelligence, taste and skilled technical leadership."[1]

The 32-year-old native of Brussels conducted more than fifty orchestras on four continents before he arrived in St. Louis. Since 1951 he had been conductor of the Belgian National Orchestra. Van Remoortel was a member of a well-known Belgian family; his father was a senator and represented his country in the United Nations, and his second cousin was Paul-Henri Spaak, the Secretary General of NATO. In 1960 King Baudouin made Van Remoortel a Knight of the Order of Leopold II for his contributions to the arts.

Van Remoortel served as permanent conductor of the St. Louis Symphony until Eleazar De Carvalho replaced him at the beginning of the 1963-1964 season. The Belgian conductor was brilliant, but managed to generate much animosity from the musicians because of his moves to replace many of the players with musicians of his own choosing.

Eleazar De Carvalho, a native of Brazil, attended the University of Brazil at Rio de Janeiro, where he received a doctorate in music. He conducted the Brazilian Symphony Orchestra and the orchestra of the Teatro Municipal in Rio de Janeiro. He was a member of the staff of the Berkshire Music Center at Tanglewood, Massachusetts, under Serge Koussevitsky, and served for a time as guest conductor of the Boston Symphony. His last position before arriving in St. Louis was that of permanent conductor of the Brazilian Symphony Orchestra.

De Carvalho enjoyed a reputation as a composer and as a champion of new music. When he assumed his new duties in St. Louis he said, "I cannot stay in a community where we have to keep playing Tchaikovsky."[2] The conductor succeeded in bringing in new works to the repertoire of the orchestra, and soon acquired the reputation of an

The Belgian conductor Edouard Van Remoortel succeeded Vladimir Golschmann in 1958. He stayed in St. Louis as permanent conductor for five seasons. (St. Louis Symphony)

Maestro Van Remoortel made special seating arrangements for the orchestra tours. (St. Louis Symphony)

Cellists Pasquale De Conto and Leslie Parnas sometime in the late fifties. (St. Louis Symphony)

Some of the musicians in the early sixties. Left to right seated: Melvin Ritter, James Krohn, Ernest Walker, Jr., Sol Kranzberg, Israel Borouchoff, Carl Sonik, Earl Bates, Henry Sigismonti, Robert Wisneskey, Howard Colf, Rosemary Goldsmith, Herbert Van den Burg. Standing: Henry Loew and Assistant Conductor Edward Murphy. (St. Louis Symphony)

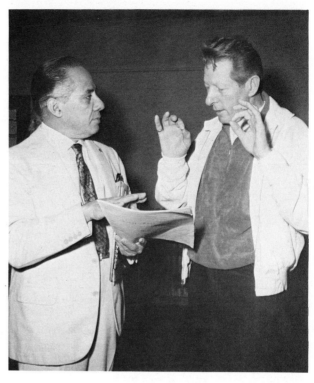

Maestro De Carvalho and Danny Kaye making plans for a concert by the orchestra at which the comedian appeared. (St. Louis Symphony)

Eleazar De Carvalho conducted the Symphony for five controversial years, 1963 to 1968. (St. Louis Symphony)

experimenter in the concert hall. At the conclusion of De Carvalho's first season with the St. Louis Symphony, Thomas Sherman wrote,

> The record does not support the charge that the concert hall was turned into a laboratory. The avant-garde material was restricted to about ten per cent of the whole season's offerings. And if art music is to be regarded as a living phenomenon and not an antiquarian's demonstration, a conscientious conductor cannot ignore the cultural trends of his own time. [3]

But many St. Louis music patrons did not appreciate such things as electronic music and recorded sounds during their concerts. They preferred the established works with which they were familiar. One 1964 letter to the newspaper from an audience member demonstrates this hostility,

> If Mr. De Carvalho enjoys this sort of thing let him play it on his own tape recorder but not at the expense of concert-goers who paid their money to hear music. If this is music, then someone is certainly playing a joke on the human race. [4]

De Carvalho generally enjoyed rapport with the members of the orchestra. In fact, one of the most important considerations which the Symphony Society made in hiring him was the fact that the players voted for him over the other men who had guest-conducted during the 1962-1963 season. And many patrons remember the exciting performances of the Verdi and Berlioz Requiems staged under De Carvalho's direction. But growing opposition to the conductor's programming led to his replacement at the conclusion of the 1967-1968 season.

Eleazar De Carvalho, shown here before he joined the St. Louis Symphony, was a native of Brazil and a champion of new music. (St. Louis Symphony)

Three prominent members of the Symphony Society in 1964 were, from left: William Zalken, Secretary; Stanley Goodman, member of the Board of Directors; Orrin S. Wightman, Jr., President. (St. Louis Symphony)

The next year saw the native Czech, Walter Susskind, arrive in St. Louis to assume the duties of permanent conductor of the Symphony. Born in Prague, Susskind studied piano, composing, and conducting at the State Conservatory in that city. Before he headed the St. Louis Symphony he was conductor of the Scottish Orchestra, the Victoria Symphony of Melbourne, the Toronto Symphony, and the Aspen Music Festival in Colorado.

Under Walter Susskind, the Symphony established a reputation that it had not enjoyed since the best years of the Golschmann era. Susskind increased the orchestra to ninety-six musicians, with special emphasis on the string section. Attendance rose during his tenure from 263,400 to 500,000. [5] Season subscriptions went from 5,200 to 14,300, and the number of subscription concerts rose from fifty-six to eighty-three. [6]

Because of a desire to devote more time to composing and guest-conducting elsewhere, Susskind retired at the conclusion of the 1974-1975 season and turned the permanent directing duties of the orchestra over to Jerzy Semkow.

The new permanent conductor of the St. Louis Symphony was born in Poland. He arrived in St. Louis in 1975 with past experience as conductor of the Royal Opera House and the Royal Danish Symphony Orchestra of Copenhagen, the Bolshoi Theatre of Moscow, and the National Opera of Warsaw. Semkow inherited, at the start of the 1975-1976 season, a St. Louis Symphony Orchestra of better musical quality and of greater financial stability than any orchestra in the organization's proud history.

Jerzy Semkow's first season proved successful. His opening concert began with Mozart's Overture to *The Abduction from the Seraglio*. And with its playing, the audience observed a precise and disciplined performance. The season brought such outstanding soloists as Zara Nelsova, Pinchas Zuckerman, Itzhak Perlman, and Eileen Farrell (in a concert version of *Tristan und Isolde*) to St. Louis, and two favorites of the Golschmann era returned again--Isaac Stern and Claudio Arrau. The orchestra's musicians appreciated the new conductor's demands for perfection and his goal to further enhance the reputation of the ensemble.

One of the greatest musical artists of modern times, Isaac Stern has been appearing with the Symphony for well over three decades. (St. Louis Symphony)

Soprano Eileen Farrell has delighted St. Louis audiences with her Wagnerian performances. (St. Louis Symphony)

Jerzy Semkow joined the Symphony as permanent conductor in 1975. The 1978-1979 season marks the end of his tenure in that position. (St. Louis Symphony)

Walter Susskind was permanent conductor of the Symphony from 1968 to 1975. (St. Louis Symphony)

Maestro Semkow and some of the musicians during one of the Eastern tours. (St. Louis Symphony)

Today the Symphony plays in a building that is one of the most beautiful music halls anywhere. Powell Symphony Hall is the first permanent home in the history of the orchestra. In January 1968 the musicians presented the first concerts in Powell Hall.

Several years before, Oscar Johnson, Jr. again responded to the needs of the Symphony, as he had done so many times in the past, by donating $500,000 for the construction of a new home for the orchestra.[7] As previously noted, Kiel Auditorium was no longer suitable for the regular concerts, and the Symphony Society was eager to have its own home. The Ford Foundation offered the Symphony two million dollars with the stipulation that the Symphony raise the same amount in matching funds, and so in 1966 the organization started the first capital fund-raising drive in its history, and Mrs. Walter S. Powell, widow of a St. Louis shoe manufacturing executive, donated one million dollars to the campaign.[8] When the St. Louis Theatre on North Grand Avenue, a vaudeville and movie house opened in 1925, became available to the Symphony, the organization bought the building at a cost of $388,475 and spent another two million dollars to renovate it.[9] The process was much less expensive than the construction of a new building would have been, and represented a pioneering effort at re-cycling a beautiful old structure.

The program for the opening gala concert in the new 2,685-seat hall included Gunther Schuller's *Fanfare for St. Louis* (which the Symphony commissioned and the composer conducted), Benjamin Britten's *The Building of the House*, and *Petrouchka* by Stravinsky. Eleazar De Carvalho and Schuller conducted the program. Isaac Stern, who played in the opening pair of regular concerts at the hall, said of Powell Hall, "It ranks with Carnegie Hall in New York and Symphony Hall in Boston."[10]

In 1977 the stage area of the hall was remodeled. The stage ceiling was lowered ten feet which enabled the musicians to hear their own sounds better. In addition to improved stage lighting, plans called for the addition of humidity controls and stage air conditioning. This work was supervised by Dr. Cyril Harris of Columbia University, the acoustical consultant for the conversion of the building into a symphony hall. Dr. Harris also directed the renovation of the concert halls at Kennedy Center in Washington, D.C., the Avery Fisher Hall and Metropolitan Opera House in New York, and Orchestra Hall in Minneapolis.

The St. Louis Theatre, shown here about 1950, became Powell Symphony Hall, the permanent home of the orchestra, in 1968. (Missouri Historical Society)

(Left) The audience arriving on Symphony night at Powell Hall. (St. Louis Symphony)

(Right) Much planning and hard work went into the transformation of the St. Louis Theatre into Powell Hall. (St. Louis Symphony)

A major force in the success of a large symphony orchestra is a talented and dedicated management staff. As previously noted, the Symphony had usually been fortunate in this regard. One of the most important reasons for the growing success of the St. Louis Symphony during the 1970s was its executive director, Peter Pastreich. A native of New York City and a graduate of Yale University, Pastreich had done management work with the Denver Symphony, Baltimore Symphony, Greenwich Village Symphony, Nashville Symphony, and Kansas City Philharmonic before arriving in St. Louis in 1966 at the age of twenty-eight to be associate manager. That same year he was named manager of the orchestra, and in 1971 became executive director of the organization. Pastreich soon established himself as one of the most able administrators in the arts. When in 1977 he announced that he was moving to San Francisco to take a similar position with the orchestra of that city, it could be noted that during his tenure in St. Louis every facet of the Symphony's operation had improved dramatically. The number of concerts per year had increased from 136 to 217. Attendance had increased three-fold to 600,000. The annual budget increased from $862,000 to $4,700,000, and the orchestra's endowment increased to $6,000,000 from only $50,000.[11] Commenting on the Pastreich years in St. Louis, Ben Wells, then president of the Symphony Society, said that "the era of Peter Pastreich has been one of remarkable progress in quality, performance and service of the orchestra. Everything became greater every year."[12]

Pastreich was succeeded as executive director by David J. Hyslop, the 35-year-old manager of the Oregon Symphony in Portland. A native of Schenectady, New York, Hyslop attended Ithaca College and participated in the arts management program of the American Symphony Orchestra League. Before heading the Oregon Symphony, he was assistant managing director of the Minnesota Orchestra, and he presently serves on the board of directors of the American Symphony Orchestra League. His tenure in Oregon was marked by a dramatic increase in the number of concerts, the audience, and the budget of that orchestra, and he looked forward to heading the St. Louis Symphony Orchestra as it approached its centennial anniversary.

Peter Pastreich served as executive director of the Symphony from 1971 to 1978. He now heads the San Francisco Symphony. (St. Louis Symphony)

Gunther Schuller's **Fanfare for St. Louis** was one of the works which the orchestra played in the gala opening concert of Powell Hall in 1968. (St. Louis Symphony)

Some of the decorations which make Powell Hall one of the most beautiful symphony halls in the United States. (St. Louis Symphony)

 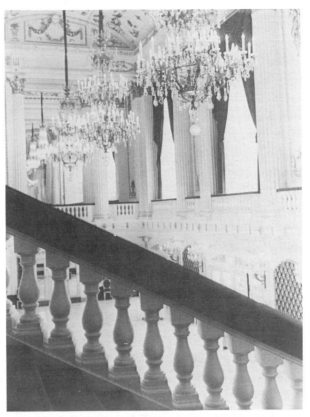

The magnificent main lobby of Powell Hall. (St. Louis Symphony)

One of the most familiar figures seen by Symphony patrons in recent years has been Leonard Slatkin. Brought to St. Louis in 1968 by Walter Susskind as an assistant conductor, he served as principal guest conductor during the 1976-1977 season. Just 24 years old when he began his conducting duties in St. Louis, Slatkin endeared himself to audiences with his enthusiasm and his explanations of new works which he delivered to the audiences from the podium. He founded the St. Louis Symphony Youth Orchestra, and was responsible for the introduction of much American music to St. Louis audiences. In 1977 Slatkin was appointed music director of the New Orleans Philharmonic, and continued to enhance his reputation as one of the leading young conductors in America.

In the spring of 1978 Jerzy Semkow announced that he would serve with the Symphony through the next season, and then leave his permanent position in St. Louis. Thus, the Symphony Society began the search for a new permanent conductor to begin with the 1979-1980 season, the year when the orchestra would begin its centennial anniversary celebration. The organization hired Leonard Slatkin for the job. Thus, an already familiar figure to St. Louis music patrons would take on an even more important role in the history of the St. Louis Symphony.

The St. Louis Symphony has employed many fine concertmasters throughout its long history. We have already seen how Scipione Guidi and Harry Farbman contributed to the musical excellence of the orchestra during the Golschmann period. Farbman retired as concertmaster in 1961 and was succeeded by Melvin Ritter. In 1965 Max Rabinowitsj assumed that role with the orchestra, and has been a familiar figure in St. Louis musical circles ever since.

Like Edouard Van Remoortel, Rabinowitsj was born in Brussels. He entered the Royal Conservatory of Music there at the age of ten, and studied at the New School of Music at Philadelphia and the University of Miami in Florida. After attending Curtis Institute of Music, he served as concertmaster of the Ottawa Philharmonic in Canada and played with the New Orleans Philharmonic and the Cincinnati Symphony before joining the orchestra in St. Louis. He had also been concertmaster of the Santa Fe Opera Company.

At the conclusion of the 1976-1977 season, Max Rabinowitsj retired from the St. Louis Symphony to become director of the St. Louis Conservatory of Music. During the following season Jacques Israelievitch, the 28-year-old assistant concertmaster of the Chicago Symphony, was named concertmaster in St. Louis. A native of Le Mans, France, he graduated from the Paris Conservatory at the age of sixteen, and he brought the experiences of frequent appearances throughout Europe and Canada with him to his new position.

The principal chair of the second violin section since 1968 has been occupied by Fryderyk Sadowski. This native of Poland, and former concertmaster of the Polish National Symphony, came to St. Louis when Walter Susskind learned that he was being forced to leave Poland. Sadowski spent time during the Second World War in a concentration camp, and perhaps owes his life to the fact that he was a musician. His SS guard saw to it that he had enough food; for this privilege he had to serenade the guard with his violin each evening.

Leonard Slatkin will become the permanent conductor of the orchestra at the beginning of the 1979-1980 season. (St. Louis Symphony)

A native of Belgium, Max Rabinovitsj was concertmaster of the orchestra from 1965 to 1977. (St. Louis Symphony)

Frederyk Sadowski has been principal of the second violin section since 1968. (St. Louis Symphony)

A native of France, Jacques Israelievitch joined the orchestra as concertmaster during the 1977-1978 season. (St. Louis Symphony)

The members of the St. Louis String Quartet several years ago consisted of Symphony musicians Max Rabinovitsj, John Korman, John Sant' Ambrogio, and Darrel Barnes. Korman is presently Associate Concertmaster and Sant' Ambrogio is Principal Cellist. (St. Louis Symphony)

A rehearsal for the orchestra, the chorus, and solo vocalists under the direction of Leonard Slatkin.
(St. Louis Symphony)

As previously noted, for a brief time during the 1930s the Symphony used its own chorus. In 1977 this practice was revived, and the orchestra was one of only six in the United States to employ its own choral group; the others being in Chicago, Cleveland, San Francisco, Cincinnati, and Atlanta. The new chorus director in St. Louis was Thomas Peck, who also served as Director of Choruses for the Cincinnati May Festival, and Founder and Director of the Grant Park Symphony Chorus in Chicago. The chorus was used for the first time when the Symphony performed Thomas Colgrass' *Theatre of the Universe* and the *Alexander Nevsky* Cantata by Sergei Prokofiev in 1977. Thereafter, the 146-member chorus performed in the Symphony's rendition of Verdi's *Four Sacred Pieces*, John Knowles Paine's *Mass in D*, and other works. It appeared as though the new chorus would enjoy a bright future.

As was true during earlier times, matters of finance continued to demand attention from those interested in Symphony affairs during the post-Golschmann era. Two musicians' strikes occurred during that time; in the fall of 1968 and 1976. But music patrons had cause to be optimistic about the financial situation of the St. Louis Symphony. In 1977 the Symphony Society announced the beginning of a

special fund-raising campaign to coincide with the orchestra's centennial in 1980. Known as the "Fund for a Second Century," the goal of the campaign was to raise $13,719,547. [13] These funds would be used to renovate Powell Hall, to cover annual operating expenses, to eliminate accumulated budget deficits, and to triple the Symphony's endowment. With the announcement in February 1978 that Emerson Electric Company had donated $500,000 to the Fund (the largest corporate gift in the orchestra's history), the amount of money raised for the project totaled more than five million dollars. [14] That firm's gift was to be used as an endowment for annual Emerson Electric Company Season Opening Concerts, beginning with the 1978-1979 season.

In 1977 the Symphony was awarded two very significant challenge grants. The Andrew W. Mellon Foundation announced a grant of $350,000 to the Symphony. This was one of the largest that the foundation awarded to twenty-seven orchestras. [15] And also during that year the National Endowment for the Arts awarded a grant to the Symphony of one million dollars, to be matched in new or increased income from contributions to the orchestra on the basis of at least three dollars for every grant dollar. This money was to be raised by the end of 1979. The St. Louis Symphony was one of only six orchestras in the nation to be awarded the maximum sum of one million dollars. [16]

(**Upper left**) In 1973 Susan Slaughter became the first woman to be appointed principal trumpet of a major American orchestra. (St. Louis Symphony)

(**Upper right**) Roland Pandolfi has been the principal horn player since 1966. (St. Louis Symphony)

(**Above**) George Silfies has been principal of the clarinets in the orchestra since 1970. (St. Louis Symphony)

The 1970s saw the creation of several principal chair endowments in the orchestra. These included the Eloise and Oscar Johnson, Jr. Concertmaster chair, the Louis D. Beaumont Associate Concertmaster chair, the Dr. Frederick Eno Woodruff Principal Second Violin chair, the Frank Y. and Katherine G. Gladney Principal Cello chair, the Elizabeth Eliot Mallinckrodt Principal Harp chair, the Symphony Women's Association Principal Trumpet chair, the Florence G. and Morton J. May Principal Keyboard Instruments chair, and the anonymously-endowed Walter Susskind Principal Clarinet chair and Principal Percussion chair.

In its efforts to raise funds and to increase ticket sales, the Symphony Society employed many of the methods which had been successful in the past. The Women's Association continued to be of invaluable assistance in this field.

For the first time in its history, the Symphony organized a "Music Marathon" in 1978. To raise money for operating expenses, the Women's Association, radio station KFUO-FM, and the Plaza Frontenac shopping center staged the event over a three-day period. Interested persons were invited to make purchases from among hundreds of items donated for the special sale. Among the premiums available were services offered by members of the orchestra, including a variety of music lessons and private concerts. The value of the premiums ranged from ten to 8,500 dollars. For the latter price, an interested patron could buy the right to conduct or be soloist with the Symphony during a special concert. Patrons could also purchase broadcast requests. The radio station played certain musical compositions of the buyer's choosing. This method of raising funds had been successful in other cities, and there was reason to believe that it would be no less successful in St. Louis. More than $52,000 was raised as the result of the event.[17] A similar event was planned for 1979.

One of the criteria for measuring the success of an orchestra is the number and variety of concerts presented during a year. Beginning in 1969 the St. Louis Symphony inaugurated a series of musical programs which increased the employment for the musicians and served to present a greater variety of musical programming to the orchestra's patrons.

Many of the nation's leading orchestras spend part of the summer season performing away from their usual concert halls, usually in a semi-rural setting. In June 1969 the St. Louis Symphony inaugurated its participation in the Mississippi River Festival on the campus of Southern Illinois University at Edwardsville. The orchestra played the normal classical literature on weekends over a six-week season in a large tènt with a seating capacity of 1,850. There was also room for ten thousand persons on an adjoining lawn outside the tent. During the week the Festival employed a variety of pop and folk artists. Some of the major instrumental soloists appeared with the orchestra during Festival concerts, including such musicians as Van Cliburn, Gary Graffman, and Eugene Istomin. Outstanding singers such as Ezio Flagello made appearances. And guest conductors included Aaron Copland, Andre Kostelanetz, Henry. Mancini, Mitch Miller, Michel Legrand, Leroy Anderson, and Arthur Fiedler. The Mississippi River Festival provided an opportunity to hear great music and outstanding guest artists in a relaxing atmosphere. In recent years, for financial reasons, Symphony participation in the Festival has been reduced.

The 1969-1970 season saw the inauguration of the Baroque Orchestra series at Powell Hall. The regular Symphony musicians play in the Baroque series, with assistance from such outstanding guest conductors and soloists as Alexander Schneider, Jean-Pierre Rampal, Szymon Goldberg, and Janos Starker.

During a 1977 series of all-Mozart concerts, pianist Eugene Istomin played that composer's **Concerto No. 21** with the orchestra. (St. Louis Symphony)

Alexander Schneider has conducted the Symphony in its popular Baroque series. (St. Louis Symphony)

Ezio Flagello, the operatic bass, is one of the many artists who have appeared with the orchestra at the Mississippi River Festival. (St. Louis Symphony)

The American composer Aaron Copland has conducted the orchestra in performances of his own works. They have appeared at the Mississippi River Festival. (St. Louis Symphony)

Probably the most famous flutist in the world today, Jean Pierre Rampal has appeared with the orchestra in its Baroque series. (St. Louis Symphony)

Mitch Miller has brought his popular sing-along format to Symphony concerts on many occasions. (St. Louis Symphony)

The most extensive chamber music series outside New York City, and the only one sponsored directly by a major symphony orchestra, was begun in 1973 by the Symphony.[18] Known as "A Musical Offering," the series was presented during its first three years at the Edison Theatre at Washington University, and thereafter at the Grace Methodist Church. Guest soloists who have performed at the concerts have included Rudolf Firkusny, Jeffrey Siegel, Zara Nelsova, Abbey Simon, John Browning, Walter Susskind, and Leonard Slatkin.

Some of the orchestra members playing in one of the chamber music concerts when the series was performed at the Edison Theater of Washington University. (St. Louis Symphony)

Pianist John Browning has appeared with the orchestra on a number of occasions in recent years. In 1977 he contributed to the performance of Prokofiev's **Concerto No. 3**. (St. Louis Symphony)

Pianist Abbey Simon has performed with the orchestra in St. Louis concerts and on the Rachmaninoff recordings. (St. Louis Symphony)

Interior of the Grace Methodist Church, site of the Symphony's chamber music concerts. (St. Louis Symphony)

One of the most popular innovations in the history of the Symphony was the inauguration of the St. Louis County Pops concert series in 1975. This series has been held each summer at Queeny Park and has been supported by St. Louis County and the Missouri State Council on the Arts. The 1978 season saw this popular concert series expand to several other locations in St. Louis County.

A major reason for the success of the programs has been its principal conductor, Richard Hayman. As the chief arranger for the Boston Pops Orchestra, Hayman is known as an exciting and innovative conductor and arranger, and has brought much entertainment to the patrons of the St. Louis County Pops concerts.

As previously noted, the St. Louis Symphony has had a long history of bringing good music to the youth of the St. Louis area. One of the most notable events in this field was the creation of the St. Louis Symphony Youth Orchestra in 1970. Originally under the direction of Leonard Slatkin, the orchestra in recent years has played under the baton of Gerhardt Zimmermann. Playing several concerts each season, the Youth Orchestra in 1978 was composed of 110 members. In 1976 the orchestra was accorded the honor of participating in the International Youth and Music Festival in Vienna, Austria as the Resident Orchestra. That was the first time that an American orchestra had been so honored. Sponsored by the Women's Association of the Symphony Society, the Youth Orchestra can rightly claim to be one of the finest musical ensembles of its kind anywhere.

The Youth Orchestra's Music Director and Conductor, Gerhardt Zimmermann, became Assistant Conductor of the St. Louis Symphony in 1974, and Associate Conductor in 1978. He directs the student and tour concerts, and has made guest appearances with a number of the leading orchestras of the nation. In 1978 he had the difficult job of substituting on the podium for Walter Susskind during a Symphony concert at Carnegie Hall in New York. His performance was praised by the New York music critics.

Richard Hayman's conducting and arranging have made the St. Louis County Pops series extremely successful. (St. Louis Symphony)

Gerhardt Zimmermann is the associate conductor of the Symphony and also conducts the Youth Orchestra. (St. Louis Symphony)

During the sixties and seventies soprano Elinor Ross has appeared with the Symphony in Beethoven's **Missa Solemnis**, Britten's **War Requiem**, and Verdi's **Requiem**. In 1974 she sang in the concert version of **Aida** at the Mississippi River Festival. (St. Louis Symphony)

One of the County Pops performances. (St. Louis Symphony)

The continuation of a rich tradition in the history of the Symphony--special concerts for children. (St. Louis Symphony)

During the two decades since the departure of Vladimir Golschmann from St. Louis, the Symphony continued to present many outstanding programs for the enjoyment of its patrons. The 1957-1958 season saw the orchestra's presentation of the Beethoven Cycle, including the nine symphonies performed throughout the course of the season, with Georg Solti conducting. In 1959 the orchestra gave its first performance of Berlioz' *L' Enfance du Christ*, assisted by soloists and the Washington University choruses. A performance of the Verdi *Requiem* was given in 1963 to honor the one hundred and fiftieth anniversary of the composer's birth. Soloists included soprano Elinor Ross, contralto Claramae Turner, tenor Jan Peerce, and bass-baritone Kenneth Smith.

In 1964 the Symphony participated in the celebration of the bicentennial of the founding of St. Louis by commissioning with the New Music Circle several new works by contemporary composers. And the following year the orchestra gave its first performance of the Berlioz *Requiem* with the assistance of seven choirs and tenor Casare Valletti. The 1966-1967 season saw the first performance by the St. Louis Symphony of Benjamin Britten's *War Requiem* with Elinor Ross, tenor Richard Lewis, baritone John Shirley-Quirk and singers from Washington University and Fontbonne College.

Leonard Slatkin, in an attempt to attract new young audiences to Powell Hall, conducted a series of concerts known as "Encounters in Music." The program during the 1973-1974 season employed an outer space theme, with electronic music broadcast in the foyer of the hall before and after the concert. The orchestra played Holst's *The Planets*, *Prelude Zarathustra* by Strauss, and other pieces that would appeal to young people. Another concert in the series was played in celebration of the one hundredth anniversary of the birth of the American composer Charles Ives. It also featured some electronic music.

A series known as the "Black Experience in Music" was produced in the 1970s. Sponsored by the Symphony and the St. Louis Music Association, it featured music by black composers, and performances by black conductors and soloists. Proceeds from the series of concerts went to the Association to be used for voice and piano scholarships, and to the St. Louis Symphony Youth Orchestra for scholarships.

Just as the entire nation celebrated the American Bicentennial in 1976, so did the St. Louis Symphony Orchestra. It was one of seven American orchestras to receive funds from the National Endowment for the Arts in order to commission a new composition by an American composer. Each work was introduced by a different orchestra and then performed by the other six participating members. The Symphony played a work by Jacob Druckman entitled, *Mirage*. Other orchestras in the project and their composers were the Pittsburgh Symphony (George Rochberg), the Cincinnati Symphony (Ned Rorem), the Detroit Symphony (Morton Gould), the Minnesota Orchestra (Michael Colgrass), the National Symphony (Gunther Schuller) and the San Francisco Symphony (Lorin Rush).

The Symphony's performances of Fourth of July concerts have frequently been the occasion of much enjoyment to the St. Louis public. And the orchestra's concert on July 4, 1976 was the greatest of all. An estimated audience of 800,000 witnessed the playing of American music under the Gateway Arch, followed by a spectacular fireworks display. The concert, conducted by Leonard Slatkin, attracted the largest audience ever to hear the St. Louis Symphony, and, in fact, one of the largest audiences to hear a concert anywhere.

In addition to those already mentioned, the Symphony gave a number of musical works their premier United States or world performances over the past two decades. Giovanni Pergolesi's *Concerto for Two Pianos and String Orchestra* received its first American hearing in 1959 in St. Louis, in honor of the two hundred and fiftieth anniversary of the composer's birth. In 1964 the orchestra played the American première of Arnold Schoenberg's *Three Little Pieces for Orchestra*, and in 1966 Anton Webern's *Cantata No. 2*.

Several original works have been commissioned by the Junior Division of the Women's Association. Among them was Vincent Persichetti's *Seventh Symphony*, played in 1959, in honor of the eightieth anniversary of the founding of the orchestra. The same composer's *A Lincoln Address* was given its world premiere in 1973 in St. Louis. The composition was written for President Richard Nixon's Second Inaugural concert but was not used on that occasion.

(**Above**) One of the joys of a St. Louis summer is to attend an outdoor concert by the Symphony. Here the scene is Art Hill in Forest Park. (St. Louis Symphony)
(**Below and right**) A crowd gathers to hear the Symphony play under the Gateway Arch on the St. Louis riverfront. (St. Louis Symphony)

The orchestra played the same piece, with William Warfield doing the narration, in a concert at Carnegie Hall that same season.

An unusual experience for local music patrons occurred in 1977 when the Symphony played the first complete performance of David Del Tredici's *Final Alice*, a work based on the *Alice in Wonderland* story.

A number of compositions by members of the orchestra's "family" received their first hearing in St. Louis. Among several works by Leonard Slatkin premièred by the Symphony was his *Dialogue for Two Cellos and Orchestra*, first played in 1975. The composer conducted the performance and his mother and brother were featured in the solo roles.

Walter Susskind wrote his *Passacaglia for Timpani and Chamber Orchestra* especially for Richard Holmes, the orchestra's timpanist, and the work was premièred in St. Louis in 1977. Susskind's *Improvisation and Scherzo for Flute and Small Orchestra* was especially written for the Symphony's Jacob Berg, and premièred in St. Louis in 1978. The first playing of these and other works continued the tradition of the St. Louis Symphony in bringing forth new musical compositions.

The practice of taking the orchestra on tours to various parts of the country was continued by all of the conductors during the past two decades. As in earlier times, the tours further enhanced the reputation of the St. Louis Symphony and brought much enjoyment to music lovers who would not otherwise have been exposed to the playing of the orchestra. As in the past, most of the tours concentrated on the midwestern and southern sections of the country. A typical review was written by a Florida critic after the orchestra played there in 1961:

> The St. Louis Symphony is one of the nation's top orchestras....and it fully lived up to its reputation....Van Remoortel squeezes every bit of music out of his players....The orchestra held the audience spellbound with a flawless and deeply moving rendition of Beethoven's seldom-heard *Symphony No. 4*....The concert was a memorable event....[19]

In 1966 the orchestra ventured to the West, for a tour including performances in California, Oregon, Washington, Idaho, and Nevada. Of a concert in San Francisco, a critic in that city wrote,

> Be informed, O blasé San Francisco, that St. Louis is not a stop-off on the road to nowhere, it's the home of a sharp and solid orchestra with balanced talent....With authority and orchestral know-how, De Carvalho can bring out of the musicians strong performances.[20]

The following season commenced with a 2,550-mile tour of the Midwest under the baton of Arthur Fiedler, conductor of the Boston Pops Orchestra.

As noted earlier, the Symphony's first performance in New York's Carnegie Hall, which occurred in 1950 with Vladimir Golschmann conducting, was a brilliant success. The orchestra returned to that fabled stage in the course of a tour during the 1967-1968 season, this time under the baton of Eleazer De Carvalho, and Itzhak Perlman as violin soloist. The music critic for the *New York Post* wrote, "It was over before we knew it and this is a high compliment to his (De Carvalho's) skill. The large audience was uninhibited in enthusiasm."[21] That concert marked the beginning of what has become an annual tradition for the St. Louis Symphony. The orchestra's visits to New York consistently bring favorable reviews from the critics.

On a visit to Carnegie Hall the next season, Walter Susskind conducted a performance of the original orchestration of the Schumann piano concerto with Malcom Frager as soloist. The orchestra also played Shostakovich's *Symphony No. 10*. Of the latter work, Raymond Ericson of the *New York Times* wrote of the "strong, brilliant performance of the St. Louis Symphony."[22] Another concert in that season's tour of the East prompted a critic to write, "Every section of the orchestra is superb and the solo and ensemble work is of the highest quality. The St. Louis Symphony is, in short, one of America's finest orchestras."[23]

To celebrate the centennial of the birth of the British composer Ralph Vaughan Williams, the Symphony brought performances of *A Sea Symphony* in 1972 to Hartford, New York City, and

Richard Holmes has been the timpani
player of the orchestra since 1969.
(St. Louis Symphony)

Principal flutist Jacob Berg joined the
orchestra in 1969. (St. Louis Symphony)

Violinist Itzhak Perlman is one of the
outstanding musical artists to appear
with the orchestra in recent years.
His 1977 appearance featured the
Stravinsky violin concerto. (St. Louis
Symphony)

Van Cliburn during an appearance
with the Symphony at a concert for
employees of the Monsanto Chemical
Company in 1960. (St. Louis Symphony)

Pianist Malcolm Frager, a native of
St. Louis, first appeared with the
orchestra in one of the student concerts. (St. Louis Symphony)

Pianist Philippe Entremont is one of
the outstanding musicians who has
appeared with the orchestra.
(St. Louis Symphony)

Pianist Daniel Barenboim is one of the many guest artists who have contributed to the success of the orchestra's concerts. (St. Louis Symphony)

One of the prominent young pianists of the international concert circuit, Vladimir Ashkenazy has been very popular with St. Louis audiences. (St. Louis Symphony)

A close personal friend of Golschmann's, violinist Nathan Milstein has been playing with the orchestra for over forty-five years. (St. Louis Symphony)

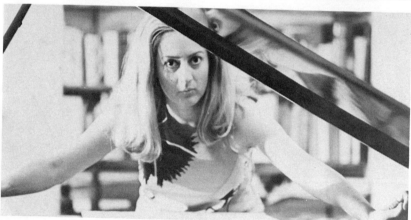

Brazilian pianist Jocy De Oliveira appeared with the orchestra while her husband, Eleazar De Carvalho, was permanent conductor. (St. Louis Symphony)

The Soviet violinist David Oistrakh was among the world's greatest musicians to make guest appearances with the Symphony. In 1970 he was the soloist for the Bach **Concerto No. 1** and the Brahms **Concerto in D.** (St. Louis Symphony)

Violinist Henryk Szeryng appeared with the orchestra in 1977 for performances of Szymanowski's **Concerto No. 2** and Mozart's **Concerto No. 3**. (St. Louis Symphony)

Josef Suk is one of the finest of the concert violinists to appear with the orchestra over the past few years. In 1971 he played Berg's concerto. (St. Louis Symphony)

Marian Anderson made her debut with the orchestra during the Van Remoortel period. (Missouri Historical Society)

Native St. Louisan Grace Bumbry made her American orchestral debut with the hometown orchestra. (St. Louis Symphony)

Violinist Pinchas Zukerman has established himself as one of the great visiting artist to appear with the orchestra in recent years. In 1975 he played Sibelius' **Concerto in D**. (Photo courtesy New York Philharmonic; Boris)

Washington, D. C. After a performance of the work at the Kennedy Center in the nation's capital, Paul Hume of the *Washington Post* commented, "The Orchestra proved itself repeatedly a flexible ensemble, instant in response and handsome in tone. The concert will long be remembered for having given the Kennedy Center one of its most memorable evenings." [24]

One of the most notable tours in the history of the St. Louis Symphony occurred in September 1978. At that time the orchestra made its first European trip. It was invited to give three concerts at the 2000-year-old Herodes Atticus Theatre in Athens, Greece as part of the Athens Music Festival. Jerzy Semkow conducted an all-Tchaikovsky program (with Isaac Stern playing the violin concerto) and a concert featuring works by Ives, Mozart, and Brahms. Leonard Slatkin was on the podium for a program of works by Bartók, William Schuman, and Mendelssohn (with Stern performing the latter's violin concerto). The St. Louis Symphony Orchestra thus joined the ranks of the nation's best orchestras in participating in foreign travel, and the event promised to begin a new tradition in an important phase of the organization's history.

We have seen that the greatest soloists in the world came to St. Louis to appear with the Symphony during the Golschmann period. That tradition continued after his departure, and is certainly being maintained today.

Van Cliburn made his first appearance with the St. Louis Symphony in 1958, playing the same two piano concerti which he played in the Tchaikovsky Competition in Moscow that same year; the Tchaikovsky First and the Rachmaninoff Third. His several guest appearances with the orchestra since that time never failed to evoke favorable responses from the local music patrons. Eugene Istomin appeared for the first time with the orchestra during that same year. He played Schumann's *Concerto in A minor*. A native St. Louisan, Malcolm Frager, has made frequent guest appearances with the orchestra. As a boy, he had played with the Symphony in an elementary school concert. During the 1960-1961 season Glenn Gould played the Beethoven series of piano concerti with the orchestra, and also played the

Beethoven *Triple Concerto* (with Harry Farbman and Leslie Parnas). He, too, has since returned.

Some of the other pianists who have appeared with the Symphony over the past two decades, many of whom started coming during the Golschmann era, were Robert and Gaby Casadesus, Geza Anda, Arthur Rubinstein, Gary Graffman, John Browning, Leonard Pennario, Gina Bachauer, Philippe Entremont, Rudolf Firkusny, Claudio Arrau, Daniel Barenboim, Andre Watts, Rudolf Serkin, Anton Kuerti, Vladimir Ashkenazy, Beveridge Webster, Jeffrey Siegel, Abbey Simon, and Alicia de Larrocha. The Brazilian pianist Jocy De Oliveira, wife of Eleazar De Carvalho, also played with the Symphony during the time that her husband was its conductor.

Among returning violinists who had already been familiar to local concertgoers were Isaac Stern, Zino Francescatti, Nathan Milstein, Yehudi Menuhin, and Ruggiero Ricci. David Oistrakh, Henryk Szeryng, Itzhak Perlman, Jaime Laredo, Josef Suk, Gyorgy Pauk, and Pinchas Zukerman were also among the outstanding violinists to play with the orchestra during the past two decades.

St. Louis music patrons also heard many fine vocalists during the past twenty years. Grace Bumbry, a native of St. Louis, made her American orchestral debut with the Symphony during the 1962-1963 season. Marian Anderson sang with the orchestra for the first time during the 1958-1959 season, singing, among other selections, Brahms's *Alto Rhapsody*. Rosalind Elias appeared in Bartók's one-act concert version of *Bluebeard's Castle* during the 1968-1969 season. And during the same season Eleanor Steber appeared in the Symphony's presentation of Mahler's *Symphony No. 4*. The soprano Eileen Farrell has made a number of appearances with the Symphony over the past few years. She helped open the 1966-1967 season with her performance in the concert version of *Fidelio*. She has since appeared in concert versions of *Götterdämmerung* and *Tristan und Isolde*.

Some of the returning singers to perform with the orchestra during the sixties and seventies include tenors Jan Peerce and John McCollum, baritone William Warfield, and mezzo-soprano Jennie Tourel. And a number of other outstanding vocal artists made their debuts with the Symphony during the

Violinist Gyorgy Pauk appeared with the Symphony in 1975 in Mozart's **Concerto #4** under guest conductor Alexander Gibson. (St. Louis Symphony)

Mezzo-soprano Claudine Carlson made her recording debut with the orchestra in their presentation of Prokofiev's **Alexander Nevsky**. (St. Louis Symphony)

Mezzo-soprano Mignon Dunn sang with the orchestra in the United States première of Sommer's **Vocal Symphony** in 1971. (St. Louis Symphony)

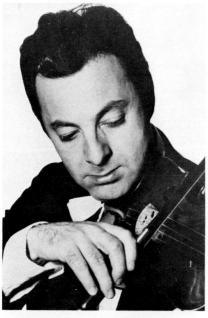

Marilyn Horne appeared with the orchestra at the Mississippi River Festival in 1972 and sang selections from the operas **Samson et Dalila**, **Les Huguenots**, and **The Siege of Corinth**. (St. Louis Symphony)

The permanent conductor of the National Symphony in Washington, D.C., cellist Mstislav Rostropovich played with the St. Louis Symphony in 1975. (St. Louis Symphony)

Rosalind Elias, the mezzo-soprano, sang in the concert version of **Bluebeard's Castle** during the Susskind period. (St. Louis Symphony)

(**Above and below**) Classical guitarists Andres Segovia and Carlos Montoya have both appeared with the orchestra. (St. Louis Symphony)

(**Above**) Sitarist Ravi Shankar's unusual music has contributed to the success of the Symphony's series of pop concerts in recent years. (St. Louis Symphony)
(**Below**) Organist Virgil Fox has appeared with the orchestra. (St. Louis Symphony)

130

post-Golschmann era, including Jean Madeira, Marilyn Horne, Martina Arroyo, Mignon Dunn, Claudine Carlson, and Elinor Ross.

In 1975 the cellist Mstislav Rostropovich performed Haydn's *Concerto in C* and Dvorak's *Concerto in B minor* with the orchestra at a special musicians' pension fund concert. Other outstanding cellists to appear with the orchestra in more recent years have been Leonard Rose, Zara Nelsova, and the former principal cellist of the orchestra, Leslie Parnas. Guitarists Andres Segovia and Carlos Montoya have appeared with the Symphony, as well as such outstanding musicians as sitarist Ravi Shankar and organist Virgil Fox.

The Symphony continued to attract famous guest conductors to its podium. After Vladimir Golschmann retired from his permanent position in St. Louis he returned on several occasions to appear with the orchestra which he had served so long and well. He conducted an especially notable set of concerts during the 1965-1966 season with Rudolf Firkusny at the piano playing the Beethoven *Concerto No. 3*. And former conductor Rudolph Ganz

returned for an appearance with the orchestra in 1960. Other familiar figures who returned to make guest conducting appearances in St. Louis over the past two decades included Pierre Monteux, Richard Rodgers, Georg Solti, Leopold Stokowski, Igor Stravinsky, Andre Kostelanetz, and Arthur Fiedler. Edouard Van Remoortel, Eleazar De Carvalho, and Walter Susskind all returned on at least one occasion to direct their former orchestra.

In addition to the familiar faces, St. Louisans also saw such famous musical personalities as Aaron Copland, Josef Krips, Sir John Barbirolli, Zubin Mehta, Sixten Ehrling, Andre Previn, Antal Dorati, Lukas Foss, Sir Michael Tippett, Sergiu Comissiona, James Levine, Alexander Gibson, Rafael Frühbeck de Burgos, and Louis Lane. At the beginning of the 1977-1978 season the native Missourian Sarah Caldwell, director of the Opera Company of Boston, conducted the St. Louis Symphony in three special performances of Beethoven's *Ninth Symphony*.

In addition to the regular classical music literature which is traditionally played by the Symphony, the audiences in St. Louis were able to hear much

Ella Fitzgerald, one of the many show business personalities who have made the orchestra's pop concerts successful. (St. Louis Symphony)

Andre Previn during a guest-conducting appearance with the Symphony in the 1961-1962 season. (St. Louis Symphony)

Sergiu Comissiona, permanent conductor of the Baltimore Symphony, guest-conducted the St. Louis orchestra in 1974 with Rafael Arozco at the piano. (St. Louis Symphony)

Rafael Frühbeck de Burgos guest-conducted the Symphony in 1974 in concerts featuring the local première of **Suite Española** by Albéniz. (St. Louis Symphony)

Alexander Gibson has guest-conducted the orchestra on several occasions. In 1971 he was joined by Gina Bachauer in a performance of the "Emperor" Concerto. (St. Louis Symphony)

Louis Lane, formerly the resident conductor of the Cleveland Orchestra, was on the podium with the St. Louis Symphony for two concerts during the 1970-1971 season. (The Cleveland Orchestra)

popular music, and were able to see the performances of many persons whose careers do not normally take them to the stages of concert halls. Over the past two decades the Symphony played more "pop" concerts than it had ever played in its history. Such show business personalities as Henry Mancini, Danny Kaye, Skitch Henderson, Ella Fitzgerald, Victor Borge, and George Shearing have contributed to the success of these events, along with so many other well-known public figures that it would be difficult to mention them all. The musical compositions that require a narrator have drawn such people as actor Vincent Price (a native of St. Louis) and news commentator Walter Cronkite to share the stage with the St. Louis Symphony. And comedian (and violinist) Jack Benny appeared in St. Louis at special benefit concerts with the orchestra to help raise money for the organization.

We have seen that in earlier days the St. Louis Symphony had participated in radio broadcasts. This method of introducing good music to a great audience was expanded during the sixties and seventies. In 1963 radio station KMOX began broadcasting tape recordings of some of the regular concerts; the first time in the history of the orchestra that this had been done on a regular basis. Each broadcast was accompanied by a ten-minute talk about the concert by Laurent Torno, former member of the Symphony. In 1975 station KWMU-FM began a weekly presenation of recordings of the orchestra's concerts. The commentator for the programs was Ronald Arnatt, professor and director of the choral groups at the University of Missouri-St. Louis. In addition to these, other St. Louis radio stations presented various programs which dealt with the affairs of the Symphony.

But St. Louis Symphony concerts are not only heard over the radio in the orchestra's home city; they are heard throughout much of the United States and Europe. Beginning in 1976, the Symphony was heard on twenty-seven radio stations across the United States. Parkway Productions, a Washington, D. C. company, began circulating weekly recordings of the concerts by the Symphony on a nationwide network which included such major cities as Chicago, New Orleans, Pittsburgh, Detroit,

Baltimore, and Minneapolis. And beginning in 1977 these recordings were available to the British Broadcasting Corporation, which broadcast them throughout the United Kingdom and parts of Western Europe. Thus, the St. Louis Symphony is one of only six major orchestras whose concerts are syndicated for radio broadcasts in the United States. And the orchestra has a worldwide listening audience each week of one million. [25]

One of the criteria for judging the quality of a symphony orchestra is the extent to which it make recordings. We have seen that the St. Louis Symphony has made records during the time when Rudolph Ganz and Vladimir Golschmann served as its conductors. Since then it has continued that tradition. In 1974 the Symphony signed a contract with Vox Productions, Inc. It thus joined the ranks of only five other American orchestras to have phonograph recording contracts; and only two others record for American companies (New York and Philadelphia). Conductors for these new recordings include Walter Susskind, Jerzy Semkow, and Leonard Slatkin. They have proven to be very successful, and are distributed throughout America, Europe, and Japan. The recordings have served to further enhance the reputation of the St. Louis Symphony, and of the Symphony the president of Vox Productions said, "I most sincerely believe that the orchestra has reached the point where it ranks among the finest orchestras not only in the United States, but in the whole world." [26]

Recognition of the quality of the new series of recordings became evident early in 1979 when two of the releases received three Grammy Award nominations. The orchestra's rendition of Prokofiev's *Alexander Nevsky*, featuring the St. Louis Symphony Chorus, was nominated both for best choral performance and for best engineering. The recording of the Rachmaninoff *First Symphony* received the honor for best orchestral performance. Both records were conducted by Leonard Slatkin and, although they did not actually win the Grammy Awards, their nominations brought much deserved favorable attention to the St. Louis Symphony.

Victor Borge during rehearsal for a concert with the orchestra in the 1962-1963 season. (St. Louis Symphony)

Newscaster Walter Cronkite participated in the orchestra's presentation of Copland's **A Lincoln Portrait** in 1975. (St. Louis Symphony)

Vincent Price, a native of St. Louis, has returned home to appear in narrative pieces with the Symphony. (St. Louis Symphony)

Jack Benny last appeared with the orchestra in 1970 in a benefit concert to raise money for the Symphony Society. (St. Louis Symphony)

Skitch Henderson conducting the orchestra during a 1961 "beer and pretzel" concert at the Exposition Hall of Kiel Auditorium. (St. Louis Symphony)

Thus, what began as a choral society in 1880 evolved into a major symphony orchestra. People of St. Louis, and music lovers in many places far from it, have reason to regard the history of the St. Louis Symphony with fond memories. But the future of this fine institution will probably be just as exciting as its past.

The entrance of a new conductor always brings anticipation and hope for even more improvement for the future. With the announcement of the appointment of Leonard Slatkin as permanent conductor of the orchestra for the 1979-1980 season, the young conductor expressed his hope that the orchestra would be able to participate in more foreign tours, commission more musical compositions, and play more American works and lesser-known works by the major composers.

The year 1980 will mark the centennial of the founding of the St. Louis Symphony Orchestra. Such landmark occasions always bring celebration and pride in accomplishments of the past, and the centennial of the premier St. Louis musical organization will be no exception. It is hoped that the second hundred years of the orchestra's existence will prove to be as successful as its first century.

A capacity crowd fills Powell Hall. (St. Louis Symphony)

APPENDIX I

MEMBERS OF THE ORCHESTRA,
1907-1908 through 1978-1979

First Violins

Name	Season
Akagi, Teruko	1956-1957 to 1959-1960
Altman, Baruch	1941-1942
Antrim, Gladys	1967-1968
(Lang, Gladys)	1968-1969 to 1969-1970
Apple, Darwyn	1971-1972 to 1978-1979
Aquino, Marciano D.	1919-1920 to 1921-1922
Armellini, Mario	1909-1910
Arnesen, Arne	1918-1919
Auffarth, Armin	1916-1917 to 1919-1920
Austria, Leonard	1955-1956
Baicher, Lucy	1948-1949 to 1953-1954
Bakalor, Joseph	1943-1944 to 1949-1950;
	1952-1953 to 1955-1956
Barnett, Morris	1917-1918
Baron, Arthur	1915-1916 to 1917-1918;
	1928-1929 to 1952-1953
Becker, Wanda	1966-1967 to 1970-1971
Beiler, Jonathan	1975-1976
Bergmann, Carl M.	1919-1920
Berman, Louis	1921-1922
Berne, Robert	1911-1912
Bernreuter, Alfred	1921-1922 to 1923-1924
Bittner, David, Jr.	1917-1918; 1919-1920 to 1923-1924
Bizet, Yvonne	1947-1948

Blumberg, Jacob	1913-1914 to 1917-1918
Brandt, Harry	1922-1923
Braun, Alfred	1907-1908 to 1908-1909
Briesmeister, Ernestine	1950-1951
Brown, William	1910-1911 to 1917-1918; 1920-1921
Burger, Robert	1916-1917; 1921-1922 to 1923-1924
Buzatesco, Max	1929-1930
Cale, Charles A.	1917-1918
Campione, Eugene	1946-1947
Catarnichi, Joseph	1919-1920 to 1923-1924
Charbulak, Victor	1921-1922
Claiborne, Frederic	1920-1921 to 1923-1924
Clark, Charlene	1973-1974 to 1978-1979
Clark, Rex	1942-1943 to 1948-1949
Clay, Benjamin F.	1907-1908 to 1913-1914; 1918-1919 to 1922-1923
Cohen, Isadore	1916-1917; 1919-1920
Conforto, Marcella	1943-1944 to 1948-1949
Curto, Joseph	1920-1921; 1922-1923
Dastich, Vincent	1921-1922 to 1922-1923
Davidson, Alfred	1907-1908 to 1919-1920
De Granada, Alvaro O.	Assistant Concertmaster: 1963-1964 to 1965-1966
Diamond, Lawrence	1970-1971 to 1978-1979
Druzinsky, Louis	1919-1920 to 1922-1923; 1924-1925 to 1926-1927
Ehrenwerth, Gizella	1943-1944; 1946-1947
Eisenberg, Irwin	1941-1942
Fabiani, Aurelio	1914-1915
Faerber, Joseph	1924-1925 to 1938-1939
Farbman, Harry	Concertmaster: 1942-1943 to 1960-1961
Feld, Ben	1923-1924
Foester, William	1916-1917
Freiermuth, John	1911-1912 to 1930-1931
Frederick, Kirk	1924-1925 to 1925-1926
Gebhard, Richard J.	1916-1917 to 1917-1918
Gieselmann, Harry	1915-1916 to 1916-1917
Gill, Andrew J.	1919-1920 to 1920-1921
Gill, Joseph	1916-1917; 1918-1919
Gimbel, Barbara Ann	1962-1963
Gimpel, Joel E.	1962-1963
Gimprich, Robert	1959-1960; 1962-1963 to 1968-1969
Gittelson, Franklin M.	Assistant Concertmaster: 1961-1962
Gluck, Joseph	1960-1961 to 1962-1963
Gold, Harry	1918-1919 to 1925-1926

Goodsell, Ben	1925-1926
Gosman, Lazar	Acting Associate Concertmaster: 1977-1978; Second Associate Concertmaster: 1978-1979
Gottschalk, Earl	1919-1920 to 1923-1924
Gottschalk, Max	1909-1910 to 1910-1911; 1913-1914 to 1917-1918
Greenberg, Isadore	1915-1916 to 1916-1917
Greenstein, Sidney	1937-1938 to 1940-1941
Grosbayne, Benjamin	1925-1926
Gross, Robert	1945-1946
Grossman, Isadore	1921-1922 to 1926-1927; 1928-1929 to 1970-1971
Guidi, Scipione	Concertmaster: 1931-1932 to 1941-1942
Gunder, Ludwig	1928-1929 to 1930-1931
Gusikoff, Michel	Concertmaster: 1917-1918 to 1925-1926
Haber, Joseph	1944-1945 to 1946-1947
Halbmann, Michael	1917-1918
Halk, John	1923-1924
Hanley, William	1957-1958
Haux, Ray	1953-1954 to 1957-1958
Henry, Dayton M.	1916-1917
Hladky, Frank	1917-1918
Hochman, David	1921-1922 to 1926-1927
Holguin, David	1953-1954 to 1954-1955
Howell, Ruth	1945-1946 to 1946-1947
Howie, Joan	1957-1958 to 1958-1959
(Siegel, Joan Howie)	1959-1960
Hudson, Ronald	1955-1956; 1958-1959
Hyna, Edward J.	1923-1924 to 1924-1925
Hyna, Joseph E.	1922-1923
Israelievitch, Jacques	Concertmaster: 1977-1978 to 1978-1979
Iticovici, Silvian	1977-1978 to 1978-1979
Jerabek, Frantisek	1921-1922
Johnson, Joseph	1925-1926 to 1928-1929; 1930-1931
Jones, Francis E.	1929-1930 to 1941-1942; 1945-1946; Assistant Concertmaster: 1946-1947 to 1949-1950; 1951-1952
Jones, Jenny Lind	1974-1975 to 1978-1979
Kafka, Rudolf	1916-1917
Kampouris, Louis	1955-1956 to 1957-1958
Kaplan, Burton B.	1960-1961
Karp, Philip	1958-1959

Kataoka, Eiko	1971-1972 to 1978-1979
Kaub, Charles A.	1907-1908 to 1933-1934
Kellenberger, Frank	1915-1916 to 1917-1918; 1919-1920
Kellogg, Virginia	1961-1962
Kendrie, Frank E.	1913-1914
Kern, Carl F.	1918-1919; 1922-1923
Kesner, Edouard	1950-1951
Kilb, Oliver	1916-1917
Knebel, Theodora	1956-1957
Korman, Joan	1971-1972 to 1972-1973
Korman, John	Associate Concertmaster:
	1971-1972 to 1977-1978; 1978-1979
	Acting Concertmaster:
	1977-1978
Kowalewski, Joseph	1950-1951 to 1952-1953
Kozak, Mary	1966-1967
Krachmalnick, Jacob	1942-1943
Kranzberg, Sol	1927-1928 to 1936-1937
Krohn, A. James	1960-1961 to 1978-1979;
	Assistant Concertmaster:
	1971-1972 to 1978-1979
Krolick, Leah	1952-1953 to 1954-1955
Kuettner, Otto	1915-1916 to 1922-1923
Lang, Gladys	1968-1969 to 1969-1970
(Antrim, Gladys)	1967-1968
Lange, Ernst	1907-1908 to 1908-1909
Lanznar, Herman	1918-1919
Lascowitz, Samuel	1909-1910 to 1910-1911;
	1915-1916 to 1916-1917;
	1920-1921 to 1921-1922
Lathrop, F. C.	1924-1925 to 1925-1926
Legate, William L.	1962-1963 to 1967-1968
Lehwaldt, Otto H.	1918-1919
Lepske, Jules	1919-1920
Levine, Jacob	1926-1927 to 1932-1933;
	1934-1935 to 1970-1971
Levinson, Herbert	1947-1948 to 1949-1950
Levy, Ellis	1910-1911 to 1913-1914;
	1915-1916 to 1935-1936;
	Assistant Concertmaster:
	1924-1925 to 1925-1926
Lewis, Gerald	1950-1951 to 1952-1953
Lichtenstein, Victor	1907-1908 to 1909-1910
Lind, Jenny	1972-1973 to 1974-1975
(Jones, Jenny Lind)	1974-1975
Lippi, John	1963-1964 to 1978-1979
Loebker, Joseph	1923-1924

Lookofsky, Harry	1936-1937 to 1937-1938
Lucia, Anthony	1972-1973 to 1975-1976
Makris, Andreas	1959-1960 to 1960-1961
Mamlock, Theodore	1956-1957 to 1957-1958; 1962-1963
Mandel, Harry	1920-1921 to 1923-1924
Mark, Oscar, Jr.	1915-1916 to 1920-1921
Markowski, G. R.	1923-1924
Maurer, Clarence	1918-1919 to 1921-1922
Melnikoff, Harry	1937-1938 to 1941-1942
Menga, Robert	1957-1958 to 1960-1961
Meyrowitz, Jasha	1956-1957
Mikelsons, Rudolfs O.	1963-1964 to 1978-1979
Milstein, Joseph	1921-1922 to 1922-1923
Milton, Blair	1973-1974 to 1974-1975
Moradian, George	1966-1967 to 1967-1968
Mucci, Victor S.	1959-1960
Nagel, Carl	1927-1928
Nagy, Ladislav	1927-1928 to 1940-1941
Nagy, Laszlo	1942-1943 to 1943-1944
Nasalski, Bogdon	1960-1961 to 1961-1962
Nastri, Geremia	1914-1915
Neiberg, Morris	1961-1962
Nickerson, Tommy	1961-1962
Nies, Edwin	1919-1920 to 1920-1921; 1923-1924; 1926-1927 to 1927-1928
Noack, Sylvain	Concertmaster: 1926-1927 to 1928-1929
Noland, Keylor	1953-1954 to 1954-1955
Olk, Hugo	Concertmaster: 1907-1908 to 1916-1917
Osmolovsky, G.	1945-1946
Oswald, Joseph F.	1912-1913
Oswald, Joseph F., Jr.	1931-1932 to 1935-1936
Pack, Ernest	1910-1911 to 1911-1912
Patterson, Ronald	Assistant Concertmaster: 1966-1967 to 1970-1971
Pepper, Joseph	Assistant Concertmaster: 1952-1953 to 1954-1955
Perez, Heinz	1958-1959
Pesold, Arnold	1907-1908 to 1910-1911
Petremont, Charles	1960-1961
Pettigrew, Thomas	1963-1964 to 1969-1970
Picone, Benjamin	1958-1959
Pistorius, George	1915-1916 to 1916-1917
Pitaro, Llaro	1957-1958; 1960-1961
Pitaro, Mario M.	1960-1961
Pokrasov, Norman	1956-1957 to 1957-1958

Poles, Simon	1923-1924
Preusse, Carl A.	1910-1911 to 1912-1913;
	1921-1922 to 1923-1924
Rabinovitsj, Max	Concertmaster:
	1965-1966 to 1976-1977
Rader, Benjamin	1917-1918; 1919-1920 to 1923-1924
Raffaelli, Gino	1949-1950
Rafferty, J. Patrick	1971-1972
Ramos, Manuel	1977-1978 to 1978-1979
Reinert, Otto	1919-1920
Rhodes, John F.	1915-1916
Ritter, Melvin	Assistant Concertmaster:
	1955-1956 to 1960-1961;
	Concertmaster:
	1961-1962 to 1964-1965
Rizzo, David	1927-1928 to 1932-1933;
	1943-1944 to 1948-1949
Robbins, Rena	1946-1947
Robinson, Donald	1961-1962
Rosa, Gerard, Jr.	1959-1960
Rosen, Irvin	1939-1940 to 1941-1942
Rosen, Jerome	1926-1927
Rublowsky, John	1952-1953 to 1954-1955
Rudnitsky, Alvin	Assistant Concertmaster:
	1950-1951
Salomon, David	1926-1927 to 1928-1929;
	1934-1935 to 1944-1945
Sarli, Dominic	1908-1909; 1917-1918
Scheda, Oton	1918-1919
Schillinger, Frederick	1915-1916
Schoen, Isaac L.	1910-1910
Schoenbrun, Josef	1955-1956 to 1958-1959;
	1960-1961 to 1962-1963
Schoenbrun, Teruko	1960-1961 to 1962-1963
Schmitt, August C.	1915-1916
Schneider, Alfred	1951-1952 to 1954-1955
Schrickel, Carl	1915-1916
Schultz, Rudolph	1949-1950 to 1953-1954;
	1955-1956 to 1956-1957; 1958-1959;
	1961-1962 to 1962-1963
Schumitzky, Meyer	1931-1932 to 1943-1944
Schure, Esther	1954-1955 to 1955-1956
Selwitz, Jascha	1920-1921
Seymour, Charles A., Jr.	1915-1916
Shalett, Edward	1927-1928 to 1940-1941
Shklar, Helen	1970-1971 to 1971-1972; 1978-1979
Siegel, Bert (Berton)	1955-1956 to 1959-1960

Siegel, Joan Howie	1959-1960
(Howie, Joan)	1957-1958 to 1958-1959
Silberberg, Jules A.	1915-1916
Silberberg, Julius F.	1907-1908 to 1908-1909
	1912-1913 to 1914-1915
Simon, Louis F.	1953-1954 to 1954-1955
Siranossian, Eleanor	1959-1960
Slatkin, Felix	1933-1934 to 1936-1937
Sorgenfrei, Arthur	1916-1917
Speyer, Maurice	1907-1908; 1920-1921
Steck, William	1958-1959 to 1960-1961
Steer, Charles Burrell	1927-1928
Steindel, Albin	1919-1920 to 1920-1921
Steindel, Walter	1956-1957; 1963-1964 to 1968-1969
Stern, Hellmut	1958-1959 to 1959-1960
Striplin, Joseph	1969-1970 to 1971-1972
Sugitani, Takaoki	Second Assistant Concertmaster:
	1967-1968 to 1970-1971;
	Assistant Concertmaster;
	1971-1972 to 1978-1979
Swain, Robert	1964-1965 to 1978-1979
Swindells, James E.	1964-1965
Takaroff, Theodore	1937-1938
Tarack, Gerald	1947-1948 to 1949-1950
Tartasky, Max	1937-1938 to 1944-1945
Tatian, Carol W.	1962-1963 to 1964-1965
Teicher, Anthony	1954-1955 to 1957-1958
Teicher, Aron	1953-1954
Thiede, Alexander	Concertmaster:
	1929-1930 to 1930-1931
Triska, Charles	1917-1918
Tryon, Millard N., Jr.	1950-1951 to 1952-1953
Tung, Helen	1972-1973 to 1977-1978
Turner, Saul (Sol)	1931-1932 to 1942-1943
Van Raalte, Francis	1919-1920
Viher, Miran	1970-1971 to 1978-1979
Voldrich, Richard	1963-1964 to 1966-1967
Vollrath, Emil	1907-1908 to 1926-1927
Waddington, Bette Hope	1962-1963 to 1965-1966
Waechtler, Arno	1907-1908 to 1919-1920
Walker, L. Ernest, Jr.	1934-1935 to 1942-1943
Watanabe, Haruka	1968-1969 to 1978-1979
Weisman, Vladimir	1954-1955
Weiss, John	1923-1924
Weiss, Sidney	1949-1950
Wexler, Max	1949-1950 to 1950-1951
Wild, Fred J.	1947-1948 to 1949-1950

Winter, Joe	1919-1920 to 1923-1924
Woeckener, Fred	1960-1961 to 1961-1962
Woloschuk, Elvira	1947-1948 to 1949-1950
Yoshida, Hiroko	1976-1977 to 1978-1979
Zivers, Alfred	1950-1951 to 1955-1956

Second Violins

Name	Season
Adair, James	1929-1930
Akagi, Teruko	1952-1953 to 1954-1955
Akins, Brent	Assistant Principal: 1978-1979
Ambrogio, Anthony	1927-1928
Bakalor, David E.	1952-1953 to 1959-1960
Bakalor, Joseph	1941-1942 to 1942-1943
Banks, Devonie	1967-1968
Baron, Arthur	1913-1914 to 1914-1915
Bates, Margaret	1959-1960 to 1960-1961
Beardon, Lowell G.	1954-1955 to 1956-1957
Beasley, Beverly Anne	1957-1958
(Robbins, Beverly Beasley)	1962-1963 to 1963-1964
(Schiebler, Beverly Beasley)	1964-1965 to 1974-1975
	Associate Principal: 1968-1969 to 1974-1975
Beiler, Jonathan	1974-1975
Berger, Anne	1947-1948
Bergsterman, Guido	1907-1908 to 1909-1910
Bittner, David, Jr.	1924-1925
Bloom, Deborah	1973-1974 to 1978-1979
Boyle, Charles	1959-1960 to 1960-1961
Brandt, Harry	1907-1908 to 1908-1909
Brown, Ethel Joy	1945-1946 to 1946-1947
Burger, Robert	1912-1913; 1924-1925 to 1941-1942
Cale, Charles A.	1907-1908; 1913-1914 to 1914-1915
Campione, Eugene	1942-1943
Carkeek, Lois	1953-1954 to 1954-1955
Catarnichi, Joseph	1924-1925
Claiborne, J. F.	1924-1925 to 1925-1926
Clark, Charlene	1968-1969 to 1972-1973
Clark, Rex	1949-1950 to 1952-1953
Claunch, Judith	1972-1973 to 1973-1974
Crowder, Elizabeth	1966-1967 to 1978-1979
Denos, Carol Wolowsky	1975-1976 to 1978-1979

Diamond, Lawrence	1969-1970
Dierker, Otto H.	1907-1908
Druzinsky, Louis	Principal:
	1927-1928 to 1944-1945
Eghian, Louis	1957-1958
Ehlin, Herman	1961-1962
Eichorn, Erich	Principal:
	1967-1968
Eisenberg, Irwin	1937-1938 to 1940-1941
Elman, Harry	1924-1925
Etzkow, Louis	1928-1929 to 1957-1958
Falzone, Francis F.	1926-1927 to 1927-1928
Fein, Israel	Principal:
	1926-1927
Ferber, Henry	1949-1950 to 1951-1952
Ficocelli, Carmine	1963-1964 to 1971-1972
Fielderman, Jack	1924-1925 to 1925-1926
Foley, Jane	1945-1946
Gebhard, Richard J.	1909-1910; 1912-1913
Gieselmann, Harry	1907-1908 to 1912-1913; 1914-1915
Gimprich, Robert	1960-1961 to 1961-1962
Glass, Lorraine	1972-1973 to 1978-1979
Gluck, Joseph	1959-1960
Goffstein, Daniel	1951-1952 to 1953-1954
Gottschalk, Earl	1924-1925 to 1927-1928
Gottschalk, Max	1911-1912
Greenberg, Isadore G.	1913-1914 to 1914-1915
Grossheider, M. Louise	1962-1963 to 1978-1979
Halbman, Michel	1925-1926 to 1927-1928
Halk, John	1924-1925 to 1927-1928
Harrington, H. Scott	1907-1908
Hikawa, Dale Andrea	1977-1978 to 1978-1979
Howell, Ruth	1944-1945
Howie, Joan	1955-1956 to 1956-1957
Hudson, Nancy P.	1958-1959
Hugo, Carl A.	1927-1928 to 1931-1932
Hugo, Victor	1913-1914
Johnson, Joseph	1966-1967
Jump, Marcia	1945-1946
Kampouris, Louis N.	1949-1950 to 1951-1952;
	1966-1967 to 1978-1979
Karam, Stephan	1957-1958
Kaub, Charles A.	1934-1935 to 1936-1937
Kellenberger, Frank	1908-1909 to 1914-1915
Kesner, Edouard	1946-1947 to 1948-1949
Kippel, Samuel	1907-1908
Knebel, Theodora	1955-1956

Kodesh, Raya	1976-1977 to 1978-1979
Kovalenko, Oleg	1963-1964 to 1965-1966
Kranzberg, Sol	1943-1944 to 1971-1972
Kraut, Oscar	1946-1947 to 1948-1949
Krohn, A. James	1959-1960
Krolick, Leah	1948-1949 to 1951-1952
Kuettner, Otto	1908-1909 to 1914-1915
Lanznar, Herman	1913-1914
Lascowitz, Samuel	1911-1912 to 1914-1915
LeVeck, Thomas	1973-1974 to 1978-1979
Levine, Jacob	1971-1972
Lewis, Marjorie	1946-1947 to 1951-1952
Lipsitz, Meyer	1928-1929 to 1945-1946
Loebker, Joseph	1924-1925 to 1926-1927
Logan, Michael G.	1963-1964 to 1965-1966
Lookofsky, Harry	1933-1934 to 1935-1936
Mader, Frank	1962-1963 to 1967-1968
Magin, Rudolph J.	1929-1930 to 1958-1959
Mark, Oscar	1912-1913
Maurer, Clarence E.	1931-1932 to 1933-1934
Mendes, Cesar	1961-1962
Moebius, Muriel	1972-1973 to 1975-1976; Assistant Principal: 1975-1976
Morris, Sam	1924-1925 to 1925-1926
Nadler, Albert	1967-1968
Nagel, Carl	1926-1927; 1928-1929 to 1952-1953
Neiberg, Morris	1959-1960 to 1960-1961
Nieman, Aaron	1962-1963 to 1966-1967
Nies, Edwin	Principal: 1924-1925 to 1925-1926
Oswald, Joseph F., Jr.	1936-1937 to 1948-1949
Patmagrian, Rudie M.	1961-1962
Perez, Heinz	1955-1956
Perry, Robert	1956-1957
Pettigrew, Thomas	1970-1971 to 1978-1979
Pistorius, George	1914-1915
Pocost, Ben	1961-1962; 1963-1964 to 1964-1965
Poles, Simon	1924-1925 to 1948-1949
Preusse, Carl A.	1925-1926 to 1936-1937
Ramos, Manuel	1975-1976
Riediger, Judith	1962-1963 to 1964-1965; 1974-1975 to 1978-1979
Rishoi, Roy	1928-1929
Rizzo, David J.	1934-1935 to 1942-1943; 1949-1950 to 1957-1958; 1962-1963

Robbins, Beverly Beasley	1962-1963 to 1963-1964
(Schiebler, Beverly Beasley)	1964-1965 to 1974-1975
	Associate Principal:
	1968-1969 to 1974-1975
(Beasley, Beverly Anne)	1957-1958
Rosen, Irvin	1932-1933 to 1938-1939
Rosen, Jerome	1934-1935 to 1965-1966
Rossow, Paul	1908-1909 to 1911-1912
Sacks, Maurice	1925-1926 to 1926-1927
Sadowski, Fryderyk	Principal:
	1968-1969 to 1978-1979
Saito, Hiroko	1974-1975 to 1975-1976
Schankman, Leon	1951-1952 to 1964-1965;
	1966-1967 to 1977-1978
Schiebler, Beverly Beasley	1964-1965 to 1976-1977
	Associate Principal:
	1968-1969 to 1978-1979
(Beasley, Beverly Anne)	1957-1958
(Robbins, Beverly Beasley)	1962-1963 to 1963-1964
Schillinger, Frederick	1908-1909 to 1912-1913; 1914-1915
Schmit, A. C.	1909-1910
Schopp, Valentin	1907-1908 to 1908-1909
Schrieber, Paul	1925-1926 to 1946-1947;
	1963-1964 to 1972-1973; 1975-1976
Schrickel, Karl	1907-1908; 1910-1911
Schultz, Rudolph	1947-1948; 1971-1972 to 1976-1977
Schumitzky, Meyer	1926-1927 to 1928-1929
Schwartzberg, Harry	1913-1914
Score, Alvin	1958-1959
Seymour, Charles M.	1913-1914 to 1914-1915
Shankman, Leon	1978-1979
Shapiro, Ivan	1912-1913
Siemer, Harry	1909-1910
Siranossian, Eleanor	1958-1959
Sorgenfrei, Arthur	1912-1913 to 1913-1914
Spinosa, Frank	1955-1956 to 1956-1957
Stanick, Louise Mahaffy	1958-1959; 1960-1961 to 1961-1962
Steinkuehler, Carl	1907-1908 to 1912-1913
Stocker, Louis F.	1907-1908
Striplin, Joseph	1968-1969
Sugitani, Takaoki	Principal: 1966-1967
Swain, Robert W.	1962-1963
Swindells, James E.	1965-1966
Teicher, Anthony	1958-1959
Teicher, Aron	1950-1951 to 1952-1953
Tishkoff, Gary B.	1960-1961 to 1961-1962
Velten, Robert	1959-1960

von Fursch, Ludwig	1911-1912
Votava, Anton	1924-1925; 1928-1929 to 1930-1931
Waddington, Bette Hope	1958-1959 to 1961-1962
Walker, L. Ernest, Jr.	1930-1931 to 1933-1934;
	1968-1969 to 1971-1972
	Principal:
	1945-1946 to 1965-1966
Weiss, Samuel	1937-1938
Wexler, Max	1948-1949
Wilcox, Marka	1976-1977 to 1978-1979
Wild, Fred J.	1959-1960 to 1961-1962
Willheim, Imanuel	1949-1950 to 1950-1951
Wolowsky, Carol	1968-1969 to 1974-1975

Violas

Name	Season
Appel, Toby	Assistant Principal:
	1970-1971
Barnes, Darrel	Principal:
	1971-1972 to 1976-1977
Berman, Mark H.	1955-1956
Boeck, Hans	1917-1918
Boehmen, John	1907-1908
Breslaw, Irene	1973-1974 to 1975-1976
Burnau, Sally	1959-1960; 1962-1963
Buttrey, Gertrude	1944-1945 to 1952-1953; 1954-1955
Chase, Ben	1953-1954
Congdon, Herbert	1967-1968 to 1975-1976
Dickler, Hyman	1937-1938 to 1940-1941
Dierich, Franz	1916-1917
Dinkin, Alvin	1934-1935 to 1943-1944
Druzinsky, Louis	1946-1947; 1959-1960 to 1960-1961
Dumm, Thomas	Principal: 1978-1979
Elson, Joseph	1959-1960
Evans, Nelda	1963-1964 to 1964-1965
Falkenhainer, Henry J.	1907-1908 to 1940-1941
Fiasca, John	1945-1946
Fleminger, Gerald	1971-1972 to 1978-1979
Fradkin, Jules	1956-1957 to 1957-1958
Frost, Felix	1956-1957
Giacobbe, Stellario	1929-1930 to 1965-1966
Glazer, Robert	1967-1968 to 1969-1970;
	Co-Principal:
	1968-1969 to 1969 to 1970

Goldsmith, Rosemary	1946-1947 to 1966-1967
Goldstein, George	1927-1928 to 1931-1932
Gronemeyer, Lee	1961-1962 to 1978-1979
Gross, Frances	1945-1946
Gutman, Leonid	1976-1977 to 1978-1979
Hagopian, Richard G.	1945-1946 to 1946-1947
Hague, Lynn	1973-1974 to 1978-1979
Hartl, John	1921-1922 to 1945-1946
Hugo, Victor	1917-1918; 1919-1920 to 1958-1959
Iwig, Henry E.	1955-1956
Kaltenthaler, William A.	1907-1908 to 1909-1910
Katz, David	1932-1933
Kielsmeyer, Louis	1907-1908 to 1922-1923
King, Sylvia	1967-1968 to 1978-1979
Kippel, Sam	1944-1945 to 1953-1954
Knebel, Arthur	1955-1956 to 1964-1965; 1966-1967
Knudsen, Christen	1910-1911 to 1926-1927
Korman, Joan	Assistant Principal: 1973-1974 to 1978-1979
Liota, Vincent	1957-1958 to 1958-1959
Lowe, Thomas D.	1965-1966
Lowenthal, Robert	1963-1964 to 1964-1965
Magers, William	1958-1959 to 1962-1963
Martin, William	1976-1977 to 1978-1979
Mattis, Kathleen	Acting Principal: 1977-1978; Associate Principal: 1978-1979
Mende, Paul	1916-1917
Metz, Reuben	1935-1936
Morgulis, George	1937-1938 to 1942-1943
Moss, Linda	1971-1972 to 1972-1973 Assistant Principal: 1972-1973
Nagy, Laszlo	1941-1942
Neeter, Philip	Principal: 1929-1930 to 1930-1931
Olk, Hugo	1919-1920 to 1922-1923
Ormond, Edward	1948-1949 to 1958-1959
Parnas, Richard	1954-1955
Pearson, Nils	1908-1909 to 1920-1921
Perich, Guillermo	Principal: 1968-1969 to 1970-1971
Powell, Paul	1942-1943
Ray, Jacques	1933-1934
Riediger, Walter	1937-1938 to 1970-1971
Roehrborn, Walter S.	1931-1932 to 1941-1942

Rossow, Paul	1912-1913 to 1922-1923;
	1924-1925 to 1926-1927
Salomon, Margaret	1966-1967 to 1978-1979
Schwartz, Murray	1947-1948 to 1954-1955
Sher, Hyman	1927-1928 to 1928-1929
Silberstein, Erich	1943-1944 to 1944-1945
Skernick, Abraham	1946-1947 to 1947-1948
Tholl, Carl A.	1907-1908 to 1940-1941
Thumser, Oswald	1907-1908 to 1930-1931
Trembly, Sally	1963-1964 to 1964-1965
Tushinsky, Jacques	1923-1924 to 1928-1929;
	Principal:
	1924-1925 to 1928-1929
Van den Burg, Herbert	1931-1932 to 1970-1971;
	Principal:
	1931-1932 to 1967-1968
Venittelli, Salvatore	1960-1961 to 1961-1962
Verme, Anthony	1947-1948 to 1978-1979
Vernon, Robert	Associate Principal:
	1972-1973 to 1975-1976
Walker, Ernest	1966-1967 to 1967-1968
Weiser, Charles E.	1965-1966 to 1978-1979
White, Garry	1931-1932 to 1936-1937

Violincellos

Name	Season
Albers, Frederick G.	1907-1908
Ammann, Walter	1910-1911 to 1911-1912;
	1913-1914; 1925-1926
Anderson, Paul	1945-1946 to 1950-1951
Anton, P. G.	1907-1908 to 1908-1909;
	1917-1918 to 1918-1919
Bandy, John	1952-1953
Bartles, Alfred H.	1960-1961
Beabout, Marilyn	1958-1959 to 1978-1979
Beidel, Richard	1927-1928
Blatt, Robert	1967-1968
Bodenhorn, Aaron	1943-1944
Bosker, Gregory	1944-1945 to 1945-1946
Braverman, Terry	Assistant Principal:
	1970-1971 to 1973-1974
Brewer, Richard	1967-1968 to 1978-1979
Callies, Richard	1911-1912

Cherry, Philip	1951-1952
Ciechanski, Aleksander	1969-1970 to 1978-1979
Clay, Edward	1907-1908 to 1923-1924
Colf, Howard D.	Principal: 1962-1963
Davis, Douglas	Principal: 1963-1964
De Conto, Pasquale	1923-1924 to 1929-1930;
	1931-1932 to 1959-1960
de Frank, Vincent	1947-1948 to 1949-1950
Downes, Warren	1953-1954 to 1955-1956
Draper, Barbara	1953-1954 to 1954-1955
Durell, Mary	1968-1969
Fabrizio, Enrico	1915-1916 to 1916-1917
Feldin, Dodia	Principal:
	1951-1952 to 1953-1954
Fletcher, Katherine	1946-1947
Geffen, Igor	1927-1928 to 1943-1944
Gottlieb, Paul	1909-1910
Graul, Ewald	1914-1915 to 1917-1918
Gruppe, Paulo	1915-1916
Hagel, George	1908-1909 to 1910-1911
Halbman, Jacob	1919-1920
Hamilton, Raymond	1920-1921; 1922-1923
Hendrickson, R. E.	1921-1922 to 1922-1923
Jellen, Gabriel	1955-1956 to 1957-1958
Jones, LaVara Farmer	1961-1962 to 1964-1965
Jump, Dorothea	1945-1946
Kagan, Gerald	1958-1959 to 1961-1962;
	Associate Principal:
	1961-1962
Kataoka, Masayoshi	1969-1970 to 1978-1979
Katsuta, Soichi	1969-1970
Kayaloff, Anna	1944-1945 to 1946-1947
Keller, Gustaf	1928-1929 to 1936-1937
Kern, Joseph	1907-1908
Kessler, Abe	1920-1921 to 1924-1925; 1926-1927;
	1934-1935 to 1942-1943; 1944-1945
Knebel, Celia	1960-1961 to 1964-1965; 1966-1967
(Koch, Celia)	1956-1957 to 1959-1960
Koch, Celia	1956-1957 to 1959-1960
(Knebel, Celia)	1960-1961 to 1964-1965; 1966-1967
Lake, Martin	1939-1940 to 1941-1942
La Marchina, Antonio	1928-1929 to 1943-1944; 1945-1946;
	1951-1952 to 1956-1957
Lavin, Avram	Principal:
	1949-1950 to 1951-1952
Lehr, Catherine	Assistant Principal:
	1974-1975 to 1978-1979

Levine, Daniel	1965-1966 to 1966-1967
Levy, Frank	1952-1953
Lustgarten, Edgar	Principal:
	1946-1947 to 1948-1949
Lydzinski, K. A.	1961-1962 to 1966-1967
Lydzinski, Sallie	1961-1962 to 1970-1971
(WeMott, Sallie)	1971-1972 to 1974-1975
Malosek, Michael	1921-1922
Mayer, Charles	1907-1908 to 1920-1921
McGill, Allen	1960-1961
Menges, Frank	1916-1917 to 1917-1918; 1921-1922
Milner, Madeleine	1952-1953 to 1954-1955
Parnas, Leslie	Principal:
	1954-1955 to 1961-1962
Perkins, James	1955-1956
Pinckney, Kenneth	1958-1959 to 1978-1979;
	Assistant Principal:
	1968-1969 to 1969-1970
Pleier, Ludwig	1914-1915 to 1916-1917
Post, Emil	1911-1912 to 1913-1914
Rossow, Carl	1923-1924 to 1949-1950
Rubinstein, Sascha	1967-1968
Sant' Ambrogio, John	Principal:
	1968-1969 to 1978-1979
Schenkman, Peter	Principal:
	1965-1966 to 1966-1967
Schmit, Lucien	1911-1912
Schon, Gerald	1912-1913; 1914-1915
Schumacher, Donovan	1946-1947 to 1950-1951
Schuster, Savely	1977-1978 to 1978-1979
Schwartz, Bernice Tobin	1949-1950 to 1955-1956
(Tobin, Bernice)	1956-1957
See, William J.	1914-1915
Sharon, Andre	1927-1928
Sher, Richard	Principal: 1967-1968
Siegert, Bernard W.	1912-1913
Silverman, Robert	1966-1967 to 1978-1979
Simon, Emile	1928-1929 to 1930-1931
Slutsky, Bernice	1947-1948 to 1948-1949
Sottile, Domenick	1922-1923; 1924-1925 to 1926-1927;
	1937-1938 to 1969-1970
Steindel, Max	1912-1913 to 1913-1914;
	1917-1918 to 1959-1960;
	Principal: 1924-1925 to 1945-1946
Steppi, Carl	1930-1931 to 1966-1967
Stolarchyk, Peter	1957-1958
Taglialavoro, Joseph	1927-1928

Name	Season
Tatian, Hrant G.	1962-1963 to 1964-1965; Acting Principal: 1964-1965
Teicholz, Martin	1935-1936 to 1938-1939
Tobin, Bernice	1956-1957
(Schwartz, Bernice Tobin)	1949-1950 to 1955-1956
Tonar, Joseph	1928-1929 to 1941-1942
Torgove, Abraham	1910-1911; 1913-1914 to 1927-1928
Torgove, Leo	1919-1920 to 1926-1927
Tower, Frank S.	1913-1914
Tung, Yuan	Associate Principal: 1970-1971 to 1978-1979
Warner, Ninian	1916-1917; 1920-1921
Watson, Leonard	1912-1913 to 1913-1914
WeMott, Sallie	1971-1972 to 1978-1979
(Lydzinski, Sallie)	1961-1962 to 1970-1971
Wlaschek, Frank	1950-1951
Zilboorg, Olga	1957-1958 to 1960-1961

Double Basses

Name	Season
Albright, Philip H.	1950-1951 to 1957-1958
Altschuh, George	1927-1928 to 1931-1932
Andel, J. S.	1926-1927
Arnold, Eugene A.	1927-1928
Auer, Karl P.	1925-1926 to 1952-1953; Principal: 1927-1928 to 1935-1936
Balkin, John	1960-1961 to 1961-1962
Bartolamasi, Albert	1946-1947 to 1948-1949
Benfield, Warren	1937-1938 to 1941-1942; Principal: 1938-1939 to 1941-1942
Brachman, A.	1924-1925
Brewster, H. Stevens, Jr.	1958-1959 to 1959-1960
Brodine, Russell	1949-1950 to 1972-1973; Assistant Principal: 1968-1969 to 1972-1973
Broeckaert, Henry	1907-1908 to 1909-1910
Buckley, Carolyn	Associate Principal: 1978-1979
Buhl, Robert	1907-1908 to 1936-1937
Burkhart, Herman	1946-1947 to 1948-1949; 1951-1952 to 1953-1954
Campione, Salvatore	1919-1920 to 1923-1924; 1925-1926 to 1926-1927; 1931-1932 to 1950-1951

Carson, Christopher	Assistant Principal:
	1974-1975 to 1978-1979
Casertani, Andrea	1928-1929 to 1935-1936
Casey, Robert	1944-1945
Claunch, Warren L.	1962-1963 to 1964-1965;
	1968-1969 to 1978-1979
Cunnington, Syd E.	1917-1918
Dean, Henry	1920-1921
De Angelis, Joseph	1926-1927 to 1927-1928
De Fulvio, Vincent	1944-1945 to 1945-1946
de Palma, Emilio	1946-1947
Dietrichs, William H.	1913-1914 to 1915-1916
Essa, Philip W.	1955-1956 to 1958-1959
Freiermuth, Fritz	1907-1908
Fuller, B. F.	1921-1922
Greenburg, Henry	1952-1953 to 1955-1956
Grimaldi, Vincent	1937-1938 to 1958-1959;
	Principal: 1943-1944 to 1949-1950
Harnach, Fred	1947-1948 to 1949-1950
Helmholz, Waldemar F.	1929-1930 to 1939-1940
Hildreth, J. H.	1921-1922
Hochman, Sania	1916-1917; 1920-1921
Hough, Howard	1917-1918
Hyna, Earl	1924-1925 to 1925-1926;
	1927-1928 to 1943-1944
Hyna, Otto	1923-1924
Jamitz, Reuben	Principal: 1942-1943
Kippenberger, Terrence M.	1962-1963 to 1972-1973
Kleeman, Joseph C.	1958-1959 to 1978-1979
Klima, John	1932-1933 to 1936-1937
Koch, David	1938-1939 to 1941-1942
Kolmschlag, Joseph	1916-1917
Kovar, Alfred J.	1922-1923 to 1923-1924
Krause, Oswald	1910-1911 to 1911-1912
Krausse, Joseph	1922-1923 to 1926-1927;
	Principal: 1924-1925 to 1926-1927
Loew, Henry L.	1949-1950 to 1978-1979;
	Principal: 1950-1951 to 1978-1979
Maisel, Ralph R.	1959-1960 to 1978-1979
Maisel, Robert	1957-1958 to 1958-1959
Mannie, Carl J.	1946-1947 to 1949-1950
Manning, Clinton	1935-1936 to 1941-1942
Martin, Donald R.	1962-1963 to 1978-1979
Mayer, Charles	1907-1908 to 1908-1909; 1917-1918
Mayland, Marilyn	1956-1957
Mehlsack, A.	1909-1910
Miller, Jesse	1954-1955 to 1955-1956

Monohan, Thomas S., Jr.	1959-1960
Muehlmann, Richard K.	1965-1966 to 1978-1979
Murphy, Janice Roberts	1974-1975 to 1978-1979
(Roberts, Janice A.)	1958-1959 to 1973-1974
Neubauer, Julius	1912-1913
Norton, Lew	1957-1958
Oatman, Ole	1913-1914 to 1919-1920
Orzechowski, Henry	1952-1953 to 1953-1954
Osmak, John	1918-1919 to 1919-1920; 1921-1922
Pacht, Newton	1950-1951 to 1951-1952
Pitchersky, Meyer	1925-1926 to 1926-1927
Previati, Louis J.	1922-1923
Ravagnani, Albert	1921-1922 to 1925-1926
Reinhold, Arno	1914-1915
Roberts, Janice A.	1958-1959 to 1973-1974
(Murphy, Janice Roberts)	1974-1975
Rosander, R.	1912-1913
Rose, John	1942-1943; 1945-1946
Rotenberg, June	1943-1944 to 1951-1952
Salkowski, John	1961-1962
Schoenfeld, Carl	1926-1927 to 1930-1931
Seydel, Theodore	1928-1929
Shaevitz, Samuel	1956-1957
Siegel, Michael	1943-1944
Sklar, Martin	1959-1960 to 1960-1961
Smith, Charles	1954-1955 to 1955-1956
Soehnlin, William, Jr.	1920-1921 to 1921-1922
Stein, William	1919-1920
Svendsen, Johan	1923-1924
Thiel, Carl	1908-1909
Thul, Carl	1907-1908; 1909-1910 to 1910-1911
Toenges, Karl L.	1953-1954 to 1954-1955
Torgove, Louis	1908-1909 to 1923-1924
Torgove, Saul	1924-1925
Trovato, Valentino	1907-1908 to 1915-1916; 1918-1919
Uray, Joseph	1957-1958
Van Reck, Alfons	1924-1925
Vopatek, Fred	1920-1921
Walter, Sylvia	1945-1946
Whistler, Albert	1940-1941 to 1941-1942
White, Carolyn	1973-1974 to 1977-1978;
	Assistant Principal:
	1973-1974;
	Associate Principal:
	1974-1975 to 1977-1978
Zimmerman, Oscar G.	Principal: 1936-1937 to 1937-1938
Zottarelle, Joseph	1911-1912 to 1913-1914;
	1915-1916 to 1922-1923

Harps

Name	Season
Conti, Amelia	1930-1931
Delledonne, Ida	1910-1911 to 1922-1923
Flach, Albertina	1952-1953 to 1957-1958
Ghio, Adelia	1908-1909 to 1909-1910
Hearn, Laura	1966-1967
Lowe, Wilhelmina	1907-1908 to 1909-1910;
(Speyer, Wilhelmina Lowe)	1923-1924 to 1926-1927
Marriott, Laura	1963-1964
Muribus, Maria	1960-1961 to 1963-1964
Pampari, Graziella	1923-1924 to 1929-1930;
	1931-1932 to 1959-1960
Pfeil, Walter	1964-1965 to 1969-1970
Pinckney, Maria	1967-1968 to 1969-1970;
	1971-1972; 1974-1975 to 1977-1978
Speyer, Wilhelmina Lowe	1923-1924 to 1926-1927
(Lowe, Wilhelmina)	1907-1908 to 1909-1910
Valasek, Joseph	1922-1923
Watanabe, Ayako	1971-1972; 1974-1975 to 1977-1978
Woodhams, Frances	Principal: 1970-1971 to 1978-1979

Oboes

Name	Season
Angelo, Peter	1959-1960 to 1960-1961
Antonucci, Joseph	1929-1930 to 1957-1958
Arner, Leonard	1948-1949 to 1954-1955;
	Principal: 1949-1950 to 1954-1955
Bertram, Adolph	1919-1920 to 1921-1922
Bowman, Peter	Principal: 1977-1978 to 1978-1979
Combatente, Ralph	1921-1922
Corne, Rene	1931-1932 to 1933-1934
Crowley, David H.	1961-1962 to 1963-1964
de Castro, Robert	1961-1962
Doucet, Louis	1911-1912
Dutton, David	1964-1965
Enkells, Elizabeth	1968-1969 to 1973-1974;
	Acting Principal: 1968-1969;
	Associate Principal: 1969-1970;

(Lucia, Elizabeth)	Assistant Principal: 1970-1971 to 1973-1974
Fantilli, August L.	Assistant Principal: 1974-1975 1958-1959
Genovese, Alfred J.	Principal: 1956-1957 to 1958-1959
Goltzer, Albert	Principal: 1946-1947 to 1947-1948
Goltzer, Doris D.	1947-1948
Gomberg, Harold	1939-1940 to 1942-1943; Principal: 1942-1943
Gordon, Marc	1972-1973 to 1978-1979
Herr, Barbara	Assistant Principal: 1976-1977 to 1978-1979
Hicks, Alfred H.	1926-1927 to 1946-1947
Holmes, John A.	Principal: 1944-1945 to 1945-1946
Horn, Paul	1965-1966
Hoxie, Burton W.	1922-1923
Hussey, George A.	1955-1956 to 1960-1961; Principal: 1959-1960 to 1960-1961
Jaeger, Laura	1966-1967 to 1967-1968
Jakez, Carlos	1917-1918
Keller, August	1964-1965 to 1967-1968; 1969-1970 to 1971-1972
Kellersberger, Anton J.	1920-1921
Kessler, Walter	1948-1949 to 1954-1955
Leoncavallo, Joseph	1922-1923 to 1923-1924
Lucia, Elizabeth	Assistant Principal: 1974-1975 to 1975-1976
(Enkells, Elizabeth)	1968-1969 to 1973-1974 Acting Principal: 1968-1969 Associate Principal: 1969-1970 Assistant Principal: 1970-1971 to 1973-1974
Majori, Olivo	1928-1929
Mathieu, Pierre	1934-1935 to 1940-1941; Assistant First: 1939-1940 to 1940-1941
McConathy, James S.	1907-1908 to 1913-1914
Miglionico, Attilio	1916-1917; 1918-1919
Parkes, Thomas	1968-1969 to 1978-1979
Rifici, Vincent	1923-1924 to 1925-1926
Russell, Myron E.	1927-1928
Schipilliti, Vincento	1910-1911
Simonazzi, Ermete	Principal: 1924-1925 to 1930-1931
Sluyter, Harris	Principal: 1955-1956
Smith, Colin G.	1962-1963 to 1963-1964
Sonik, Carl	Principal: 1961-1962 to 1967-1968
Spada, Joseph	1923-1924 to 1926-1927

Standke, Paul	1912-1913 to 1919-1920;
	1921-1922 to 1922-1923
Wagner, Samuel G.	1920-1921
Wann, Lois	Principal: 1943-1944
Ward, Arthur	1908-1909 to 1909-1910;
	1914-1915 to 1915-1916
Woodhams, Richard	Principal: 1969-1970 to 1976-1977
Worrell, Claude	1959-1960 to 1960-1961
Wouters, Jacques	1907-1908 to 1918-1919

English Horns

Name	Season
Angelo, Peter	1959-1960 to 1960-1961
Bertram, Adolph	1920-1921
Combatente, Ralph	1921-1922
Crowley, David H.	1961-1962
Doucet, Louis	1911-1912
Goltzer, Doris D.	1947-1948
Gordon, Marc	1972-1973 to 1978-1979
Hicks, Alfred H.	1926-1927 to 1946-1947
Hoxie, Burton W.	1922-1923
Hussey, George A.	1955-1956 to 1958-1959
Keller, August	1964-1965 to 1965-1966;
	1968-1969 to 1971-1972
Kellersberger, Anton J.	1920-1921
Kessler, Walter	1948-1949 to 1954-1955
McConathy, James S.	1908-1909 to 1913-1914
Rifici, Vincent	1924-1925 to 1925-1926
Schipilliti, Vincento	1910-1911
Smith, Colin G.	1962-1963 to 1963-1964
Standke, Paul	1912-1913 to 1918-1919
Wagner, Samuel G.	1920-1921
Wouters, Jacques	1907-1908 to 1913-1914; 1919-1920

Flutes

Name	Season
Altmeyer, Peter	1924-1925 to 1926-1927
Amerina, Albert P.	1907-1908
Berg, Jacob	Principal: 1969-1970 to 1978-1979

Borouchoff, Israel	Principal: 1958-1959 to 1965-1966
Broeckaert, Leopold	1907-1908 to 1909-1910
Close, L. Mack	1907-1908 to 1931-1932
Coleman, Janice	1965-1966 to 1978-1979
Di Sevo, Oresti	1944-1945 to 1945-1946
Gilbert, Joseph Jean	1911-1912
Gippo, Jan	1972-1973 to 1978-1979
Kiburz, John F.	1907-1908 to 1910-1911;
	1912-1913 to 1939-1940
Kiburz, John F., Jr.	1940-1941 to 1967-1968;
	1969-1970 to 1970-1971
Klump, Robert W.	1954-1955 to 1956-1957
Leifer, Lyon	1964-1965
Lutes, Carl W.	Principal: 1956-1957 to 1957-1958
Moskovitz, Harry H.	1932-1933 to 1941-1942
Neff, Oscar W.	1918-1919 to 1923-1924;
	1928-1929 to 1931-1932
Nelson, Joseph	1912-1913 to 1917-1918
Niosi, Emil J.	1942-1943 to 1943-1944
Sauter, John	1927-1928
Schmit, Gustave Adolph	1911-1912
Scott, Janet	1962-1963 to 1963-1964
Shostac, David	Principal: 1968-1969
Sillars, Janet	1957-1958 to 1961-1962
Skowronek, Felix	Principal: 1966-1967 to 1967-1968
Smith, Janice	Assistant Principal:
	1968-1969 to 1978-1979
Tipton, Albert N.	Principal: 1946-1947 to 1955-1956
Torno, Laurent	1932-1933 to 1953-1954;
	Principal: 1942-1943 to 1945-1946

Piccolos

Name	Season
Amerina, Albert P.	1910-1911
Close, L. Mack	1910-1911 to 1931-1932
Di Sevo, Oresti	1944-1945 to 1945-1946
Gilbert, Joseph Jean	1911-1912
Gippo, Jan	1972-1973 to 1978-1979
Kiburz, John F.	1907-1908 to 1910-1911;
	1931-1932 to 1939-1940
Kiburz, John F., Jr.	1940-1941 to 1942-1943;
	1946-1947 to 1965-1966;
	1968-1969 to 1970-1971

Neff, Oscar W.	1918-1919 to 1924-1925
Nelson, Joseph	1912-1913 to 1917-1918
Niosi, Emil J.	1943-1944
Schmit, Gustave Adolph	1911-1912
Smith, Janice	1971-1972

Clarinets

Name	Season
Adler, Wolf	1956-1957 to 1958-1959
Amodeo, Charles	1912-1913
Bates, Earl	Principal: 1949-1950 to 1962-1963
Burgio, Michael E.	1956-1957 to 1959-1960
Camacho, Charles E. (Carlos)	1923-1924 to 1954-1955
Coleman, Robert	1960-1961; 1962-1963 to 1978-1979; Assistant Principal: 1970-1971 to 1978-1979
Crisanti, Andrew J.	Principal: 1963-1964 to 1964-1965; Associate Principal: 1969-1970
DeSantis, Louis	Principal: 1925-1926
Ewing, Glen	1909-1910 to 1911-1912
Forlani, Nicola R.	1910-1911 to 1916-1917
Freeman, Stephen	1958-1959
Gesner, Clarence L.	1922-1923 to 1953-1954
Gray, Gary	1964-1965 to 1965-1966
Greenburg, Lloyd A.	1961-1962
Guentzel, Gustav	1907-1908
Halbmann, Alexander	1917-1918 to 1921-1922
Harder, Erwin E.	1921-1922
Mazzocchio, Alfred J.	1950-1951 to 1955-1956
Meyer, James	1966-1967 to 1967-1968; 1969-1970 to 1978-1979
Moses, John	Principal: 1968-1969
Munger, Leland	Principal: 1965-1966 to 1967-1968
Politzer, David	1948-1949 to 1949-1950; 1954-1955 to 1955-1956
Sarli, Antonio	1907-1908 to 1908-1909; 1912-1913 to 1916-1917; 1919-1920
Schultes, Arthur	1908-1909 to 1909-1910
Scott, Leslie	1959-1960 to 1963-1964
Siebenmann, William J.	1918-1919
Silfies, George	Principal: 1970-1971 to 1978-1979
Trovato, Valentino	1907-1908; 1911-1912 to 1914-1915
Ward, Christine	1970-1971 to 1978-1979

Warner, Melvin
Zottarelle, Rocco M.

Assistant Principal: 1968-1969
1917-1918; 1920-1921 to 1924-1925;
1926-1927 to 1948-1949;
Principal: 1926-1927 to 1930-1931;
1942-1943 to 1948-1949

Bass Clarinets

Name	Season
Adler, Wolf	1956-1957 to 1958-1959
Amodeo, Charles	1912-1913
Camacho, Charles E. (Carlos)	1922-1923 to 1954-1955
Ewing, Glen S.	1911-1912
Forlani, Nicola Romeo	1911-1912 to 1914-1915
Gray, Gary	1964-1965 to 1965-1966
Guentzel, Gustave	1907-1908
Harder, Erwin	1919-1920 to 1921-1922
Meyer, James	1968-1969 to 1978-1979
Politzer, David	1955-1956
Sarli, Anthony	1912-1913 to 1914-1915
Scott, Leslie	1960-1961 to 1963-1964
Trovato, Valentino	1908-1909 to 1918-1919

Bassoons

Name	Season
Beilfuss, Herman	1925-1926
Berry, George E.	Principal: 1962-1963 to 1978-1979
Buckley, Bradford	1969-1970 to 1978-1979
Cantor, Lester	Principal: 1958-1959 to 1961-1962
Cibulka, William G.	1908-1909 to 1909-1910
Cunnington, Henry	1934-1935 to 1943-1944
Delledonna, Domenico	1910-1911 to 1922-1923
Eisenman, Robert	1945-1946
Ferrell, John E.	1926-1927 to 1958-1959
Fischer, Frederick	1907-1908 to 1921-1922
Fuhrman, Max	Principal: 1924-1925 to 1928-1929
Grapengeter, Harry	1910-1911
Gravell, Sam	1959-1960 to 1967-1968
Hebert, Emil	Principal: 1943-1944

Herzberg, Norman	1938-1939 to 1941-1942; Principal: 1946-1947 to 1952-1953
Jeffries, Daniel	1909-1910
Kasow, Norman	Principal: 1953-1954
Kruse, William H.	1924-1925
Litke, Paul	1923-1924
Lorr, Ralph	1944-1945
Martenson, Robert D.	Principal: 1954-1955 to 1957-1958
Masters, Ralph	Principal: 1944-1945
Mosbach, Joseph	Principal: 1942-1943
Mottl, Robert	Assistant Principal: 1968-1969 to 1978-1979
Pietrini, Louis	Principal: 1929-1930 to 1933-1934
Poepping, Noel	1907-1908 to 1908-1909; 1911-1912 to 1933-1934
Reines, Nat	1934-1935 to 1937-1938
Sage, Octave	1922-1923
Selig, Gabriel P.	Principal: 1945-1946
Weary, M. B.	1923-1924
Wisneskey, Robert	1946-1947 to 1978-1979

Contra Bassoons

Name	Season
Buckley, Bradford	1968-1969 to 1978-1979
Delledonne, Domenico	1911-1912 to 1914-1915
Ferrell, John E.	1934-1935 to 1958-1959
Fischer, Frederick	1911-1912 to 1913-1914
Gravell, Sam	1959-1960 to 1965-1966
Poepping, Noel	1907-1908 to 1909-1910; 1911-1912 to 1933-1934

Horns

Name	Season
Babbe, Oscar A.	1918-1919 to 1919-1920
Brown, Ralph W.	1923-1924 to 1924-1925
Burnham, William R.	1912-1913
Di Lecce, Pietreangelo	1912-1913
Dolan, John B.	1932-1933 to 1941-1942; 1945-1946 to 1955-1956

Dorfman, Herman	1942-1943
Erickson, Frank O.	1914-1915 to 1917-1918
Eymann, Charles	1909-1910 to 1911-1912
Friedel, Kaid	1963-1964 to 1978-1979; Principal: 1963-1964 to 1966-1967
Gardner, Julius	1920-1921
Gebhardt, William C.	1914-1915; 1928-1929 to 1932-1933
Gilcher, Albert A.	1915-1916 to 1919-1920
Gustat, Robert	1927-1928 to 1965-1966
Helmholz, Waldemar	1909-1910; 1913-1914 to 1919-1920; 1921-1922 to 1922-1923
Henniger, Frank	1920-1921
Hoefer, Franz	1907-1908
Kunze, Arthur	1908-1909
Lecce, Pellegrino	1919-1920 to 1926-1927; Principal: 1924-1925 to 1926-1927
Lind, Hans	1915-1916
Martin, Philip H.	1931-1932
Messenger, Archie H.	1912-1913
Miller, William	1925-1926 to 1927-1928
Minsel, Robert	1923-1924
Mountz, John	1933-1934 to 1941-1942
Muenzer, Frank	1922-1923
Murphy, Edward A.	1930-1931 to 1933-1934; 1936-1937 to 1966-1967; Principal: 1930-1931; 1942-1943 to 1965-1966
Nadaf, George	1957-1958
Newell, Thomas E., Jr.	1955-1956 to 1956-1957
Pandolfi, Roland	Principal: 1966-1967 to 1978-1979
Peter, Karl	1907-1908
Rapini, Vincent	1946-1947 to 1954-1955
Rescigno, Joseph	1921-1922 to 1928-1929; Principal: 1927-1928 to 1928-1929
Sansone, Lorenzo	1912-1913 to 1914-1915
Schaub, Frederick	1920-1921
Schiebler, Carl	1963-1964 to 1978-1979
Schinner, Carl	1907-1908 to 1911-1912; 1920-1921 to 1921-1922
Schmitt, James	1957-1958
Schmitter, Albert W.	1958-1959 to 1962-1963
Scholz, Adolph	1911-1912; 1913-1914
Schrickel, Carl	1908-1909
Schultz, Kenneth	1958-1959 to 1978-1979
Scott, George L.	1928-1929 to 1930-1931
Shaw, Boone F.	1954-1955

Sigismonti, Henry	1956-1957; 1959-1960 to 1962-1963; Assistant Principal: 1962-1963
Stagliano, James	1934-1935 to 1935-1936
Stango, Emilio	1923-1924 to 1930-1931
Strieby, Lawrence	1967-1968 to 1978-1979; Assistant Principal: 1968-1969 to 1978-1979
Thaens, Paul	1908-1909 to 1911-1912
Ugrin, John	1917-1918 to 1919-1920; 1921-1922 to 1922-1923
Vegna, Joseph	1931-1932 to 1953-1954
Waerle, Jean	1910-1911
Walk, James E.	1955-1956 to 1957-1958
Zaenglin, George	1907-1908
Zoellner, Albert	1913-1914

Trumpets and Cornets

Name	Season
Bambridge, John	1909-1910
Barton, Leland S.	1916-1917
Blackburn, Roger	Acting Co-Principal: 1972-1973
Carione, Joseph	1919-1920 to 1941-1942; 1944-1945 to 1956-1957
Dastich, Vincent	1921-1922 to 1922-1923
Glessner, George	1907-1908 to 1915-1916
Glickstein, David	1919-1920
Goetting, Chandler	Principal: 1966-1967 to 1971-1972
Goodrich, Andrew	1917-1918
Grossheider, Roger	1961-1962 to 1978-1979
Gustat, Joseph	1920-1921 to 1943-1944; Principal: 1924-1925 to 1930-1931
Hartl, John	1915-1916; 1921-1922 to 1924-1925; 1927-1928 to 1941-1942; 1943-1944
Hebs, William	1910-1911 to 1914-1915
Hugo, Carl F.	1927-1928 to 1931-1932
Jeffers, Edward	1918-1919
Krauss, Samuel G.	1936-1937 to 1943-1944; Principal: 1942-1943 to 1943-1944
Lambiase, Thomas	1918-1919
Loebker, Joseph	1923-1924 to 1924-1925
McDuffee, Malcolm	Assistant Principal: 1973-1974 to 1978-1979
Mellon, Edward K.	1916-1917

Miller, Frank	1934-1935 to 1968-1969
Pearson, Nils	1907-1908 to 1920-1921
Rosenfeld, Seymour	Principal: 1944-1945 to 1945-1946
Schopp, John	1907-1908 to 1908-1909
Slaughter, Susan	1969-1970 to 1978-1979;
	Assistant Principal: 1971-1972
	Acting Co-Principal: 1972-1973;
	Principal: 1973-1974 to 1978-1979
Smith, Gary	1966-1967 to 1978-1979;
	Assistant Principal:
	1968-1969 to 1970-1971
Stacy, Fred	1957-1958
Stolz, Donald R.	1958-1959 to 1965-1966;
	Principal: 1961-1962 to 1965-1966
Tarrantino, Noah	1907-1908 to 1908-1909
Weatherly, Robert	Principal: 1946-1947 to 1960-1961
Willbrandt, Adolph	1909-1910

Trombones

Name	Season
Bittner, David	1907-1908 to 1918-1919
Davenport, Roger	1964-1965; 1967-1968 to 1978-1979
De Vincenzo, Salvatore	1937-1938 to 1942-1943;
	Principal: 1942-1943
Dittert, Merrit W.	1934-1935 to 1936-1937
Forkert, Oswald	1907-1908 to 1908-1909
Hallback, Oscar	1907-1908 to 1939-1940;
	Principal: 1924-1925 to 1930-1931
Jernigan, Melvyn	1959-1960; 1966-1967 to 1978-1979
Kahila, Kauko	1944-1945
Kiefer, Eugene	1909-1910 to 1919-1920
Kirsch, Clifford W.	1943-1944
Lorr, Flori	1944-1945 to 1950-1951
McCulloh, Byron	1952-1953 to 1955-1956
Meier, Charles F.	1920-1921 to 1942-1943
Merello, George T.	1945-1946 to 1955-1956
Miller, Robert	1966-1967
Oventrop, Edward C.	1923-1924; 1931-1932 to 1933-1934
Palladino, Louis	Principal: 1943-1944
Richardson, William W., Jr.	1965-1966
Rudy, Milton S.	1956-1957
Schneider, Bernard	1956-1957 to 1978-1979;
	Principal: 1958-1959 to 1978-1979

Name	Season
Sloan, Glenn	1957-1958 to 1958-1959
Valetic, Joseph	1924-1925 to 1930-1931
Vegna, Paul	1919-1920 to 1921-1922
Ziegler, Dorothy	1944-1945 to 1963-1964;
	Principal: 1944-1945 to 1957-1958

Tubas

Name	Season
Adam, Eugene	1947-1948 to 1954-1955
Bambridge, John	1936-1937 to 1946-1947
Beatty, Clarence	1907-1908 to 1908-1909
Brown, Burt	1917-1918 to 1918-1919
Dietrichs, William H.	1913-1914 to 1916-1917
Emde, James	1955-1956; 1957-1958 to 1961-1962
Hildreth, J. H.	1921-1922
MacEnulty, John III	1962-1963 to 1978-1979
Spiller, Adam	1927-1928; 1931-1932 to 1935-1936
Vanni, Vincenzo	1922-1923 to 1926-1927
Waldeck, Lewis	1956-1957
Walker, Ralph E.	1919-1920 to 1920-1921
Wisecup, Clarence	1909-1910 to 1912-1913

Timpani

Name	Season
Albers, William G.	1909-1910
Ehrlich, William	1926-1927 to 1957-1958
Espino, Eugene	1966-1967
Friedlander, Edward L.	1959-1960
Hobbs, Albert	1967-1968 to 1968-1969
Holmes, Richard	1969-1970 to 1978-1979
Johnson, J. Massie	1960-1961 to 1964-1965
Kain, Dennis	1965-1966
Kristufek, Otto	1910-1911 to 1920-1921
Makowski, Raymond	1958-1959
Manzer, Lawrence W.	1908-1909
Vet, Charles H.	1907-1908
Vitto, Ben	1921-1922 to 1925-1926

Percussion

Name	Season
Albers, William G.	1913-1914; 1922-1923 to 1941-1942
Bambridge, John	1914-1915 to 1916-1917
Bank, Dorothy Davison	1947-1948
(Davison, Dorothy)	1945-1946 to 1946-1947
Burg, Adolph	1907-1908 to 1917-1918
Catin, Charles B.	1952-1953 to 1955-1956
Clark, William G.	1963-1964 to 1971-1972
Conner, Jack	1948-1949; 1958-1959
Davison, Dorothy	1945-1946 to 1946-1947
(Bank, Dorothy Davison)	1947-1948
Eckhardt, George	1911-1912 to 1912-1913
Ehrlich, William	1958-1959 to 1962-1963
Gesner, Elmer	1917-1918 to 1957-1958
Gilcher, William	1909-1910 to 1910-1911
	1919-1920 to 1921-1922
Kasica, John	1971-1972 to 1978-1979
Klieber, Albert	1908-1909; 1918-1919
Makowski, Ray	1956-1957 to 1957-1958
Matson, Robert	1949-1950 to 1950-1951
O'Donnell, Richard L.	1959-1960 to 1978-1979;
	Principal: 1965-1966 to 1978-1979
Rizzo, David J.	1940-1941 to 1941-1942;
	1943-1944 to 1944-1945;
	1949-1950 to 1969-1970
Schick, Louis H.	1927-1928 to 1930-1931
Seymour, Charles A., Jr.	1916-1917
Stubbs, Thomas	1970-1971 to 1978-1979
Vollrath, Emil	1919-1920 to 1921-1922
Waechtler, Moritz	1907-1908 to 1908-1909

Piano and Celesta

Name	Season
Allen, Jane	1962-1963 to 1963-1964
Covelli, John	1970-1971
Frederick, Corinne	1935-1936 to 1941-1942
Glazer, Gilda	1967-1968 to 1969-1970
Gruen, Rudolph	1918-1919
Liberman, Barbara	1971-1972 to 1978-1979

Matson, Robert	1949-1950 to 1950-1951
Mottl, Mary	1971-1972 to 1973-1974
Norris, Mary	1952-1953 to 1955-1956
Oswald, Joseph F., Jr.	1931-1932 to 1948-1949
Rizzo, David J.	1947-1948 to 1948-1949
Slatkin, Leonard	1968-1969 to 1971-1972
Steindel, Walter	1957-1958 to 1959-1960;
	1964-1965 to 1966-1967
Ziegler, Dorothy	1959-1960 to 1963-1964

Librarians

Name	Season
Gesner, Clarence L.	1943-1944 to 1956-1957
Gesner, Elmer	1920-1921 to 1966-1967
Grossheider, Roger	1967-1968 to 1975-1976
Kiefer, Eugene	1915-1916 to 1919-1920
McConathy, James S.	1907-1908 to 1913-1914
Stone, David	Assistant: 1977-1978 to 1978-1979
Tafoya, John	1977-1978 to 1978-1979
Ward, Arthur	1914-1915

Personnel Managers

Name	Season
Fischer, Frederick	1907-1908 to 1930-1931
Kleeman, Joseph	Assistant: 1977-1978 to 1978-1979
Loew, Henry	1967-1968 to 1976-1977
Murphy, Edward	1961-1962; 1963-1964
Schiebler, Carl	1977-1978 to 1978-1979
Schreiber, Paul	1964-1965 to 1966-1967
Steindel, Max	1931-1932 to 1960-1961; 1962-1963

Assistant and Associate Conductors

Name	Season
Cleve, George	1967-1968
Farbman, Harry	1942-1943 to 1960-1961

Fischer, Frederick	1907-1908 to 1930-1931
Guidi, Scipione	1931-1932 to 1941-1942
Kovalenko, Oleg	1965-1966
Murphy, Edward	1961-1962 to 1967-1968
Slatkin, Leonard	1968-1969 to 1975-1976
	Principal Guest Conductor:
	1977-1978
Zimmermann, Gerhardt	1974-1975 to 1978-1979

APPENDIX II

WORKS PREMIERED BY THE ORCHESTRA,
1907-1908 through 1977-1978

dall'Abaco, Evaristo Felice, *Concerto da Chiesa*

                        November 27-28, 1936   US

Adomian, Lan, *Suite for Orchestra*

                        January 26-27, 1951   W

Albinoni, Tomaso, *Adagio for Strings and Winds*

                        June 2, 1973   W

Alexander, Josef, *Andante and Allegro for String Orchestra*

                        February 20-21, 1953   W

Amfitheatrof, Daniele, *"Il Miracolo delle Rose:" Legenda Francescana*
("The Miracle of the Rose:" A Franciscan Legend)

                        January 27-28, 1928   US

Antheil, George, *"Tom Sawyer," A Mark Twain Overture*

                        February 18-19, 1950   W

Antheil, George, *Waltzes from "Spectre De La Rose"*

                        November 6-7, 1948   W

Antheil, George, *Nocturne from "Decatur at Algiers"*

                        December 10-11, 1944   W

Antheil, George, *Capriccio*

                        December 9-10, 1932   US

Arambarri, Jesus, *Prelude to a Fairy-Tale*

                        March 11-12, 1932   US

Arrigo, Girolamo, *Thumos, for Wind Instruments and Percussion*

                        March 17-18, 1967   US

Aubert, Louis, *Feuille D'Images*

                        January 10-11, 1948   US

Auric, Georges, *Symphonic Suite, Phedre* (from the Ballet)

                        February 9-10, 1957   US

Bach, J. S. (orchestrated by Claude Levy), *Partita in E minor*

                        January 21-22, 1949   W

US = United States; W = World première.

Bach, J. S. (orchestrated by Alexander Tansman), *Tocata in D minor*

                                                               December 20-21, 1935   W

Bach, J. S. (arranged by Alexander Tansman), Two chorales: *"Through Adam Came Our Fall;" "Now Comes the Gentiles' Savior"*

          December 1-2, 1939   W

Bach, J. S. (orchestrated by Amadeo de Filippi), *Wachet Auf, Ruft Uns Die Stimme*

          January 8-9, 1953   W

Baker, Robert, *Six Variations on Each Other*

          February 19-20, 1966   W

Balch, George, *Portrait of an Actress*

          March 3, 1946   W

Barraud, Henri, *Offrande A Une Ombre*

          January 10-11, 1947   US

Barraud, Henri, *Overture for Numance*

          October 29-30, 1949   W

Bartók, Bélla, *Divertimento for String Orchestra*

          November 8-9, 1940   US

Bartók, Bélla, *Mikrokosmos Suite*

          November 20-21, 1943   W

Berio, Luciano, *Allelujah II, for Five Instrumental Groups*

          November 25-26, 1966   US

Binkerd, Gordon, *Symphony No. 4*

          October 12-13, 1963   W

Bliss, Arthur, *Mêlée Fantasque*

          February 28-29, 1924   US

Blumenfeld, Harold, *A Festival Overture*

          1961-1962 season   W

Blumenfeld, Harold, *Symphony, Amphitryon 4*

          November 12-13, 1965   W

Boccherini, Luigi, *Symphonie Concertante*

          November 12-13, 1965   US

Brenta, Gaston, *Symphony*

          January 29-30, 1965   US

Brod, Max, *Two Rustic Israeli Dances*

          September 24-25, 1971   US

Brott, Alexander, *Fancy and Folly*

          January 16-17, 1948   W

Casella, Alfredo, *Suite in C*

          December 28-29, 1917   US

Converse, Frederick, *"Ave et Vale," Tone Poem for Orchestra*

          January 26-27, 1917   W

Coppola, Piero, *Symphonic Poem: "La Ronde Sous la Cloche"*

          November 6-7, 1936   US

Couperin, Francois (transcribed and arranged by Darius Milhaud), *Overture and Allegro*

          January 17-18, 1941   W

Couperin, Francois, *Suite in C minor*

          April 9-11, 1936   W

Delannoy, Marcel, *"Cendrillon," Suite for Grand Orchestra*

February 28-29, 1936 US

De Los Rios, Waldo, *Concierto Para la Guitarra Criolla*

October 27, 1974 US

Del Tredici, David, *Final Alice*

December 15-17, 1977 (First complete performance) W

Desplanes, Jean-Antoine, *Grave*

March 14-15, 1952 W

Druckman, Jacob, *Mirage*

March 4-6-7, 1976 W

Durante, Francesco (transcribed by Adriano Lualdi), *Concerto in F minor for String Orchestra*

October 17-18, 1952 US

Erb, Donald, *Concerto for Trombone and Orchestra*

March 11-12-13, 1976 W

Fischer, Irwin, *Choral Fantasy for Organ and Orchestra*

December 23-26, 1954 W

Fitelberg, George, *Tone Poem, "The Song of the Falcon"*

December 6-7, 1912 US

Fourestier, Louis, *A Saint Valery*

November 16-17, 1934 US

Garofalo, Carlo, *Romantic Symphony*

February 12-13, 1915 US

Gaubert, Philippe, *Concerto in F for Orchestra*

November 30-December 1, 1934 US

Goldsmith, Jerry, *Music for Orchestra*

February 18-19, 1972 W

Gould, Morton, *Anniversary Quadrille*

October 23-24, 1954 W

Gould, Morton, *Harvest*

October 27-28, 1945 W

Guarnieri, Carmago, *Brasiliana Suite*

January 31-February 1, 1953 US

Harsanyi, Tibor, *Danses variees*

January 3-4, 1953 US

Harsanyi, Tibor, *Divertimento No. 2 for String Orchestra and Trumpet*

December 6-8, 1947 US

Harsanyi, Tibor, *"La Joie de Vivre:" Divertissement for Orchestra*

March 8-9, 1935 US

Honegger, Arthur, *Pastorale d'Eté*

November 17-18, 1922 US

Hovhaness, Alan, *Mountain of Prophecy*

October 21-22, 1961 W

Howard, Robert, *Gateway Overture*

July 4, 1978 W

Inghelbrecht, D. E., *Sinfonia Breve*

December 2-3, 1938 US

Jaubert, Maurice, *Suite Francaise*

           November 10-11, 1933 W

Johnston, Benjamin Burwell, *Quintet for Groups*

           March 24-25, 1967 W

Kabalevsky, Dmitri, *Suite from the opera "Colas Breugnon"*

           March 18, 1956 US

Kanitz, Ernst, *Ballet Music*

           December 16-17, 1938 US

Kanitz, Ernest, *Sinfonia Seria*

           October 17-18, 1964 W

Kessler, John, *Introduction and Fugue*

           December 11-12, 1936 W

Kessler, John, *Poeme for Orchestra*

           February 19-20, 1932 W

Kessler, John, *Soliloquy*

           January 20-21, 1954 W

Kessler, John, *Two Symphonic Sketches: "Avalon"*

           January 19-20, 1934 W

Klein, Lothar, *Design for Percussion and Orchestra*

           December 10-11, 1971 W

Konstantinoff, Kostia, *Wien*

           December 28-29, 1934 W

Korngold, Erich, *Concerto in D Major for Violin and Orchestra*

           February 15-16, 1947 W

Kroeger, Ernest, *Symphonic Poem, "Mississippi"*

           February 19-20, 1926 W

Labunski, Witkor, *Two Movements from the Symphony in G minor*

           January 8-9, 1944 W

Landowski, Marcel, *Poeme Symphonique, "Edina"*

           February 27-28, 1948 US

Lazarus, Daniel, *Excerpts from the Symphonic Poem, "Symphonie Avec Hymne"*

           November 24-25, 1934 W

Legley, Victor, *La Cathedrale d' Acier*

           March 21-22, 1964 US

Legley, Victor *Dyptique*

           May 12-13, 1967 US

Levy, Ellis, *Valse de Concerto*

           February 22, 1925 W

Lourié, Arthur-Vincent, *Suite from the Opera, "The Blackmoor of Peter the Great"*

           November 25-26, 1961 W

Lovreglio, Eleuthere, *Spectres*

           December 13-14, 1935 US

Malipiero, G. Francesco, *Concerto for Cello and Orchestra*

           December 15-16, 1950 US

Manfredini, Francesco, *Prelude and Fugue*

           November 10-11, 1939 US

Manuel, Roland, *Peña de Francia*

March 4-5, 1938 W

Marcello, Benedetto, *Introduzione, Ari and Presto for String Orchestra*

March 1-2, 1940 US

Martinu, Bohuslav, *Suite Concertante for Violin and Orchestra*

December 28, 1945 W

Middendorf, J. William, *Violin Concerto in D minor*

November 18-20, 1977 W

Mihalovici, Marcel, *Sequences*

January 29-30, 1949 US

Milhaud, Darius, *Concerto for Marimba and Vibraphone*

February 12-13, 1949 W

Milhaud, Darius, *Fanfare*

March 21-23, 1940 W

Mulé, Giuseppe, *Two Excerpts from the Symphonic Suite "Sicilia Canora" a) "Una Notta A Taormina" b) "Fioriscono gli aranci"*

January 4-5, 1929 US

Nordoff, Paul, *Suite for Orchestra*

December 6-7, 1940 W

Ornstein, Leo, *Nocturne and Dance*

February 12-13, 1937 W

Pendleton, Edmund, *Alpine Concerto for Flute and Orchestra*

February 9-10, 1951 US

Pergolesi, Giovanni, *Concerto For Two Pianos And String Orchestra*

November 27-28, 1959 US

Perkins, John Macivor, *Music for Orchestra*

April 9-10, 1965 W

Persichetti, Vincent, *A Lincoln Address*

January 25-27, 1973 W

Persichetti, Vincent, *Seventh Symphony*

October 24-25, 1959 W

Pisk, Paul A., *Three Ceremonial Rites*

January 7-8, 1966 W

Rathaus, Karol, *Overture to "Salisbury Cove"*

January 21-22, 1950 W

Rathaus, Karol, *Suite for Full Orchestra*

November 25-26, 1932 US

Rieti, Vittorio, *Sinfonia Tripartita*

December 16-17, 1944 W

Rivier, Jean, *Overture Pour Une Opérette imaginaire*

November 23-24, 1935 US

Robb, John Donald, *Symphony No. 3 in One Movement*

October 20-21, 1962 W

Rochberg, George, *Time-Span for Orchestra*

October 22-December 4, 1960 W

Rosenthal, Manuel, *Les Petits Métiers*

March 6-7, 1936 US

Rosenthal, Manuel, *Magic Manhattan*

January 13-14, 1950 W

Rossini, Gioacchino (transcribed by Ottorino Raspighi), *Rossiniana*

March 23-24, 1956 US

San Juan, Pedro, *Ritual Symphony, "La Macumba"*

December 14-15, 1951 W

Santoliquido, Francesco, *Suite Sinfonica, "Acquarelli"*

February 24, 1924 US

Santoro, Claudio, *Symphony No. 6*

November 29-30, 1963 W

Santoro, Claudio, *Symphony No. 8*

November 14-15, 1964 W

Scarlatti, Domenico, *Concerto No. 5 in D minor for String Orchestra with Piano Obbligato*

February 5-6, 1937 US

Scarlatti, Domenico, *Toccata, Bourée and Gigue*

January 11-12, 1935 US

Schickele, Peter, *American Birthday Card*

July 17, 1976 W

Schickele, Peter, *A Zoo Called Earth*

June 27, 1970 W

Schoenberg, Arnold, *Three Little Pieces for Orchestra*

November 21-22, 1964 US

Schumann, Robert, *Concerto in D minor for Violin and Orchestra*

December 23-26, 1937 US

Shostakovitch, Dmitri, *Five Preludes*

February 21-22, 1948 W

Simoni, Wolfgang, *Suite Sefardi*

January 24-25, 1941 W

Slatkin, Leonard, *Absurd Alphabedtime Stories* (Verses by Julius Hunter)

March 14, 1976 W

Slatkin, Leonard, *Dialogue for Two Cellos and Orchestra*

February 23, 1975 W

Slatkin, Leonard, *Extensions I*

April 16-21, 1974 W

Slatkin, Leonard, *The Raven*

May 2, 1971 W

Slatkin, Leonard, *Rhymes and Sonnets*

December 1, 1974 W

Stockhausen, Karlheinz, *Punkte ("Points")*

May 6-7, 1966 US

Stoehr, Richard, *Suite for String Orchestra*

February 17-18, 1911 US

Stoessel, Albert, Suite from the Opera, *"Garrick"*

February 4-5, 1938 W

Susskind, Walter, *Improvisation and Scherzo for Flute and Small Orchestra*

February 9-11-12, 1978   W

Susskind, Walter, *Passacaglia for Timpani and Chamber Orchestra*

February 24-26, 1977   W

Swafford, Jan, *Passage for Piccolo and Orchestra*

March 1, 1977   W

Tansman, Alexander, *Adagio for String Orchestra*

December 18-19, 1936   US

Tansman, Alexander, *Concertino for Piano and Orchestra*

December 18-19, 1936   US

Tansman, Alexander, *Deux Moments Symphoniques*

January 6-7, 1933   W

Tansman, Alexander, *Ricercari*

December 22-23, 1949   W

Tansman, Alexander, *Serenade No. 3 for Orchestra*

November 10-11, 1945   W

Tansman, Alexander, *Symphony No. 7*

October 24-25, 1947   W

Tansman, Alexander, *Triptyque for String Orchestra*

November 6-7, 1931

Tansman, Alexander, *Variations on a Theme of Frescobaldi*

November 12-13, 1937   W

Tartini, Giuseppe, *Concerto in F Major, No. 58, for Two Oboes, Two Horns, and String Orchestra*

November 26-27, 1948   US

Tavares, Mario, *Introduction and Brazilian Dance*

October 24-25, 1953   US

Tharichen, Werner, *Concerto for Voice and Orchestra*

February 12-13, 1959   US

Thirlet, Maurice, *Poème, for Small Orchestra*

February 26-27, 1937   W

Tuthill, Burnet, *"Come Seven," Rhapsody for Orchestra*

February 19-20, 1944   W

Valentina, Giuseppe, *Concerto Grosso, Opus 11, No. 7 for String Orchestra*

February 23-24, 1940   W

Verley, Albert, *Chanson Tourangelle*

February 16-17, 1946   W

Verley, Albert, *Cloches dan la Vallée*

February 7-8, 1936   W

Verley, Albert, *Pastel Sonore*

November 25-26, 1938   W

Vitali, Tommaso, *Chaconne*

January 30-31, 1948   W

Vivaldi, Antonio, *"Autunno" e "Inverno" dalle "Quatro Stagione" ("Autumn" and "Winter" from the "Four Seasons") for String Orchestra, Organ and Cembalo*

January 27-28, 1928   US

Vivaldi, Antonio, *"Estate" dalle "Quatro Stagione" ("Summer" from the "Four Seasons")* for String Orchestra, Organ and Cembalo

January 13-14, 1928 US

Vivaldi, Antonio, *"Primavera" dalle "Quatro Stagione" ("Spring" from the "Four Seasons")* for String Orchestra, Organ and Cembalo

January 6-7, 1928 US

van der Voort, Antoni, *Sinfonietta*

November 22-23, 1940 W

Webern, Anton Von, *Cantata No. 2*

April 16-17, 1966 US

Weinberger, Jaromir, *Preludes réligieux et profanes*

January 14-15, 1956 US

Wykes, Robert, *"Adequate Earth" A Symphonic Setting of Seven Poems by Donald Finkel*

February 5-6-7, 1976 W

Wykes, Robert, *Fanfare for BHAM*

June 24, 1976 W

Wykes, Robert, *"Letter to an Alto-Man"* (Poem: Donald Finkel)

May 19-20, 1967 W

Wykes, Robert, *The Shape of Time*

April 2-3, 1965 W

Wykes, Robert, *Toward Time's Receding*

April 7-8, 1972 W

Xenakis, Yannis, *"Strategie," for Two Orchestras and Two Conductors*

February 26-27, 1965 US

Ysaye, Theophile, *Fantasie on a Popular Walloon Theme*

January 8-9, 1915 US

APPENDIX III

DISCOGRAPHY OF THE ORCHESTRA

Selection	Number	Date Recorded
Bartók: *Piano Concerto No. 3* Leonard Pennario, piano (with Prokofiev Concerto No. 3) Conductor: Golschmann	Capitol P-8253	1953
Beethoven: *Choral Fantasy*, "Elegiac Song," *Calm Sea and Prosperous Voyage*	Vox	1977 1978
Bernstein: *Jeremiah Symphony* Nan Merriman, soprano (3 78s) Conductor: Leonard Bernstein	Victor M/DM-1026 Reissued on Camden CAL-196	1947
Binkerd: *Symphony No. 1* (with Wagner *Siegfried Idyll*, not by St. Louis Symphony) Conductor: Van Remoortel	MS-6291 Columbia ML-5691	1959
Bizet: *Carmen Suite* (with ballet music from Gounod *Faust*) Conductor: Golschmann	Capitol P-8288 Reissued on Pickwick S-4020	1954
Bolzoni: *Minuet* (with Rimsky-Korsakov *Song of India*) Conductor: Ganz	Victor 45531	1925
Britten: *Sinfonia da Requiem* (with Copland *Red Pony Suite*) Conductor: Andre Previn	Columbia ML-5983 MS-6583	1963
Chopin: Romantic Music (orchestral arrangements) (with Respighi *Rossiniana*) Conductor: Golschmann	Columbia ML-5161	1956
Copland: *Red Pony Suite* (with Britten *Sinfonia da Requiem*) Conductor: Andre Previn	Columbia ML-5983 MS-6583 Reissued on Odyssey Y-3106	1963

Corelli: Adagio from *Sonata Op. 5, No. 5*, arranged by Filippi (final side in 78 album of Schoenberg Verklärte Nacht, 4 discs) Conductor: Golschmann	Victor M/DM-1005	1947
Couperin: *La Sultane* (see under Milhaud)		
d'Albert: Overture from *The Improvisator* (78) (with Sinding *Rustle of Spring, Op. 32, No. 3*) Conductor: Ganz	Victor 45389	1920s
Dardanus: *Airs de Ballet* from *Second Suite* Conductor: Golschmann	Columbia 68887-D	1935
Debussy: *La Mer* (with Ravel *La Valse* and *Valses nobles et sentimentales* Conductor: Golschmann	Columbia ML-5155	1956
de Falla: *Nights in the Gardens of Spain* Arthur Rubinstein, piano (with Mozart *Piano Concerto in A*, K. 488) Conductor: Golschmann	Victor LM-1091	1949
de Falla: Ballet suite from *Three-Cornered Hat* (with Prokofiev *Chout*) Conductor: Golschmann	Capitol P-8257	1954
de Falla: *La Vida breve--Spanish Dance No. 1* (with Shostakovich *Age of Gold*) Conductor: Golschmann	Victor 11-8592	1942
Delibes: Suites from the ballets *Coppélia* and *Sylvia* (with Easdale *The Red Shoes* and Weber *Invitation to the Dance*) Conductor: Golschmann	Columbia ML-5254 MS-6028 Reissued on Odyssey 32 16 0338	1957
Delius: *Walk to the Paradise Garden* Conductor: Golschmann	Victor	1942
Dvořák: *Cello Concerto in B minor, Silent Woods Rondo in G minor;* Zara Nelsova, cello *Violin Concerto in A minor, Romance in F minor, Mazurek in E minor;* Ruggiero Ricci, violin *Piano Concerto in G minor* Rudolf Firkusny, piano Conductor: Susskind (3 discs)	Vox Box QSVBX-5135	1974 1975

Dvořák: *Piano Concerto in G minor*   Turnabout   1975
Rudolf Firkusny, piano   QTV 34691
Conductor: Susskind

Dvořák: *Violin·Concerto in A minor, Romance in*   Turnabout   1975
F minor, Mazurek in E minor Ruggerio Ricci, violin   QTV 34700
Conductor: Susskind

Dvořák: *Slavonic Dances Nos. 1 and 3* (78)   Victor 11-8566   1942
Conductor: Golschmann

Easdale: Ballet music from *The Red Shoes*   Columbia ML-5254   1957
(with Delibes suites from the ballets *Coppélia*   MS-6028
and *Sylvia* and Weber *Invitation to the Dance*   Reissued on
Conductor: Golschmann   Odyssey 32 16 0338

Franck: *Symphony in D minor*   Capitol P-8221   1953
Conductor: Golschmann   Reissued on
    Pickwick S-4012

German: Three Dances from *Nell Gwyn* (78)   Victor 9009   1920s
Conductor: Ganz

Gershwin: All works for orchestra and for piano   Vox Box   1974
and orchestra (3 discs) Jeffrey Siegel, piano   QSVBX-5132
Conductor: Slatkin

Gershwin: *An American in Paris, Catfish Row,*   Turnabout   1974
Promenade Barbara Liberman, piano   QTV-S 34594
David Mortland, banjo
Conductor: Slatkin

Gershwin: *Concerto in F, Rhapsody in Blue, "I Got*   Turnabout   1974
Rhythm" Variations   QTV 34703
Jeffrey Siegel, piano
Conductor: Slatkin

Gounod: Ballet music from *Faust*   Capitol P-8288   1954
(with Bizet *Carmen Suite*)   Reissued on
Conductor: Golschmann   Pickwick S-4020

Haydn: *Symphony No. 103 in E-flat*   Columbia M-221   1935
("Drum Roll") (4 78s)
Conductor: Golschmann

Holst: *The Planets*   Turnabout   1974
Conductor: Susskind   QTV-S 34598

Kabalevsky: Suite from *Colas Breugnon* (with Shostakovich *Symphony No. 1*) Conductor: Golschmann	Columbia ML-5152	1956
Lalo: *Symphonie espagnole* Nathan Milstein, violin (with Prokofiev *Violin Concerto No. 1*) Conductor: Golschmann	Capitol P-8303	1954
Lassen: *Festival Overture* (78) Conductor: Ganz	Victor 55202	1923
Mendelssohn: *Fingal's Cave Overture* (78) Conductor: Ganz	Victor 9013	1926
Milhaud: *Suite provencale* (78) (reissued with Schoenberg *Verklärte Nacht* on Camden CAL-178) Conductor: Golschmann	Victor DM-951	1942
Milhaud: *La Sultane*, after Couperin (78) Conductor: Golschmann	Victor 11-8238	1942
Mozart: *Piano Concerto in A*, K. 488 Arthur Rubinstein, piano (with de Falla *Nights in the Gardens of Spain*) Conductor: Golschmann	Victor LM-1091	1949
Mozart: *Symphony No. 38 in D*, K. 504 ("Prague") (78) (Reissued with Sibelius *Symphony No. 7* on Bluebird LBC-1067) Conductor: Golschmann	Victor M/DM-1085 Reissued on Victor LM-27	1948
Mussorgsky: *Night on Bald Mountain*, arranged by Rimsky-Korsakov Mussorgsky/Ravel: *Pictures at an Exhibition* Conductor: Slatkin	Turnabout QTV-S 34633	1975
Paine: *Mass in D* Carmen Balthrop, soprano Joy Blackett, mezzo-soprano Vinson Cole, tenor John Cheek, bass-baritone Conductor: Gunther Schuller	New World NW 262/263	1977
Prokofiev: *Alexander Nevsky* Claudine Carlson, mezzo-soprano Conductor: Slatkin	Candide QCE 31098	1977

Prokofiev: *Chout* (with de Falla *Tricorne*) Conductor: Golschmann	Capitol P-8257	1953
Prokofiev: *Lieutenant Kije, Ivan the Terrible*		
Prokofiev: Suite from *The Love For Three Oranges,* *Sycthian Suite* Conductor: Van Remoortel	Columbia ML-5462 MS-6132 Reissued on Odyssey 32 16 0344	1959
Prokofiev: *Piano Concerto No. 3* Leonard Pennario, piano (with Bartók *Concerto No. 3*) Conductor: Golschmann	Capitol P-8253	1953
Prokofiev: *Symphony No. 1* ("Classical") (78) Conductor: Golschmann	Victor M/DM-942	1942
Prokofiev: *Violin Concerto No. 1* Nathan Milstein, violin (with Lalo *Symphonie espagnole*) Conductor: Golschmann	Capitol P-8303	1954
Rachmaninoff: *Isle of the Dead*		1976
Rachmaninoff: *Piano Concertos Nos. 1, 2, 3, and 4,* *Variations on a Theme of Paganini* Abbey Simon, piano Conductor: Slatkin	Vox QSVBX 5149	1975 1976
Rachmaninoff: *Piano Concerto No. 2, Rhapsody on a* *Theme of Paganini* Abbey Simon, piano Conductor: Slatkin	Turnabout QTV-S 34658	1975 1976
Rachmaninoff: *Piano Concerto No. 2* Leonard Pennario, piano Conductor: Golschmann	Capitol P-8302 Reissued on Pickwick S-4030	1954
Rachmaninoff: *Piano Concerto No. 3* Abbey Simon, Piano Conductor: Slatkin	Turnabout QTV-S 34682	1976
Rachmaninoff: *Symphony No. 1* Conductor: Slatkin	Candide QCE 31099	1977
Rachmaninoff: *Symphony No. 2* Conductor: Slatkin	Vox	1978
Rachmaninoff: *Symphony No. 3, Vocalise* Claudine Carlson, mezzo-soprano Conductor: Slatkin	Vox	1976

Ravel: *La Valse, Valses nobles et sentimentales* (with Debussy *La Mer*) Conductor: Golschmann	Columbia ML-5155	1956
Respighi: *Rossiniana* (with Chopin Romantic Music orchestral arrangements) Conductor: Golschmann	Columbia ML-5161	1956
Rimsky-Korsakov: *Scheherazade* Conductor: Semkow	Turnabout QTV-S 34667	1976
Rimsky-Korsakov: *Song of India* (with Bolzoni *Minuet*) Conductor: Ganz	Victor 45531	1925
Rossini: Overture to *Barber of Seville* Conductor: Ganz	Victor 55290	1925
Schoenberg: *Verklärte Nacht* (with Corelli *Adagio* on 4 78s) (Reissued with Milhaud *Suite provencale* on Camden CAL-178) Conductor: Golschmann	Victor M/DM-1005	1945
Schumann: *Symphony Nos. 1, 2, 3, and 4, Manfred Overture* Conductor: Semkow	Vox SVBX 5146	1976
Shostakovich: *Age of Gold*, Polka and Russian Dance (with de Falla *Vida breve*) (78) Conductor: Golschmann	Victor L1-8592	1942
Shostakovich: *Symphony No. 1* (with Kabalevsky *Colas Breugnon*) Conductor: Golschmann	Columbia ML-5152	1956
Shostakovich: *Symphony No. 5* Conductor: Golschmann	Capitol P-8268 Reissued on Pickwick S-4016	1953
Sibelius: *Symphony No. 7* (Reissued with Mozart *Symphony No. 38* on Bluebird LBC-1067) Conductor: Golschmann	Victor M/DM-922	1942
Sinding: *Rustle of Spring, Op. 32, No. 3* (78) (with d'Albert Overture from *The Improvisator*) Conductor: Ganz	Victor 45389	1920s

Smetana: *Ma Vlast*, Dances from the Overture to *The Bartered Bride* Conductor: Susskind	Turnabout QTV-S 34619	1975
Strauss: *Also Sprach Zarathustra* Max Rabinovitsj, violin Conductor: Susskind	Turnabout QTV-S 34584	1974
Tansman: *Triptych for String Orchestra* (2 78s) Conductor: Golschmann	Columbia X-47	1935
Tchaikovsky: *Francesca da Rimini*, *Romeo and Juliet* Conductor: Golschmann	Capitol P-8225 Reissued on Pickwick S-4002	1953
Tchaikovsky: Excerpts from *Swan Lake* (4 78s) Conductor: Golschmann	Victor M/DM-1028 Reissued on Victor LM-1003	1945
Wagner: "Ride of the Valkyries," Prelude from *Die Meistersinger*, Preludes to Acts I and III from *Lohengrin*, Overture from *Rienzi*, "Good Friday Spell" from *Parsifal* Conductor: Semkow	Vox	1977
Weber: *Invitation to the Dance*, arranged by Berlioz Leslie Parnas, cello (Reissued with Suites from the ballets *Coppélia* and *Sylvia* by Delibes, and Easdale *The Red Shoes* on Odyssey 32 16 0338) Conductor: Golschmann	Columbia ML-5254 MS-6028	1957

NOTES

Chapter I

1. Ernst C. Krohn, *Missouri Music* (New York: Da Capo Press, 1971), p. 165.

2. *Ibid.*, p. 166.

3. Harry M. Hagen, *This Is Our St. Louis* (St. Louis: Knight Publishing Company, 1970), p. 153.

4. Thomas J. Scharf, *History of Saint Louis City and County* (2 vols.; Philadelphia: Louis H. Everts & Co., 1883), II, 1630.

5. Krohn, *Missouri Music*, p. 171.

6. *Ibid.*, p. 170.

7. *Ibid.*

8. *Ibid.*

9. Transcript of 1948 interview with John Gecks by Charles van Ravenswaay, in Music Envelope (Manuscript Collection, Missouri Historical Society, St. Louis, Missouri). Cited hereafter as Gecks interview.

10. Gecks interview.

11. St. Louis Symphony Society, *St. Louis Symphony Orchestra Diamond Jubilee Souvenir Program* (St. Louis, 1955), n.p.

12. Gecks interview.

13. St. Louis Symphony Society, *St. Louis Symphony Orchestra Diamond Jubilee Souvenir Program*, n.p.

14. *Ibid.*

15. John H. Mueller, *The American Symphony Orchestra* (Bloomington: Indiana University Press, 1951), p. 146.

16. *Ibid.*, p. 28.

17. *Ibid.*, p. 146.

18. Krohn, *Missouri Music*, p. 173.

19. From an undated *St. Louis Globe-Democrat* clipping found in the Music Papers (Manuscript Collection, Missouri Historical Society, St. Louis, Missouri). From its contents, it must be of the early 1900s.

20. Mark Bennitt and Frank Parker Stockbridge (eds.), *History of the Louisiana Purchase Exposition* (St. Louis: Universal Exposition Publishing Company, 1905), p. 703.

21. Krohn, *Missouri Music*, p. 174.

22. Thomas B. Sherman, "The Story of Music in America--9--St. Louis," *Musical America*, LXVII, no. 15 (December 1, 1947), 34.

23. Mueller, *The American Symphony Orchestra*, p. 197.

24. *Ibid.*, p. 149.

25. Letter of David Montagnon to W. H. Pommer, date unknown, in Pommer Papers (Manuscript Collection, Missouri Historical Society, St. Louis, Missouri).

26. St. Louis Symphony Society, *St. Louis Symphony Orchestra Diamond Jubilee Souvenir Program*, n. p.

27. Reprinted in *St. Louis Post-Dispatch*, February 28, 1920.

28. Homer Bassford, "Memories Linger On in Ruins of Old Odeon," *St. Louis Star-Times*, XL, no. 264 (August 8, 1935), 13.

29. *Ibid.*

30. "An Informal History of the Saint Louis Symphony Society Compiled for George D. Markham May 25, 1927," a hand-printed souvenir in the Missouri Historical Society, St. Louis, Missouri, n.p. Mrs. Parker's husband was a founder of the St. Louis Union Trust Company, Republican candidate for mayor of St. Louis in 1901, and a director of the Louisiana Purchase Exposition.

31. *St. Louis Republic*, May 28, 1916.

32. Frank Peters, "Rudolph Ganz as a Conductor," *St. Louis Post-Dispatch*, XCIII, no. 189 (July 11, 1971), 5D.

33. *Ibid.*

34. *Ibid.*

35. "Ganz Listed With the 'Greats' of Music," *Musical Leader*, XCVI, no. 8 (August 1964), 14.

36. Mueller, *The American Symphony Orchestra*, p. 149.

37. Thomas B. Sherman, "Symphony's End," *St. Louis Post-Dispatch*, XCIV, no. 205 (March 29, 1942), 5H.

38. St. Louis Symphony Society, *St. Louis Symphony Orchestra Diamond Jubilee Souvenir Program*, n.p.

39. *St. Louis Post-Dispatch*, March 16, 1927.

40. St. Louis Symphony Society, *St. Louis Symphony Orchestra Diamond Jubilee Souvenir Program*, n.p.

41. *Ibid.*

Chapter II

1. "Halfway in St. Louis," *Time*, LV, no. 12 (March 20, 1950), 62.

2. Hope Stoddard, *Symphony Conductors of the U.S.A.* (New York: Thomas Y. Crowell Company, 1957), p. 65.

3. *Ibid.*, p. 68.

4. *Ibid.*, p. 66.

5. *Ibid.*, p. 70.

6. *Ibid.*, p. 71.

7. *St. Louis Star-Times*, November 1, 1940.

8. St. Louis Symphony Society, *St. Louis Symphony Orchestra Diamond Jubilee Souvenir Program* (St. Louis, 1955), n.p.

9. Stoddard, *Symphony Conductors of the U.S.A.*, p. 72.

10. Letter of Vladimir Golschmann to the William Eisendraths, July 27, 1939, in Vladimir Golschmann Letters (Manuscript Collection, University of Missouri--St. Louis, St. Louis, Missouri).

11. Letter of Vladimir Golschmann to William Zalken, July 21, 1948, in St. Louis

Symphony Society Papers (St. Louis Symphony Society, St. Louis, Missouri). Cited hereafter as Symphony Papers.

12. *Ibid.*

13. *St. Louis Post-Dispatch*, September 15, 1941.

14. "Halfway in St. Louis," *Time*, 62.

15. There were some exceptions to the rule. Once when the orchestra was on tour Golschmann forced a particular player, whom he wanted to fire, to continually play through a piece at rehearsal until the musician was near exhaustion. When the man finally could play no longer, Golschmann charged him with incompetency. On another occasion the conductor and the pianist William Kapell had an argument, and that evening the soloist and the conductor did not perform together. People close to the orchestra also recall that Golschmann once threw the music score at the face of a singer at rehearsal and charged him with not being up to the standards demanded by a great orchestra. The soloist's appearance was canceled. These incidents were not typical of Golschmann's behavior. Interview with Herbert Van den Burg, former principal violist, September 26, 1975. Cited hereafter as Van den Burg interview.

16. "Halfway in St. Louis," *Time*, 62.

17. "On the Cover," *Musical Courier*, CXLI, no. 3 (February 1, 1950), 3.

18. Arthur W. Hepner, "He Never Loses His Head or Temper," *St. Louis Post-Dispatch*, XCVI, no. 124 (January 7, 1944), 3D.

19. Stoddard, *Symphony Conductors of the U.S.A.*, p. 71.

20. "Long-Term Conductor," *Time*, XLVII, no. 9 (February 27, 1956), 47.

21. *Atlantic City Press*, April 25, 1937.

22. *Columbus (Ohio) Citizen*, January 18, 1939.

23. *St. Louis Star-Times*, November 16, 1938.

24. Thomas B. Sherman, "Conductors on Parade," *St. Louis Post-Dispatch*, XCI, no. 195 (March 19, 1939), 5H.

25. *St. Louis Post-Dispatch*, October 22, 1940.

26. *The Mirror*, February 1932, n.d.

27. Interview with William J. Miller, Jr., Associate Professor of History, Saint Louis University, September 22, 1975. Cited hereafter as Miller interview.

28. John H. Mueller and Kate Hevner, *Trends in Musical Taste* (Bloomington: Indiana University Publications, 1942), p. 84.

29. Interview with Laurent Torno, former principal flutist, September 18, 1975.

30. Harry Burke, "Melchior Places Golschmann Among 5 Best Conductors," *St. Louis Globe-Democrat*, LX, no. 182 (November 17, 1934), 3A.

31. Van den Burg interview.

32. "Conductor's Choice," *House Beautiful*, XCI (August 1949), 123.

33. Miller interview.

34. Thomas B. Sherman, "The Story of Music in America--9--St. Louis," *Musical America*, LXVII, no. 15 (December 1, 1947), 34.

35. Van den Burg interview.

36. *Ibid.*

37. Review by Olin King in *New York Times*, reprinted in *St. Louis Globe-Democrat*, December 24, 1931.

38. Stoddard, *Symphony Conductors of the U.S.A.*, p. 71.

39. *Philadelphia Bulletin*, November 23, 1935.

40. Review in *Philadelphia Evening Public Ledger*, reprinted in *St. Louis Globe-Democrat*, November 26, 1935.

41. Review in *Philadelphia Daily News*, reprinted in *St. Louis Globe-Democrat*, November 26, 1935.

42. *Philadelphia Inquirer*, July 7, 1954.

43. *Chicago American*, January 19, 1937.

44. *Chicago Times*, January 19, 1937.

45. *Chicago Tribune*, January 19, 1939.

46. Review by Olin Downes in *New York Times*, reprinted in *St. Louis Star and Times*, April 10, 1933.

47. Stoddard, *Symphony Conductors of the U.S.A.*, p. 71.

48. "St. Louis Symphony Announces Schedule," *Musical Courier*, CXLIV, no. 5 (October 15, 1951).

49. Letter of Vladimir Golschmann to William Zalken, n.d., in Symphony Papers.

50. Review in *Alerta* (Madrid), Summer 1954, n.d., clipping in Symphony Papers.

51. Including honorary degrees from Illinois Wesleyan University in 1941, Washington University in 1951, and University of Missouri in 1954.

52. Stoddard, *Symphony Conductors of the U.S.A.*, p. 71.

Chapter III

1. *St. Louis Star*, October 13, 1931. Arthur J. Gaines continued as manager of the Symphony through the 1937-1938 season.

2. Guidi was concertmaster through the 1941-1942 season, when Golschmann dismissed him. He was quite popular with the Symphony patrons, as was another of the players whom Golschmann brought in 1931, Herbert Van den Burg, principal violist throughout the entire Golschmann tenure. A list of all the members of the orchestra from 1907 to 1979 appears in Appendix I.

3. *St. Louis Post-Dispatch*, September 28, 1931.

4. *St. Louis Globe-Democrat*, October 24, 1931.

5. *St. Louis Times*, October 24, 1931.

6. *St. Louis Post-Dispatch*, October 24, 1931.

7. Information about performances of the guest artists who appeared with the Symphony during the Golschmann era appears elsewhere in this chapter.

8. *St. Louis Post-Dispatch*, March 19, 1932.

9. *St. Louis Times*, December 31, 1931.

10. *Poplar Bluff American Republic*, March 23, 1937.

11. William B. Heyne founded the Bach Choir in 1940.

12. Letter of a student to Miss Helen Ballweg, January 29, 1954, in St. Louis Symphony Society Papers (St. Louis Symphony Society, St. Louis, Missouri). Cited hereafter as Symphony Papers.

13. *St. Louis Star-Times*, October 22, 1935.

14. The seating capacity in St. Louis was greater than in the symphony halls in Boston, Cleveland, Chicago, Detroit, and Carnegie Hall in New York.

15. We may see another problem with the auditorium as reflected in a letter from the assistant manager of the auditorium to the manager of the Symphony, "With reference to your letter regarding Mrs. Crego's refusal to renew her symphony subscription

because of moths and roaches, I'm afraid the lady does not appreciate Mr. Golschmann's effort. He certainly would not feel flattered if he knew she was watching a roach instead of him. Probably the roach was more interesting." Letter of Louis Wagner to William Zalken, September 18, 1952, in Symphony Papers.

16. Like other major American orchestras, the Symphony appeared at military posts in the area during the war. In 1945 the USO sponsored a tour of Europe by Golschmann and Farbman to conduct military bands and orchestras.

17. Review by Warren Storey Smith in *Boston Post*, reprinted in *St. Louis Post-Dispatch*, March 6, 1950.

18. Reprinted in *St. Louis Globe-Democrat*, March 9, 1950.

19. "Halfway in St. Louis," *Time*, LV, no. 12 (March 20, 1950), 62.

20. Elmer Gesner joined the Symphony in 1916 and retired in 1959. He also played in the Municipal Opera orchestra from 1920 to 1961. He tells the story of the time when a string on one of his chimes broke during a concert and the chime fell down and hit horn player Edward Murphy on the head. This occurred during the playing of Berlioz' *Symphonie Fantastique*. Interview with Elmer Gesner, September 19, 1975.

21. And near-tragedies sometimes occurred. In 1955 fourteen musicians were injured, none seriously, in a bus accident in Virginia. They canceled an Ohio concert, the first time in twenty years that a concert was canceled.

22. In 1937 Keller left the orchestra, returned to his native Europe, and died in a fire.

23. Of one town, he wrote (very much "tongue-in-cheek") to friends in St. Louis, "Dear friends, We arrived here at 6:00 after a wonderful voyage. The beauty of the city is indescribable. This post card will show better than words what I mean. Why people go to Florence, Aix-en-Provence or Rio de Janeiro is too much for me. Tomorrow we'll stay in Wheeling, West Virginia as we want to hear the lecture on modern art." Post card of Vladimir Golschmann to the William Eisendraths, n.d., in Vladimir Golschmann Letters (Manuscript Collection, University of Missouri-St. Louis, St. Louis, Missouri).

24. Bernard Schram, "When the Symphony is Crossed Up It's Usually Out Loud," *St. Louis Globe-Democrat*, LXXII, no. 182 (December 8, 1946), 1E.

25. *Chicago American*, February 14, 1938.

26. *The (Memphis) Commercial Appeal*, March 17, 1942.

27. Review by John Rosenfeld in *Dallas Morning News*, reprinted in *St. Louis Post-Dispatch*, December 8, 1952.

28. Review by Elizabeth Crocker in *Dallas Journal*, April 8, 1938.

29. Review by Pat McNealy Barnes in *Houston Post*, March 17, 1936.

30. A discography of the orchestra appears in Appendix III.

31. Thomas B. Sherman, "Off the Records," *St. Louis Post-Dispatch*, XCVIII, no. 123 (January 6, 1946), 4H.

32. Thomas B. Sherman, "Off the Records," *St. Louis Post-Dispatch*, XCVIII, no. 151 (February 3, 1946), 4H.

33. *Chattanooga Times*, October 6, 1935.

34. Interview with Herbert Van den Burg, September 26, 1975. Cited hereafter as Van den Burg interview.

35. *St. Louis Post-Dispatch*, November 10, 1934.

36. *St. Louis Star-Times*, November 5, 1938.

37. Interview with Edward Murphy, former principal horn player and assistant conductor, September 10, 1975. Cited hereafter as Murphy interview.

38. After a 1942 Milhaud performance of his own works, which he also conducted, a newspaper editorial said, "A symphony conductor...must be allowed the liberty to bring in contemporary works and first performances, at his judicious discretion, if the audiences are not to die of musical dry rot while listening interminably to eighteenth and nineteenth-century 'Masterpieces.'" *St. Louis Star-Times*, January 22, 1942.

39. *St. Louis Post-Dispatch*, March 9, 1935.

40. *St. Louis Post-Dispatch*, October 30, 1949. Mrs. Harry S Truman, Vice President Alben Barkley, and Helen Traubel were some of the celebrities who attended the concert. Golschmann sent President Truman a telegram in which he said, "Am so happy, Mr. President, to tell you of the splendid success of Miss Truman. Not only her voice but her lovely personality won the heart of all of us." Telegram of Vladimir Golschmann to President Truman, October 31, 1949, in Symphony Papers.

41. A member of the orchestra described Stravinsky, during a 1935 visit to St. Louis, as a "nervous, little man, who has an overpowering fear of sickness." The composer arrived in the city wrapped in a fur coat, scarves, and sweaters. *Chattanooga Times*, October 6, 1935.

42. A list of American and world premières played by the orchestra from 1907 to 1978 appears in Appendix II.

43. Thomas Sherman wrote that it was "an uncertainly inspired and weakly organized composition, low in content, wan in color, commonplace in its harmonies and rhythms and saved from complete mediocrity only by a typically Schumannesque second subject in the first movement and a certain display of originality in the short slow movement." *St. Louis Post-Dispatch*, December 24, 1937.

44. The announcement for the award read, "It is hoped the contest will serve to stimulate creative activity in the symphonic field. As a part of a significant celebration in the history of music in the American Middle West, it is designed to focus attention upon the increasing importance of the native composer in the symphonic repertory." *St. Louis Globe-Democrat*, September 10, 1939.

45. Programs of the St. Louis Symphony Orchestra, 1946-1947 season, p. 723.

46. Four men served as manager of the Symphony throughout the Golschmann period: Arthur J. Gaines through the 1937-1938 season, Don Foster for part of the 1938-1939 season, John S. Edwards until the conclusion of the 1941-1942 season, and William Zalken beyond the Golschmann tenure. Foster arrived in St. Louis from business duties in Cape Girardeau, Missouri. He resigned over differences with Golschmann. Edwards had worked for the *St. Louis Globe-Democrat*, and resigned over policy differences with the Symphony Society Board of Directors. He went to the Hollywood Bowl in California as associate manager. Zalken had worked for the *St. Louis Post-Dispatch*, and had been in charge of public relations work for the Symphony and Municipal Opera in St. Louis before becoming manager.

47. *St. Louis Post-Dispatch*, October 15, 1946.

48. *St. Louis Globe-Democrat*, June 1, 1949.

49. *St. Louis Globe-Democrat*, October 19, 1933.

50. Thomas B. Sherman, "Cadenza on an Economic Theme," *St. Louis Post-Dispatch*, XCIV, no. 170 (February 22, 1942), 5H.

51. "St. Loo Symph May Fold in Coin Crisis, Civic Leaders Concerned," *Variety*, CXCV, no. 9 (August 4, 1954), 48.

52. *St. Louis Post-Dispatch*, May 7, 1936.

53. *St. Louis Post-Dispatch*, December 30, 1951.

54. *St. Louis Post-Dispatch*, January 3, 1954.

55. *St. Louis Globe-Democrat*, January 23, 1958.

56. L. Warrington Baldwin served as president before the Golschmann era and through the 1931-1932 season. J. D. Wooster Lambert served for the 1932-1933 season. Edwin J. Spiegel succeeded Johnson, and served for the remainder of the Golschmann period.

57. *Poplar Bluff (Missouri) American Republic*, n.d.

58. Interview with Oscar Johnson, Jr., October 4, 1975.

59. *St. Louis Globe-Democrat*, October 15, 1941.

60. For example, in 1942 Golschmann gave $3,000. He had given $1,000 in previous years. *St. Louis Post-Dispatch*, June 9, 1942.

61. "Musicians Get Cuts Back," *Variety*, CXXXII no. 13 (December 7, 1938), 51.

62. "St. Louis Greets World Premiers [*sic*]," *Musical Courier*, CXLVII, no. 6 (March 15, 1953), 19.

63. The St. Louis Symphony was one of the few major orchestras in the country where money from special fund-raising activities was used to pay less than half of the operating expenses. With most orchestras, the normal sources of revenue (ticket sales, royalties, etc.) accounted for less than half of the money needed to pay bills. Thus, they had to rely on public appeals for money to cover more than half of their budget. In St. Louis usually between fifty and sixty per cent of operating costs were paid by natural sources of income. During the 1947-1948 season, only twelve per cent of the orchestra's expenses went for administrative staff and office space rentals. Only six per cent of expenses went for advertising and ticket sales. Eighty-two per cent of the budget was used for employment of the regular musicians, permanent conductor, and guest soloists. Such figures indicate sound business management on the part of the Symphony Society. Letter of St. Louis Symphony Society to Ray Schroeder, Deputy Comptroller of St. Louis, July 30, 1948, in Symphony Papers.

64. Supporters of the Symphony believed that the city charged too much rent for Kiel Auditorium, especially considering the financial plight of the orchestra and the relative financial security of the city during that time. In response to a letter in the newspaper favoring a more lenient policy from the city, the St. Louis deputy comptroller wrote, "I just wanted to tell you that the City of St. Louis does aid the Symphony financially. The Kiel Auditorium report for the 1947-1948 season shows receipts from the Symphony were $12,732.62 and costs $22,242.85 leaving a deficit of $9,510.23 which obviously was contributed by the City to the Symphony. During the 1946-47 season the Symphony tenancy in the Auditorium cost the City $18,523.45 and the cash payments were $10,957.28 leaving the city contributing $7,566.17. Just what the City will contribute for the season now drawing to an end is not definite but it will be similar to a year ago because salaries of City employees have increased. What our Symphony needs is some person who will write thank-you letters of appreciation for favors shown." Letter of Ray C. Schroeder to Aron G. Benesch, *St. Louis Star-Times*, February 19, 1949.

65. Public letter of Mayor Raymond R. Tucker, October 6, 1954, in Symphony Papers.

66. The Symphony was the only major American orchestra without a pension fund until 1935, when Igor Stravinsky guest-conducted a benefit concert whose proceeds were used to start such a fund. He and violinist Samuel Dushkin performed for two-thirds of their regular fee. Subsequently, several soloists appeared with the orchestra to help

raise money for the pension fund.

67. Between the 1955-1956 season and the 1957-1958 season, the orchestra experienced a forty per cent turnover in musicians. *St. Louis Post-Dispatch*, December 2, 1957.

68. Murphy interview.

69. Interview with Morton D. May, former Active Vice-President, now Chairman of the Board, of the Symphony Society, November 6, 1975. Cited hereafter as May interview.

70. *St. Louis Post-Dispatch*, December 2, 1957. Despite his disenchantment with the administrative problems, Golschmann wanted to stay with the orchestra. May interview.

71. *St. Louis Post-Dispatch*, April 9, 1958.

72. *St. Louis Globe-Democrat*, April 7, 1958.

73. Reprinted in *St. Louis Globe-Democrat*, December 16, 1933.

74. *Indianapolis Star*, January 20, 1937.

75. Thomas B. Sherman, "Orchestra's Growth," *St. Louis Post-Dispatch*, XCII, no. 82 (November 26, 1939), 5G.

76. Reprinted in *St. Louis Globe-Democrat*, March 21, 1949.

77. Thomas B. Sherman, "The Symphony Tour," *St. Louis Post-Dispatch*, CII, no. 71 (November 20, 1949), 4G.

78. Interview with Laurent Torno, former principal flutist, September 18, 1975, and Van den Burg interview. World War II affected the quality of the orchestra. During the 1941-1942 season the orchestra contained eighty-seven players. The number dropped to seventy-two during 1942-1943, increased to seventy-five the next season, went to seventy-four the following season, and during the 1945-1946 season the number increased to eighty-two. As some of the regular musicians were drafted for military service, they were replaced by players who were not always of the best quality.

A side-effect of the war was the increase in the number of women in the orchestra. Until the 1943-1944 season only two women were members (harpist Graziella Pampari and pianist Corinne Frederick). During that season the number increased to five, and the next season saw nine women in the orchestra. During the next two seasons the orchestra contained fourteen women. Women were well represented throughout the rest of the Golschmann period, and beyond it.

79. Deems Taylor, "The Ten Finest," *Holiday*, IX, no. 3 (March 1951), 67.

80. Programs of the St. Louis Symphony Orchestra, 1955-1956 season, n.p.

Chapter IV

1. *St. Louis Post-Dispatch*, December 13, 1957.

2. William F. Woo, "There's an Awful Lot of Tchaikovsky in Brazil," *St. Louis Post-Dispatch*, XXCIV, no. 287 (October 18, 1962), 3F.

3. Thomas B. Sherman, "An Enterprising Symphony Season," *St. Louis Post-Dispatch*, XXCVI, no. 109 (April 19, 1964), 5B.

4. Letter from D. W. Hiestand to *St. Louis Post-Dispatch*, April 6, 1964.

5. St. Louis Symphony Society, "A Tribute to Walter Susskind," 1973, p. 2.

6. *Ibid.*

7. *St. Louis Globe-Democrat*, December 29, 1961.

8. St. Louis Symphony Society, "Powell Symphony Hall," n.d., pp. 2-3 (mimeographed), in Symphony Papers. Walter S. Powell, born in Virginia in 1879 and

educated at M.I.T., came to St. Louis in 1926 to work for Brown Shoe Company. He was director and manager of their tanneries. In 1961, as president of the United States Figure Skating Association, he was killed in an airplane crash while accompanying the American skating team to Prague, Czechoslovakia for the international competition.

9. *Ibid.*, p. 2

10. *Ibid.*, p. 4

11. *St. Louis Post-Dispatch*, December 21, 1977.

12. *Ibid.* Ben Wells, president of the Seven-Up Company, became president of the Symphony Society with the start of the 1970-1971 season. In 1978 he was succeeded by W. L. Hadley Griffin, president of Brown Group, Inc. The two other heads of the Society during the post-Golschmann era were Orrin S. Wightman, Jr., an executive with the G. H. Walker brokerage firm (1958-1959 through 1964-1965), and Stanley J. Goodman, president of the May Company (1965-1966 through 1969-1970).

13. *St. Louis Post-Dispatch*, September 15, 1977.

14. *St. Louis Post-Dispatch*, February 14, 1978.

15. *Ibid.*

16. *Saint Louis Symphony Newsletter*, Vol. V, no. 4 (Summer 1977).

17. *Saint Louis Symphony Notes*, Vol. VII, no. 1 (Spring 1978).

18. Programs of the St. Louis Symphony Orchestra, 1973-1974 season, p. 59.

19. Review in *St. Petersburg Times*, reprinted in Programs of the St. Louis Symphony Orchestra, 1960-1961 season; p. 609.

20. Review in *San Francisco Chronicle*, reprinted in Programs of the St. Louis Symphony Orchestra, 1965-1966 season, p. 396.

21. Reprinted in Programs of the St. Louis Symphony Orchestra, 1967-1968 season, p. 533.

22. Reprinted in Programs of the St. Louis Symphony Orchestra, 1968-1969 season, p. 224.

23. *Ibid.*, p. 225.

24. Reprinted in Programs of the St. Louis Symphony Orchestra, 1972-1973 season, p. 291.

25. *Saint Louis Symphony Newsletter*, Vol. VI, no. 1 (Fall 1977).

26. Programs of the St. Louis Symphony Orchestra, 1973-1974 season, p. 277.

BIBLIOGRAPHY

Primary Sources

Archival Materials

Herbert W. Cost Scrapbook. Manuscript Collection. Missouri Historical Society, St. Louis, Missouri.

Russel Dearmont Papers. Manuscript Collection. Western Historical Manuscript Collection. State Historical Society Manuscripts, Columbia, Missouri.

Vladimir Golschmann Letters. Manuscript Collection. University of Missouri--St. Louis, St. Louis, Missouri.

"An Informal History of the Saint Louis Symphony Society Compiled for George D. Markham May 25, 1927." Manuscript Collection. Missouri Historical Society, St. Louis, Missouri.

Diaries of George D. and Mary McKittrick Markham. Manuscript Collection. Missouri Historical Society, St. Louis, Missouri.

Music Envelope. Manuscript Collection. Missouri Historical Society, St. Louis, Missouri.

Music Papers. Manuscript Collection. Missouri Historical Society, St. Louis, Missouri.

W. H. Pommer Papers. Manuscript Collection. Missouri Historical Society, St. Louis, Missouri.

Rice Family Papers. Manuscript Collection. Missouri Historical Society, St. Louis, Missouri.

St. Louis Symphony Orchestra Programs, 1904 to 1978. St. Louis Symphony Society, St. Louis, Missouri.

St. Louis Symphony Society Papers. St. Louis Symphony Society, St. Louis, Missouri.

Interviews by the Author

Becker, Mrs. William Dee. Personal interview with a patron and former member of the Board of Directors of the St. Louis Symphony Society. October 15, 1975.

Gesner, Elmer. Personal interview with a former percussionist and librarian of the St. Louis Symphony Orchestra. September 19, 1975.

Johnson, Oscar, Jr. Personal interview with a financial contributor and former president of the St. Louis Symphony Society. October 4, 1975.

Love, Martha. Personal interview with a patron of the St. Louis Symphony Orchestra. October 13, 1975.

May, Morton D. Personal interview with a former Active Vice-President of the St. Louis Symphony Society. November 6, 1975.

Miller, William J., Jr. Personal interview with a patron of the St. Louis Symphony Orchestra. September 22, 1975.

Murphy, Edward. Personal interview with a former principal horn player of the St.

Louis Symphony Orchestra. September 10, 1975.

Torno, Laurent. Personal interview with a former flutist of the St. Louis Symphony Orchestra. September 18, 1975.

Van den Burg, Herbert. Personal interview with a former principal violist of the St. Louis Symphony Orchestra. September 26, 1975.

Wolff, Mrs. Norman. Personal interview with a patron of the St. Louis Symphony Orchestra, and daughter of Mrs. Max Goldstein. October 8, 1975.

Zalken, William. Personal interview with a former manager of the St. Louis Symphony Orchestra. September 13, 1975.

Reports

Conference of Managers. Summaries of reports on symphony orchestras from 1945 to 1953.

St. Louis Symphony Society. "Powell Symphony Hall." A Description and History of Powell Symphony Hall, n.d. (Mimeographed.)

_____. *Saint Louis Symphony Newsletter*, V, no. 4, Summer 1977.

_____. *Saint Louis Symphony Newsletter*, VI, no. 1, Fall 1977.

_____. *Saint Louis Symphony Notes*, VII, no. 1, Spring 1978.

_____. *A Tribute to Walter Susskind.* 1973.

Newspapers

Scrapbooks of St. Louis and out-of-town newspaper clippings, 1931-1945. St. Louis Symphony Society, St. Louis, Missouri.

St. Louis Globe-Democrat, 1931-1961. (Daily.)

St. Louis Post-Dispatch, 1920-1978. (Daily.)

St. Louis Star, 1931. (Daily.)

St. Louis Star and Times, 1933. (Daily.)

St. Louis Star-Times, 1935-1951. (Daily.)

St. Louis Times, 1931. (Daily.)

Secondary Sources

Books

Alberti, Luciano. *Music of the Western World.* New York: Crown Publishers, Inc., 1974.

Bennitt, Mark, and Stockbridge, Frank Parker, eds. *History of the Louisiana Purchase Exposition.* St. Louis: Universal Exposition Publishing Company, 1905.

Ewen, David. *Dictators of the Baton.* Chicago: Alliance Book Corporation, 1943.

_____. *The Man With the Baton.* New York: Thomas Y. Crowell Company, 1936.

Grant, Margaret, and Hettinger, Herman S. *American Symphony Orchestras and How They Are Supported.* New York: W. W. Norton & Company, Inc., 1940.

Hagen, Harry M. *This Is Our St. Louis.* St. Louis: Knight Publishing Company, 1970.

Krohn, Ernst C. *A Century of Missouri Music.* St. Louis: Privately published, 1924. ✓

_____. *Missouri Music.* New York: Da Capo Press, 1971.

Mueller, John H. *The American Symphony Orchestra.* Bloomington: Indiana University Press, 1951.

——————, and Hevner, Kate. *Trends in Musical Taste.* Bloomington: Indiana University Publications, 1942.

Scharf, J. Thomas. *History of Saint Louis City and County.* 2 volumes. Philadelphia: Louis H. Everts & Co., 1883.

Stevens, Walter B. *St. Louis, the Fourth City, 1764-1909.* 3 volumes. St. Louis: The S. J. Clarke Publishing Co., 1909.

St. Louis Symphony Society. *St. Louis Symphony Orchestra. Diamond Jubilee Souvenir Program.* St. Louis, 1955.

Stoddard, Hope. *Symphony Conductors of the U.S.A.* New York: Thomas Y. Crowell Company, 1957.

Articles

Althoff, Shirley. "Violinist." *St. Louis Globe-Democrat Sunday Magazine*, XXCVI, no. 169 (March 19, 1961), 8.

Bassford, Homer. "Golschmann Back From Creole-Land With Fresh Zest." *St. Louis Star and Times*, XLVII, no. 105 (February 3, 1933), 22.

——————. "Memories Linger on in Ruins of Old Odeon." *St. Louis Star-Times*, XL, no. 264 (August 8, 1935), 13.

"Baton Passing." *Time*, LXX, no. 27 (December 30, 1957), 48-49.

Baumhoff, Richard G. "The Man Behind the Kettledrum." *St. Louis Post-Dispatch*, CI, no. 56 (October 31, 1948), 2G.

Bohle, Bruce. "Economics of the Symphony." *St. Louis Post-Dispatch*, CV, no. 123 (February 1, 1953), 6G.

Briggs, John. "St. Louis 'Delights' New Conductor." *St. Louis Post-Dispatch*, LXXIX, no. 346 (December 19, 1957), 2F.

Burke, Harry. "Melchior Places Golschmann Among 5 Best Conductors." *St. Louis Globe-Democrat*, LX, no. 182 (November 17, 1934), 3A.

"Conductors' Choice." *House Beautiful*, XCI (August 1949), 60, 122-123.

Cost, Herbert W. "St. Louis Hears First U.S. Performance of Camargo Guarnieri's Brasiliana Suite." *Musical America*, LXXIII, no. 5 (April 1, 1953), 33.

——————. "St. Louis Symphony Gives Many Local Premiers." [*sic*] *Musical America*, LXXII, no. 5 (April 1, 1952), 22.

Curtis, Olga. "Vladimir Golschmann, D. S." *St. Louis Post-Dispatch*, XXCVI, no. 109 (April 19, 1964), 2H.

"Ganz Listed with the Greats of Music." *Musical Leader*, XCVI, no. 8 (August 1964), 14.

"Golschmann Honored." *Musical America*, LXXI, no. 8 (June 1951), 28.

"Golschmann to Become Conductor Emeritus." *Musical America*, LXXV, no. 6 (April 1955), 6.

"Golschmann to Stay in St. Louis." *Musical America*, LXXVI, no. 8 (June 1956), 33.

"Golschmann Feted in 20th St. Louis Year." *Musical Courier*, CXLII, no. 8 (November 15, 1950), 19.

"Halfway in St. Louis." *Time*, LV, no. 12 (March 20, 1950), 62.

Hepner, Arthur W. "He Never Loses His Head or Temper." *St. Louis Post-Dispatch*, XCVI, no. 124 (January 7, 1944), 3D.

Hynds, Reed. "Bringing Good Music to St. Louis Symphony's Major Accomplishment." *St. Louis Star-Times*, LIII, no. 148 (March 24, 1939), 8.

Jackson, Martha. "Symphony Harpist." *St. Louis Post-Dispatch*, XXCIX, no. 135 (January 18, 1937), 3D.

Krohn, Ernst. "The St. Louis Symphony and its Conductors." *Focus/Midwest*, II, no. 5 (June 1963), 16-19.

"Long Term Conductor." *Time*, LXVII, no. 9 (February 27, 1956), 47.

Martyn, Marguerite. "Women and the Symphony." *St. Louis Post-Dispatch*, XXCIV, no. 215 (April 8, 1932), 2F.

Menees, Charles. "Golschmann Conducts Despite Injury." *Musical America*, LXXV, no. 3 (February 1, 1955), 8.

_____. "Golschmann to Become Conductor Emeritus." *Musical America*, LXXV, no. 6 (April 1955), 6.

_____. "St. Louis Symphony Launches 75th Anniversary Year." *Musical America*, LXXIV, no. 14 (November 15, 1954), 6.

"Muscians Get Cuts Back." *Variety*, CXXXII, no. 13 (December 7, 1938), 51.

"Novelties Given by St. Louis Orchestra." *Musical Courier*, CXL, no. 9 (December 15, 1949), 20.

"On the Cover." *Musical Courier*, CXLI, no. 3 (February 1, 1950), 3.

"Out of the West." *Newsweek*, XXXIII, no. 8 (February 21, 1949), 81.

Peters, Frank. "Rudolph Ganz as a Conductor." *St. Louis Post-Dispatch*, XCIII, no. 189 (July 11, 1971), 5D.

_____. "The St. Louis Symphony's Golschmann Years." *St. Louis Post-Dispatch*, XCIII, no. 72 (March 14, 1971), 5C.

Schram, Bernard. "When the Symphony Is Crossed Up It's Usually Out Loud." *St. Louis Globe-Democrat*, LXXII, no. 182 (December 8, 1946), 1E.

Sherman, Thomas B. "American Conductor." *St. Louis Post-Dispatch*, XXC, no. 18 (January 19, 1958), 5C.

_____. "Another Symphony Crisis." *St. Louis Post-Dispatch*, XCIII, no. 178 (March 2, 1941), 5H.

_____. "Boston Critics Praise St. Louis Symphony." *St. Louis Post-Dispatch*, CII, no. 174 (March 6, 1950), 3B.

_____. "Cadenza on an Economic Theme." *St. Louis Post-Dispatch*, XCIV, no. 170 (February 22, 1942), 5H.

_____. "Case of Symphony Absentees." *St. Louis Post-Dispatch*, XXCVI, no. 67 (March 8, 1964), 5B.

_____. "Conductors on Parade." *St. Louis Post-Dispatch*, XCI, no. 195 (March 19, 1939), 5G.

_____. "An Enterprising Symphony Season." *St. Louis Post-Dispatch*, XXCVI, no. 109 (April 19, 1964), 5B.

_____. "Glimpsing the Future." *St. Louis Post-Dispatch*, XXC, no. 25 (January 26, 1958), 5C.

_____. "Golschmann Completes a Season." *St. Louis Post-Dispatch*, XXCIV, no. 203 (March 27, 1932), 4B.

_____. "Kiel Auditorium Acoustics." *St. Louis Post-Dispatch*, LXXVIII, no. 359 (December 30, 1956), 5B.

_____. "Looming Deficits." *St. Louis Post-Dispatch*, CII, no. 77 (December 3,

1950), 6G.

_____. "Music and Music Makers." *St. Louis Post-Dispatch*, XCII, no. 201 (March 24, 1940, 5H.

_____. "Music for St. Louis Bicentennial." *St. Louis Post-Dispatch*, XXCIII, no. 140 (May 21, 1961), 5B.

_____. "New Look for Symphony Season." *St. Louis Post-Dispatch*, XXCI, no. 267 (October 11, 1959), 5B.

_____. "Off the Records." *St. Louis Post-Dispatch*, XCVIII, no. 123 (January 6, 1946), 4H.

_____. "Off the Records." *St. Louis Post-Dispatch*, XCVIII, no. 151 (February 3, 1946), 4H.

_____. "Orchestra's Growth." *St. Louis Post-Dispatch*, XCII, no. 82 (November 26, 1939), 5G.

_____. "A Report on the Student Concerts." *St. Louis Post-Dispatch*, CII, no. 131 (January 22, 1950), 4G.

_____. "The Story of Music in America--9--St. Louis." *Musical America*, LXVII no. 15 (December 1, 1947), 7, 13, 34.

_____. "Symphony Needs Larger Audiences." *St. Louis Post-Dispatch*, XXCVI, no. 39 (February 9, 1964), 5C.

_____. "The Symphony Season." *St. Louis Post-Dispatch*, XCIII, no. 192 (March 16, 1941), 5H.

_____. "Symphony's End." *St. Louis Post-Dispatch*, XCIV, no. 205 (March 29, 1942), 205.

_____. "The Symphony's Future Prospects." *St. Louis Post-Dispatch*, LXXVII, no. 92 (April 3, 1955), 6G.

_____. "Symphony's New Head." *St. Louis Post-Dispatch*, LXXIX, no. 349 (December 22, 1957), 5D.

_____. "Symphony's Perennial Crisis." *St. Louis Post-Dispatch*, XXCIII, no. 49 (February 19, 1961), 5D.

"St. Loo Symphony May Fold, Civic Leaders Concerned." *Variety*, CXCV, no. 9 (August 4, 1954), 48.

"St. Louis: A City to Emulate." *High Fidelity/Musical America*, XV, no. 7 (July 1965), 112.

"St. Louis Greets World Premiers." [*sic*] *Musical Courier*, CXLVII, no. 6 (March 15, 1953), 19.

"St. Louis Symphony Announces Schedule." *Musical Courier*, CXLIV, no. 5 (October 15, 1951), 15.

"St. Louis Symphony Celebrates 75th Season." *Musical America*, LXXIV, no. 12 (October 1954), 4.

"St. Louis Symphony Gives Many Local Premiers." [*sic*] *Musical America*, LXXII, no. 5 April 1, 1952), 22.

"The Symphony Goes Co-Ed." *Newsweek*, XXII, no. 23 (December 6, 1943), 86, 88.

"Symphony Season." *Time*, XXX, no. 16 (October 18, 1937), 53.

Taylor, Deems. "The Ten Finest." *Holiday*, IX, no. 3 (March 1951), 64-67.

"Traubel Chase Finale to Aid St. Louis Symphony." *Variety*, CXCIII, no. 7 (January 20, 1954), 64.

"Vladimir Golschmann." *International Musician*, LVI, no. 1 (July 1957), 30.

Woo, William F. "There's an Awful Lot of Tchaikovsky in Brazil." *St. Louis*

Post-Dispatch, XXCIV, no. 287 (October 18, 1962), 3F.

Yates, P. "A city to Emulate." *High Fidelity/Musical America*, XV, no. 7 (July 1965), 112-13.

INDEX